Reparation for Vic
Crimes against Hu

The healing role of reparation

Edited by Jo-Anne M. Wemmers

LONDON AND NEW YORK

First published 2014
by Routledge

2 Park Square, Milton Park, Abingdon, Oxon OX14 4RN
711 Third Avenue, New York, NY 10017, USA

Routledge is an imprint of the Taylor & Francis Group, an informa business

First issued in paperback 2016

British Library Cataloguing in Publication Data
A catalogue record for this book is available from the British Library

Library of Congress Cataloging-in-Publication Data
Reparation for victims of crimes against humanity: the healing role of reparation / edited by Jo-Anne M. Wemmers.
pages cm. – (Routledge frontiers of criminal justice; 19).
Reparations for historical injustices. 2. Crimes against humanity.
3. Genocide survivors–Legal status, laws, etc. 4. War victims–Legal status, laws, etc. I. Wemmers, Jo-Anne M., 1964- editor of compilation.
KZ6785.R47 2014
341.6'6–dc23 2013046491

ISBN 978-1-138-66536-1 (pbk)
ISBN 978-0-415-71536-2 (hbk)
ISBN 978-1-315-88186-7 (ebk)

Typeset in Times New Roman
by Wearset Ltd, Boldon, Tyne and Wear

Contents

Illustrations

Figures

Tables

Contributors

Gregory D.B. Boese received his MA in Social and Personality Psychology from the University of Manitoba in 2010. He is now completing a PhD in Social Psychology with Stephen Wright at Simon Fraser University. His research uses social and political psychology to understand intergroup relations and applied political behavior.

Yael Danieli (PhD) is a clinical psychologist, traumatologist and victimologist. Co-founder and Director of the Group Project for Holocaust Survivors and their Children, she has treated, extensively researched and advocated on the impact of crimes against humanity on victims and their families over the globe and is regularly invited worldwide to share her expertise on human rights violations and their consequences.

Danielle Gaucher holds a PhD in Social Psychology from the University of Waterloo. Her research centers on issues of social justice and social change, specifically investigating social-psychological processes that serve to maintain inequality. She is an Assistant Professor of Psychology at the University of Winnipeg, and Adjunct Professor of Psychology at the University of Manitoba.

Mariana Goetz (LLM) is Deputy Director of REDRESS, and has worked in the field of victims' rights and international justice since 1997, including at the Special Court for Sierra Leone and the International Criminal Tribunal for Rwanda. She campaigned for the establishment of the International Criminal Court leading to the Rome Conference and has taught public international law at the London School of Economics. She obtained her law degree from King's College and her Masters from the London School of Economics.

Christophe Herbert is a PhD candidate in Psychiatry at McGill University and a psychologist at the Trauma Clinic of Montreal. For ten years, he has been helping victims of all types to recover from trauma and providing psychological support to workers in dangerous occupations. He is also the founder and publication director of the *Journal international de victimologie*.

Nicholas A. Jones earned a PhD in Sociology from the University of Calgary in 2006. He is an Associate Professor at the Department of Justice Studies of the

University of Regina. His primary research interests include genocide, restorative justice, transitional justice, Aboriginal justice issues, policing and criminological theory.

Fannie Lafontaine obtained her PhD from the National University of Ireland Galway and her Masters from Cambridge University. She is a Professor of Law at Laval University and holds the Canada Research Chair on International Criminal Justice and Human Rights. She founded and directs the International Criminal and Humanitarian Law Clinic and is on the administrative board of Lawyers Without Borders Canada. Her research interests include international criminal law, international humanitarian law, Canadian and international human rights law, Canadian criminal law, and peace and security.

Amissi M. Manirabona holds a PhD in Law from the University of Montreal and is a Professor at the Faculty of Law, University of Montreal. His research interests include environmental criminal law, corporate criminal law, business law and human rights, and international criminal law.

Gabriela Manrique Rueda is a PhD candidate in Criminology at the University of Montreal. Her research interests include the issue of paramilitary groups, social control and the privatization of security in countries at war. Her dissertation focuses on the experience of the dirty work of violence by former combatants of paramilitary groups in Colombia.

Frédéric Mégret is an Associate Professor at the Law Faculty of McGill University and research chair at the Centre for Human Rights and Legal Pluralism. He obtained his PhD from the Graduate Institute of International and Development Studies in Geneva. His principal research interest is in the theoretical dimensions of international criminal justice, the laws of war and human rights.

Katelin H. Neufeld is an MA student in Social and Personality Psychology at the University of Manitoba. She is interested in applying social psychological theories to form evidence-based interventions for current social issues and social in/action. In her undergraduate thesis research, she examined factors that influence public support for providing clean running water to First Nations communities.

Stephan Parmentier (PhD) is a Professor of Sociology of Crime, Law and Human Rights at the Leuven Institute of Criminology and Secretary-General of the International Society for Criminology. His main research interests include political crimes, transitional justice, human rights and the administration of criminal justice.

Charlie Rioux is an MA student at the Department of Psychology at the University of Montreal, where she is studying the effects of temperament and parenting styles on weight gain and substance use. She is also interested in the issues of domestic and sexual violence, abuse, trauma and eating disorders.

Katherine B. Starzyk holds a PhD in Social and Personality Psychology from Queen's University. She is an Assistant Professor at the University of Manitoba in Winnipeg. She investigates the individual and social determinants of collective action. Her goals are to understand how to shift attitudes toward past and present human rights issues, as well as how various frames of such histories or issues affect intergroup relations.

Jill Strauss earned her PhD from the University of Ulster in Northern Ireland and was a Fulbright scholar. She is an Adjunct Assistant Professor teaching conflict resolution at John Jay College of Criminal Justice, City University of New York. Her research involves restorative practices and the visual interpretation of narrative and difficult histories. Jill's artistic projects have been exhibited in Northern Ireland, the United States and Canada.

Hugo van der Merwe holds a PhD in Conflict Analysis and Resolution from George Mason University. He is the Head of Research at the Centre for the Study of Violence and Reconciliation in South Africa. For more than 15 years, he has managed research, advocacy and intervention projects relating to transitional justice in South Africa and on the African continent. He is co-editor in chief of the *International Journal of Transitional Justice.*

Elmar G.M. Weitekamp obtained a PhD in Criminology from the University of Pennsylvania in 1989. He is an Associate Professor of Criminology, Victimology and Restorative Justice at the the University of Tübingen.

Jo-Anne M. Wemmers is a Professor at the School of Criminology, University of Montreal, and head of the research group Victims, Rights and Society at the International Center for Comparative Criminology. She obtained her PhD in criminology from the University of Leiden. She is also director of the journal *Criminologie* and editor of the *International Review of Victimology*. Her research focuses on victims in the criminal justice system. Central themes include victims' justice judgments and therapeutic jurisprudence.

Andrew Woolford holds a PhD in Sociology from University of British Colombia. He is Professor of Sociology and Social Justice and Criminology Research Coordinator at the University of Manitoba. He has conducted comparative research on Indigenous boarding and residential schools in the US and Canada, with a focus on schools in New Mexico and Manitoba. His research interests include genocide studies, transitional justice, informal justice, sociology of law, criminology, social movements and Aboriginal politics.

Acknowledgments

This book is the result of an international workshop, which took place in Montreal from October 25 to 27, 2012. The workshop was made possible with the kind support of the International Centre for Comparative Criminology, University of Montreal, and a Connection Grant from the Social Sciences and Humanities Research Council of Canada (SSHRC). I would like to thank all of the participants for their wonderful input, which made the workshop a success. Thanks as well to Claudine Gagnon and Marie-Eve Rousseau who helped with the organization of the workshop and the editing of the book. Thanks to Laura Westbrook at Brill for her assistance with the copyrights. Finally, I would like to thank Frank and John for their patience and support throughout this project.

Introduction

Jo-Anne M. Wemmers

Crimes against humanity are among the worst crimes known to mankind. Whereas domestic crimes are an offence against the state, crimes against humanity are considered to be so horrible that they constitute an affront against humanity. The notion can be traced back to the 1907 Hague *Convention Respecting the Laws and Customs of War on Land*, which in its preamble refers to the "laws of humanity". However, it was not until after World War II and the atrocities committed by the Nazis that the concept came into regular usage. In 1945 the Nuremburg Tribunal, which was created by the Allied forces in order to try Nazi war criminals, included crimes against humanity (United Nations 1945: Art. 6). Today, crimes against humanity are included in the *Rome Statute of the International Criminal Court*, which defines them as: "murder; extermination; enslavement; deportation or forcible transfer; imprisonment; torture; rape, sexual slavery, enforced prostitution, forced pregnancy, enforced sterilization or any other form of sexual violence; persecution against any identifiable group; enforced disappearance of persons; apartheid; and other inhumane acts of a similar character" (Art. 7). Many of these acts are also considered war crimes when they occur in the context of war. Crimes against humanity, however, constitute crimes regardless of the context in which they take place.

While the Nuremburg Tribunal may have introduced the notion of crimes against humanity, it did not include reparation for victims. Reparation aims to restore the victim and make them whole again. In the case of crimes against humanity, this task is particularly daunting. If reparation is to be healing or therapeutic, then it is not only important to consider what constitutes fair reparation; one must also consider how reparation is obtained and how it affects victims individually and collectively. Proper care must be given to procedures: they should not constitute a secondary victimization by inflicting further harm or suffering on victims. At the same time, however, reparation must respect legal rules and requirements.

In this book we consider how reparation can be healing. In order to develop responses that meet both victims' needs and strict legal criteria, we need to go beyond boundaries and reach across disciplines. A purely psychological framework views victims in isolation from the criminal justice process, and this does not deal adequately with the legal context with which victims are often faced.

At the same time, a purely legal approach fails to take into account the impact of the law on victims and their healing process. Unless consideration is given to the impact of the law on victims, a strictly legal approach could lead to secondary victimization and add insult to injury, thereby increasing victims' suffering. Working with victims means that we have to go beyond boundaries.

This book is intended to fill the existing gaps in how we approach reparation. It provides a multidisciplinary approach to reparation, which brings together the legal framework for reparation with victims' perspectives and the social context in which they live. This provides a rich and nuanced way of looking at reparation, which we feel will help change the way we think about reparation for victims of crimes against humanity and thus advance the ongoing discussions about reparation. The experts participating in this project have different backgrounds such as psychology, criminology sociology, law and human rights. Each chapter approaches reparation differently, which allows the reader to obtain a multidimensional view of reparation. By approaching the same question from different perspectives, this book contributes to the development of a shared discourse, which is multi-layered and integrates key concepts from the different disciplines.

The research presented in this book can be placed on two main axes. The first axis is a continuum based on the focus of the object of study, namely victims. At the one end of this axis lies the individual victim. At the other extreme lies the victimized group. For example, in studying Holocaust victims we could examine individual victims separately or we could examine the different social groups that were victimized, such as Jews or homosexuals.

The second axis is that of the legal versus psychological framework for approaching justice. At the one end is the purely legal approach, which focuses solely on legal principles and questions of law. At the other end is the psychological approach, which focuses purely on victims' needs and the psychosocial impact of reparation on individual and collective victims. The psychological approach is used by clinical and social psychologists and focuses on individual perceptions and group processes. In between these extremes is therapeutic jurisprudence (Wexler and Winick 1996), which considers the psychological effects of legal processes and addresses the impact of the law and legal procedures on those involved such as victims. Together these axes offer an ideal framework for examining reparation for victims of crimes against humanity.

What makes this book unique is its multidisciplinary approach to the question of reparation. It goes beyond the legal rhetoric that dominates much of the discussion on reparation for victims of crimes against humanity and considers the impact of the law and legal procedures on victims. The inadequacy of an exclusively law-driven process was made clear by victims of Canada's Indian Residential Schools, when they requested the creation of a Truth and Reconciliation Commission as part of the Indian Residential School Settlement Agreement (IRSSA) in order to allow them to share their stories with others. Up until that point the IRSSA had focused exclusively on financial reparations for victims, and this was deemed by victims to be insufficient. More recently, on August 7,

2012, the International Criminal Court (ICC) published its first decision regarding reparations for victims of crimes against humanity. That decision has since been appealed both by the defence and by victims, and the ensuing debate will be largely a legal one. In this context, the book is also timely, as it can make a positive contribution to the ongoing discussion in and around the ICC on reparation for victims.

The book is divided into four parts, which correspond with the two axes described above. In Part I, we focus on the psychology of individual victims. This section begins with the contribution by Yael Danieli in which she outlines a multidimensional framework for reparative justice. The author emphasizes that reparative justice is a process and that opportunities for reparation extend beyond the court. Next, Christophe Herbert, Charlie Rioux and Jo-Anne Wemmers present psychological problems that victims commonly develop following violent victimization and consider how such problems may affect victims' participation in reparative justice processes. Part I closes with a chapter by Jo-Anne Wemmers in which she examines the meaning of justice for victims and discusses the opportunities and limitations that this presents for the ICC and its ability to restore justice for victims.

Part II addresses issues surrounding victims and the law. It opens with a discussion by Mariana Goetz on reparative justice at the International Criminal Court. In her chapter, she argues that without developing an institution-wide understanding of key values that underpin how justice can be reparative for victims, the court is unlikely to successfully fulfill its mandate in relation to victims. Next, Amissi Manirabona and Jo-Anne Wemmers present their findings on victims' need for reparation following crimes against humanity. Based on interviews with victims, this chapter aims to give a voice to victims as it explores their attitudes and perceptions with respect to reparation. Part II closes with a chapter by Fannie Lafontaine in which she discusses the problem of prosecution by third states. While this is something that victims desire, it is problematic for many reasons and, as a result, fairly rare. She explores possible alternative justice mechanisms in order to respect a third state's obligations under international law while giving due recognition to justice, accountability and reparation for victims.

In Part III, the focus shifts to the psychology of the group. Beginning with the innovative work of Katherine B. Starzyk, Danielle Gaucher, Gregory Boese and Katelin Neufeld on people's reactions to intergroup harm and reparation, this section examines how groups or society influences the individual. Andrew Woolford examines reparation with respect to the Indian Residential Schools in Canada. Based on his research with the Truth and Reconciliation Commission of Canada, he discusses state involvement in collective healing projects and demonstrates how these processes risk maintaining old colonial relations instead of rebuilding intergroup relationships. Next, Nicholas Jones, Stephan Parmentier and Elmar Weitekamp address the issue of accountability, reparations and justice for victims. Using data from a population-based survey in Bosnia-Herzegovina, they find that the degree to which victims feel that they suffered impacts their perceptions of reparation and the need for retribution. When victims feel that they have suffered greatly, they place more importance on holding offenders to account, recognition by the offender of the harm committed and uncovering the truth than victims who feel that they suffered less. Part III ends with a chapter by Jill Strauss on her work in Northern Ireland. She describes her work with members of opposing social groups in which art combined with conflict resolution approaches is used to facilitate reparation. Through art and storytelling, participants developed new ways of understanding the other group.

Part IV addresses collective reparations and the law. In the first chapter in this section, by Frédéric Mégret, the author critiques the individualistic focus of the ongoing legal discourse regarding reparations and the ICC and argues in favor of collective reparations for victims. Next, Gabriela Manrique Rueda examines the restitution of land in Colombia and concludes that fair reparation for victims should be based on the distributive principle of equity while prioritizing victims' needs and respecting the historical and cultural importance of the land for victims. The final chapter in this part of the book, by Hugo Van der Merwe, considers reparations from three different vantage points: need; human rights and political. Using the South African situation as an example, the author demonstrates that the way reparations are framed can lead to very different priorities in terms of whom and what is repaired.

The last chapter of the book, by Jo-Anne Wemmers, brings together the ideas generated by the individual chapters. It takes into consideration both the individual and the group and how they interact with the law.

References

Convention (IV) Respecting the Laws and Customs of War on Land and its Annex: Regulations concerning the laws and customs of war on land (1907). The Hague, 18 October, available at: www.icrc.org/applic/ihl/ihl.nsf/Article.xsp?action=openDocument&document Id=BD48EA8AD56596A3C12563CD0051653F (accessed July 16, 2013).

United Nations (1945) *Charter of the International Military Tribunal – Annex to the Agreement for the prosecution and punishment of the major war criminals of the European Axis*, available at: http://avalon.law.yale.edu/imt/imtconst.asp#art6 (accessed July 16, 2013).

Wexler, D. and Winick, B. (1996) *Law in a Therapeutic Key*, Durham: Carolina Academic Press.

Part I

The victims

1 Healing aspects of reparations and reparative justice for victims of crimes against humanity[1]

Yael Danieli

This chapter proposes a theoretical framework of reparative justice that is a multidimensional, multidisciplinary, holistic conception of justice for victim/survivors of massive trauma such as crimes against humanity. This framework has been generated from the author's own field work with victim/survivors. Importantly distinguishing between outcome and process, it lays out a variety of ways victim/survivors of multiple situations worldwide have experienced and viewed both the meanings and the related processes of reparation in particular, and of justice in general.

The need for a multidimensional, multidisciplinary integrative framework

Massive trauma causes such diverse and complex destruction that only a multidimensional, multidisciplinary integrative framework is adequate to describe it (Danieli 1998). An individual's identity involves a complex interplay of multiple spheres or systems. Among these are the biological and intrapsychic; the interpersonal – familial, social, communal; the ethnic, cultural, ethical, religious, spiritual, natural; the educational/professional/occupational; the material/economic, legal, environmental, political, national and international. These systems dynamically coexist along the time dimension to create a continuous conception of life from past through present to the future. Ideally, the individual should simultaneously have free psychological access to and movement within all these dimensions of their identity. Each dimension may be in the domain of one or more disciplines, which may overlap and interact, such as biology, psychology, sociology, economics, law, anthropology, religious studies, and philosophy. Each of the many disciplines that deal with these various dimensions has its own views of human nature and it is those that inform what the professional thinks and does.

Exposure to trauma causes a rupture, a possible regression, and a state of being "stuck" in this free flow among dimensions, which I have called fixity. The time, duration, extent and meaning of the trauma for the individual, the survival mechanisms/strategies utilized to adapt to it (Danieli 1985), and post-victimization traumata, especially the conspiracy of silence (Danieli 1982) or the second wound (Symonds 1980) that ubiquitously follow all, but particularly massive, victimization, will determine the elements and degree of rupture, the disruption, disorganization and disorientation, and the severity of the fixity. The fixity may render the individual vulnerable, particularly to further trauma/ruptures, throughout the life cycle. It also may render immediate reactions to trauma (e.g., acute stress disorder) chronic, and, in the extreme, these may become (what I have termed) life-long post-trauma/victimization adaptational styles (Danieli 1985) when survival strategies generalize to a way of life and become an integral part of one's personality, repertoire of defense, or character armor, one's view of oneself and the world, and relationships with others.

These effects may also become intergenerational in that they affect families and succeeding generations (Danieli 1985, 1998). In addition, they may affect groups, communities, societies and nations. Thus, it is not only what the victim has experienced and suffered during the trauma, be it genocide, crimes against humanity, or war crimes. It is what happens after the trauma that crucially affects the long-term, including multigenerational, legacies of the trauma (Keilson 1992).

This multidimensional, multidisciplinary approach allows evaluation of each system's degree of rupture or resilience, and thus informs the choice and development of optimal multilevel intervention. Repairing the rupture and thereby freeing the flow rarely means "going back to normal". Clinging to the possibility of "returning to normal" may indicate denial of the survivors' experiences and thereby fixity. The same holds true for expecting justice (meaning legal accountability) and reparation, or any other single measure in the post-traumatic period, to "make it all OK". When conducted reparatively, justice processes should contribute to lessening the feeling of being stuck, paralyzed or frozen in time for both the survivors and their societies. When justice processes are not so conducted, the justice system may participate in the conspiracy of silence, thus exacerbating the fixity and contributing to the victim/survivor's sense of hopelessness, shame, demoralization and despair.

As Van Boven states,

> In devising strategies of justice it must be borne in mind that lack of reparation for victims and impunity for perpetrators are two sides of the same coin … all efforts and strategies aimed at strengthening the normative framework in the quest for peace and justice must reveal the clear nexus that exists between impunity of perpetrators and the failure to provide just and adequate reparation for victims.
>
> (1999: 16)

Reparative justice takes this further. It says that the justice process as a whole can be reparative, rather than reparation being merely an end result.

Post-traumatic stress disorder and other diagnosed conditions

Victims respond to trauma in rather predictable ways. They suffer shock and a sense of helplessness, and experience difficulty concentrating and sleeping, bodily tensions of all kinds, guilt and shame, anger and profound grief. They re-experience the events of the victimization that many of them dedicate their whole lives to avoiding. Sometimes they also exhibit striking resilience.

The psychological effects in the most seriously affected individuals are defined narrowly in both of the world's primary nosologies, the ICD-10 and DSM-IV. Only in 1980 did the evolving descriptions and definitions of the "survivor syndrome" in the psychiatric literature win their way into the *Diagnostic and Statistical Manual of Mental Disorders* as a separate, valid category of "mental disorder" – 309.81 Post-traumatic Stress Disorder (American Psychiatric Association 1980). My late, dear colleague, one of the only 11 Norwegian Jewish Holocaust survivors, Professor of Psychiatry Leo Eitinger, used to refer to it as "disease of despair". When conducted reparatively, justice processes can be one of the mechanisms that could contribute to lessening the sense of demoralization that is at the root of this despair.

The most directly relevant syndromes include Acute Stress Disorder (ASD) in the short term, and post-traumatic stress disorder (PTSD) in the longer term. PTSD is characterized by intrusive recollections, avoidance reactions, and symptoms of increased arousal. PTSD has been found to be associated with stable neurobiological alterations in both the central and autonomic nervous systems. Additional disorders that frequently occur after exposure to trauma include depression, other anxiety disorders, and substance abuse. Conversion and somatization disorders (expressing emotional reactions via the body) may also occur, and may be more likely to be observed in non-Western cultures (Engdahl *et al.* 1999). Complicated bereavement (Horowitz 1976) and traumatic grief (Prigerson and Jacobs 2006: 613) have been noted as additional potential effects. Shear and colleagues (2001) define "traumatic grief" as a constellation of symptoms, including preoccupation with the deceased, longing, yearning, disbelief and inability to accept the death, bitterness or anger about the death, and avoidance of reminders of the loss. Research shows that traumatic events that are man-made and intentional, unexpected, sudden and violent have a greater adverse impact than natural disasters (Norris 2002).

Exposure to trauma may also prompt review and re-evaluation of one's self-perception, beliefs about the world, and values. Although changes in self-perception, beliefs, and values can be negative, varying percentages of trauma-exposed people report positive changes as a result of coping with the aftermath of trauma (Tedeschi and Calhoun 1996). Survivors have described an increased appreciation for life, a reorganization of their priorities, and a realization that they are stronger than they thought.

The foregoing discussion reveals why it is so important to take a multidimensional approach to justice for victims. The symptoms described above would affect victims' behavior as witnesses and claimants in courts. Not less importantly, they would affect the listeners. All will need psychosocial protection before, during and after their involvement in the process of justice so that they are not vicariously traumatized and so that they do not as a result, as court staff, re-traumatize the victims. Studies of psychotherapists working with victims of massive trauma have shown how, while attempting to protect themselves against their own vicarious victimization, they too participated in the conspiracy of silence (Danieli 1982; Figley 1995). Justice professionals have responded similarly (see examples below). Indeed, the field of traumatology has recognized the necessity for specialized training to protect all involved in these horrific experiences and in bearing witness to them.

Moreover, multigenerational findings uniformly suggest that the process of redress and the attainment of justice are critical to the healing for individual victims, as well as for their families, societies and nations (Danieli 1998). Klain underscores its importance for succeeding generations, "to break the chain of intergenerational transmission of hatred, rage, revenge and guilt" (1998: 293). Thus, although a reparative judicial process, criminal or civil, is one of the healing agents, it does not obviate the need for the other psychological and social elements necessary for recovery.

Cognitive recovery involves the ability to develop a realistic perspective of what happened, what was done by whom and to whom, and accepting the reality that it happened the way it did: for example, what was and was not under the victim's control, what could not be, and why. Accepting the impersonality and randomness of the events also removes the need to attribute personal causality and consequently guilt and false responsibility. An educated and contained image of the events of victimization can potentially free victims from constructing their view of themselves and of humanity solely on the basis of those events. For example, having been helpless does not mean that one is a helpless person; having witnessed or experienced evil does not mean that the world as a whole is evil; having been betrayed does not mean that betrayal is an overriding human behavior; having been victimized does not necessarily mean that one has to live one's life in constant readiness for the re-enactment of victimization; having been treated as dispensable vermin does not mean that one is worthless; and, taking the painful risk of bearing witness does not mean that the world will listen, learn, change, and become a better place (Danieli 1988).

Integration of the trauma must take place in all of life's relevant dimensions or systems and cannot be accomplished by the individual alone. Systems can change and recover independently of other systems. Rupture repair may be needed in all systems of the survivor, in his or her community and nation, and in their place in the international community (Danieli 1998). Reparative justice is a necessary but not sufficient part of this process. In order to facilitate trauma recovery, perspective and integration through awareness and containment must be established so that one's sense of continuity and belongingness is restored. To be healing and even self-actualizing, the integration of traumatic experiences must be examined from the perspective of the totality of the trauma survivor's family and community members' lives.

Victims tell about reparation: process considerations

The importance of procedures in reparative justice and in the context of reparations in particular is illustrated by the mistakes made in the *Weidergutmachung* after World War II. *Wiedergutmachung* literally means to make something good again; in the aftermath of World War II, the term was used to refer to making amends for suffering caused by the Nazi regime. The Allied Powers issued laws restricted to restoring to the original owners property confiscated by the Nazis. This section discusses the lack of procedural considerations in the *Wiedergutmachung* as a way to illustrate the importance of procedure in reparative justice in general and in the context of reparations in particular. The process of applying for German *Wiedergutmachung* (Danieli 1992) was experienced by most survivors as yet an additional series of hardships. These laws did not take into account personal damage to victims of Nazi persecution – those who had suffered in mind and body, or had been deprived unjustly of their freedom, or whose professional or economic prospects had been summarily cut short. Nor did these laws consider assistance to the widows and orphans of those who had died as a result of Hitler's policies. The Western allies placed the responsibility for the reparation of such damages in the hands of the newly constituted German Federal States. It took over two decades of arduous struggle in both psychiatry and law, and a number of stages, for the Federal Republic of Germany to enact on 14 September 1965 the "Final Federal Compensation Law" that finally did differentiate indemnification for persecution of persons from restitution for lost property.

The implementation of the compensation law was traumatic in itself. Kestenberg (1980), a reparation lawyer, states:

> Even when most German officials showed concern and willingness to compensate Jews for the wrong done to them, their so-called "Wiedergutmachung" was only concerned with monetary matters. A moral "Wiedergutmachung" was not planned and did not exist. No one bothered to restore the survivor's dignity. On the contrary, the procedures inherent in some of the paragraphs of the Restitution Laws inflict indignities upon the claimants while at the same time German authorities are elevated to the status of superior beings who adjudge the claimants' veracity and honesty and classify them in accordance with the degree of their damage (Kestenberg 1980: 2–3). Even if the applicant had indeed been confined in a concentration camp, they behaved as if he were trying to extort money from the German government under false pretences.
>
> (Kestenberg 1980: 4)

Crucial to having a claim processed was undergoing a psychiatric examination. To be an examiner, the only requirement was that the psychiatrist be able to speak and write German, not Yiddish or Polish, which were the languages spoken by many survivors. The psychiatric examiner had to determine, and try to express in numbers, how much, or what fraction of the patient's emotional illness was, in his opinion, due to the persecution he suffered, a nearly impossible task due to the cumulative effects of trauma. The law required a minimum of 25 percent damage in order for the applicant to receive a pension (Danieli 1992).

Examiners had intense negative emotional and moral reactions to the process of interviewing and assessing claims. These reactions motivated much of their writings and were poignantly expressed in most of them (Danieli 1982). Eissler speculates that one major reason for the experts' (and the courts) "open or concealed hostility against those who have had to bear great sufferings" has to do with the "universal," archaic, pagan "contempt that man still tends to feel for the weak and humiliated, for those who have had to submit to physical punishment, suffering, and torture" (1967: 1357–8).

These statements reveal that it is essential to provide sensitization and specialized training to those conducting intakes or any other interaction with victim/survivors (Danieli 1994). Krystal and Niederland report:

> Even the hearing of the tales of the concentration camp survivors is so disturbing and traumatic, so abusive to the examiner that some are compelled to avoid obtaining the details of the victims' traumatization. They then arrived at a meaninglessly brief summary of the experiences.
>
> (1968: 341)

Hocking reports cases "where patients have been told by examiners not to describe their experiences, only their symptoms" (1965: 481). I know of some eminent judges who, similarly, instructed victims to "stop telling stories and stick to the facts" (Danieli 2002). Krystal (1971) reviewed 387 cases of restitution claimants examined by him prior to 1967 in the Detroit area. His survey

> showed that the final adjudication of the cases had very little to do with his findings or diagnosis, but correlated very highly and significantly with … where in Germany the case was handled: That is, who in Germany made the final decision.
>
> (Krystal 1971: 218)

He demonstrated that individual restitution offices favored certain types of diagnosis and that the average percentage of disability given by the various restitution offices for a given diagnosis "vary by sometimes as much as 100 percent".

These studies reveal that many process considerations were overlooked in the reparations programs for Jewish survivors of the Holocaust. In particular, those actually working in the reparations programs were inadequately prepared to take statements, let alone able to offer survivors the kind of psychosocial support they needed. These experiences with survivors, in addition to other missed opportunities with victims by the Nuremberg trials (Danieli 2006), inform my assessment that process is key to reparative justice.

Victims tell about reparation: outcome considerations

Reparations require good outcomes, not only good processes. In order to understand more fully the experience of receiving reparation and how it can be helpful to individuals and to their society, and to gain a long-term perspective, I interviewed victim/survivors of the Nazi Holocaust, Japanese and Armenian Americans, victims from Argentina and Chile, and professionals working with them, both in and outside their countries. Through the years, I augmented these with other interviews while working in South Africa, Bosnia and Herzegovina, Rwanda, and Northern Ireland, and with victims of terrorism worldwide.

The following sections briefly detail how victim/survivors view some of the specific outcome components of reparations, namely restitution, compensation, apology, education, and commemoration.

Restitution, compensation and apology

Restitution attempts to replace for the victims what was destroyed or lost. A community-based example is when a perpetrating neighbor rebuilds the house s/he destroyed. Compensation is given when restitution is not possible.

Reparation in general and compensation in particular are psychologically symbolic. Since we cannot monetize a life, any financial reparation largely offers a symbolic function. Of course, financial compensation is not enough. Some people do not need the money at all yet insist on getting financial reparation; for the many who are desperate and need the support, the check is a practical necessity. Compensation is a symbolic act because the victim can never really be compensated. It may be minor in amount but major in significance. For a family in Bhopal as little as $15 a month may make a difference, even though it's a pittance by Western standards.

How does one compensate for three and a half years in concentration camps, or for the loss of a child? It is impossible. How does one pay for a dead person? Ken Feinberg (2005) aptly named his book on the unprecedented effort to compensate the victims of 9/11 *What is Life Worth?* How does one compensate a Korean woman sexually abused by the Japanese in World War II? It's not the money but what the money signifies – vindication. It may signify the government's own admission of guilt and an apology. The actual value, especially in cases of loss of life, is, of course, merely symbolic, and should be acknowledged as such.

The money makes it concrete for the victim the confirmation of responsibility, wrongfulness, that s/he is not guilty, and that somebody cares about it. It does have at least a token meaning. Just a letter of apology does not have the same meaning. In the domestic US justice system, when damage occurs, money is paid; an apology combined with actual or financial restitution goes a long way to make the apology genuine. In Israel some idealists fought against taking money from the Federal Republic of Germany for the crimes perpetrated against them during the Nazi Holocaust:

> I refused. Today I am sorry, because I concluded that I did not succeed to change anything by refusing and the truth is that here and in Israel there are aging survivors who don't have an extended family. The steady sum enables them to go on. The fact that I gave up only left the money in the hands of the Germans. We were wrong.
>
> (quoted in Danieli 1992: 206)

For the Argentinean and Chilean parents of "disappeared" children, it was crucial that the state would admit that a horrible crime was done without any justification or reason; it was not so much about money or apology. But not only were the parents suddenly without their sons and daughters. They were also robbed of the chance of their children helping and standing by them in their old age. In such situations, they saw no place for lump sum compensation; these families needed regular, life-long payments (Danieli 1992).

In Argentina, responses of different victim groups varied. The Madres de Plaza de Mayo organization officially refused economic reparations, which they saw as the Government's attempt to buy their silence, particularly in the absence of social and historical recognition that their children had been political or social opponents, and not criminals. Conversely, the former political prisoners, especially if they had been in prison for a long time, considered economic compensation to be their rightful reparation. Most were young when imprisoned; their imprisonment had deprived them of finishing their studies, progressing in a job, or establishing their own homes and families (Danieli 1992).

Many Japanese Americans felt finally vindicated when, after 50 years, they were compensated for their internment during World War II, not as a Japanese American issue, but as an American constitutional one.

> So many of our people could now talk about it and express deep-seated feelings for the first time in 50 years. That was the positive, therapeutic side. It was only a token compensation. $20,000 won't cover what was lost: jobs, names, all properties, horrible living conditions, dignity or citizenship. It's not the money but what the money signifies. The apology was more important than the amount of money.
>
> (quoted in Danieli 1992: 208)

Legal procedures against the victimizers and financial arrangements compensating the victims are necessary steps in the aftermath of man-made calamities. However, they are not sufficient for societies to recover, which reveals the importance of looking at the societal level, not only the individual level, when talking about reparations. This is where process and outcome merge.

Financial reparations can also serve as an apology, which can also in turn be considered an outcome. The acknowledgement for the victims and survivors' loss and suffering is implied in the bystanders' impulse or effort to repair the damages. The victim is thus embraced back by the society that actively or passively allowed the harm to occur. Reparations open the door to the victim to transcend the trauma in that s/he can learn to trust that

> the same world that created the circumstances for the crime, the victimization, also has created the circumstances for good and kind and compassionate people to be there for each other, for the victims in time of need. Reparations should thus have not only a healing, but also a humanizing, effect on the victims and on society as a whole. The world is not all bad. People are there for people.
>
> (Danieli *et al.* 1996: 446)

Finally, it is important to note that cultural context also determines the success of reparation programs that focus on financial compensation. For example, returning South African activists who had been injured in the struggle against apartheid and had gone into exile, the first to receive reparations in the form of repatriation, sometimes had to fight for the reparation money with their families, who claimed possession of it. The process of giving and receiving reparations must be reparative as well. Victims in South Africa had to demonstrate in order to urge the government to pay them the reparations due.

As one young Rwandan said to me at the 16th Commemorative Conference of the Rwandan Genocide,[2] describing his experience of collecting the monthly reparation allotment for the household from the government, "She just hands you the money. She doesn't even ask me how we are" (Anonymous 2010). This young man was now an adolescent Rwandan orphan head of household and his monthly contacts with the government official were his only regular contacts with an adult. His comments reveal how aligned process and outcome are.

Education

One cannot overestimate the importance for reparation of education, in all its diverse meanings, on all levels and contexts, by all available media. Judicial processes can be useful in establishing a narrative that can be used in schools and other public discourse, to ensure that it is the truth rather than a political construct that is being taught. There should be general awareness on a high level, and information and education about the situation, how it arose, and its consequences, including through the outreach programs of the International Criminal Court (ICC). Streets and museums should be named after victims. Statues of heroes and martyrs should be erected. There should be rooms in colleges, scholarship funds, concerts and theatre performances as memorial services, and educational books.

No matter how indigent the survivors are, education should be afforded for free to their children. A stellar example is Foundation Rwanda, an organization that was established at the wishes of Rwandan women who were raped during the genocide and had a child as a result, to ensure their children born of rapes committed during the 1994 genocide receive full high school education, as do other "survivors", so that they are not discriminated against. Foundation Rwanda also links the mothers to holistic support including medical care, trauma counseling and income-generating activities.

In countries and regions that have moved out of totalitarian regimes into quasi-democratic ones (Argentina, Chile, Eastern Europe, Rwanda), victims and victimizers of the former regime go on living in the same society. As these societies do not have any social and psychological mechanisms to repair past relations, these tensions tend only to penetrate deeper, and thereby are transmitted to the next generations. Therefore, alongside legal and financial steps, in each of these countries, a socio-psychological process is required to work on the after-effects of the traumata with children of both victims and victimizers – to bring them together to think about the overall social responsibility to prevent detrimental tensions erupting again and again within those societies. And medical and psychosocial rehabilitative services should be available for free to victims and their family members for as long as they need such services.

In addition to their traditional training, all professionals, but especially those that interface with victim/survivors and the trauma they have experienced, must also be educated about their responsibilities to protect and promote the human rights of victim/survivors and to consider how their interactions may aid or harm those who have suffered from violence (Sirkin *et al.* 1999).

Commemoration

There is a need for commemoration both for the victims and for society. Rituals are very important; there is no organized society, religion or culture that does not have rituals of memory. Commemorations can fill the vacuum with creative responses and may help heal the rupture, not only internally but also the rupture that the victimization created between the survivors and their societies. This is a mutually reinforcing context of shared memory, shared mourning, a sense that the memory is preserved, that the nation has transformed that memory into a part of its global consciousness and shares the horrible pain. What may be an obligatory one-day-a-year commemorative ritual to some may be experienced by victims as a gesture of sharing and support. This is fundamental to the societal dimension of reparative justice (Danieli 2009b).

Commemoration should be done with great dignity, and with a feeling that while it honors those who suffered or died, it is also done for preventive purposes. Knowing that compensation for loss of lives, health and hopes can never be fully fulfilled, one must maintain the commitment to the "NEVER AGAIN!" motto. Commemoration opens the possibility for intergenerational dialogue, including dialogues between children of survivors and of perpetrators.

In Elie Wiesel's words, "they have no cemetery; we are their cemetery" (1985: 156). Building monuments is important to re-establishing a sense of continuity for the survivors and for the world. Much of the chronic grief, holding on to the guilt, shame, and pain of the past, has to do with these internally carried graveyards. Victim and survivors fear that successful mourning may lead to letting go and thereby to forgetting the dead and committing them to oblivion. The attempt to make these graveyards external creates the need for building monuments so that the survivors might have a place to go to remember and mourn in a traditional way.

Building monuments also has the significant functions of documentation and education – an extension of bearing witness – and of leaving a legacy so that the victims, the survivors and the trauma will not be forgotten. Indeed, perhaps the most important challenge confronting victims, especially of the massive crimes we are deliberating, is the ultimate impossibility of mourning the loss and destruction rendered by such crimes. Isabella Leitner, a Holocaust survivor, expressed it thus:

> I search the sky … in desperate sorrow but can discern no human form … There is not a trace. No grave. Nothing. Absolutely nothing. My mother lived for just a while – Potyo for less than fourteen years. In a way they did not really die. They simply became smoke. How does one bury smoke? How does one place headstones in the sky? How does one bring flowers to the clouds? Mother, Potyo … I am trying to say good-bye to you. I am trying to say good-bye.
>
> (Leitner 1985: 77)

I have read her words aloud in many presentations across the world – in South Africa, Rwanda, Bosnia, Australia, Israel, the Americas – and have been uniformly told by listeners that they have experienced her words as comforting and transforming.

Victims tell us about reparation: the reparative framework

In the following I summarize what the victims and survivors interviewed (paraphrased in part in the foregoing sections) deemed necessary components for healing in the wake of massive trauma. These components are presented as goals and recommendations, organized in a four-tier reparative framework, from the individual, societal, national, and international perspectives.

A Individual

Re-establishment of the victim's equality of value, power and esteem (dignity), the basis of reparation in the society or nation, is accomplished by 1) compensation, both real and symbolic; 2) restitution; 3) rehabilitation; and 4) commemoration.

B Societal

Relieving the victim's stigmatization and separation from society is accomplished by 1) commemoration; 2) memorials to heroism; 3) empowerment; and 4) education.

C National

Repairing the nation's ability to provide and maintain equal value under law and the provisions of justice is accomplished by 1) prosecution; 2) genuine apology; 3) establishing secure public records; 4) education; and 5) creating national mechanisms for monitoring, conflict resolution and preventive interventions.

D International

Asserting the commitment of the international community to combat impunity and provide and maintain equal value under law and the provisions of justice and redress is accomplished by 1) creating and utilizing ad hoc and permanent mechanisms for prosecution (e.g., ad hoc tribunals and the ICC); 2) establishing secure international public records to prevent future denial of the events or their records and/or their destruction (e.g., in the Hague or with UNESCO) in order to help ensure their truths for posterity; 3) education; and 4) creating international mechanisms for monitoring, conflict resolution and preventive interventions (Danieli 1992).

This comprehensive set of components, rather than presenting alternative means or "different types" of reparation, constitutes necessary complementary elements, all of which are needed in different weights in different situations, cultures, and contexts, and at different points in time. It is also crucial that victim/survivors participate in the choice of reparation measures adopted for them, as individuals or collectively (Roht-Arriaza 2004), including in the choice of commemorative and educational measures. Participation is key to ensuring that the process is both fair and perceived as fair.

Courts in general and the ICC in particular should be mindful of this complex, comprehensive reparative framework and its multidimensional implications and avoid the reductionistic impulse to consider any single measure as sufficient to fulfilling the court's reparative mandate. In this context it is important to note that the principle of including victim/survivors in all decision-making processes undertaken on their behalf was recognized by the ICC's Trial Chamber I in the principles it established, the first in the ICC's history, for providing reparations to victims in the court's first conviction, that of Thomas Lubanga Dyilo. The paramount reparative significance of including victim/survivors cannot be overemphasized, and must be implemented as a matter of course. The same is true for trust funds for victims in general and the ICC's Trust Fund for Victims in particular.

Conclusion: toward reparative justice

This chapter reviewed the complex process of the aftermath of massive victimization and the psychological and psychosocial meanings of reparations for victims of crimes against humanity. It showed that the complex nature of trauma requires an equally complex understanding of justice. To emphasize the insufficiently acknowledged significance of the process of claiming and obtaining reparations in particular, the chapter highlighted the distinction between viewing reparations merely as outcome and viewing it from both the process and the outcome perspectives.

More recently, particularly through the years leading to and after the establishment of the International Criminal Court, I have extended the reparative notion to the full judicial process to develop a framework of reparative justice which is crucial to ensuring that the victim/survivors' total experience of justice is healing rather than hurtful and dejecting, and that they are not used merely as witnesses for the case, or, worse, re-traumatized (Danieli 2009a, 2009b; Stover 2005).

Briefly, reparative justice insists that every step throughout the justice experience – from the first encounter of a court with a potential victim/witness through the follow-up of witnesses after their return home to the aftermath of the completion of the case – presents an opportunity for redress and healing. Thus, while restitution, compensation or rehabilitation may come only after the court process has concluded, there are ample opportunities along the way to engage victims of crimes against humanity reparatively throughout the process, thereby enhancing their individual healing and their family's and their community's attempts at healing, even for generations to come.

Methodologically, applying the multidimensional, multidisciplinary approach holding the victims' total experience of justice as its core is not only a mutually reinforcing professional practice, but is fundamental to realizing the true meaning of justice for victim/survivors of the worst crimes.

Notes

1 Parts of this chapter have previously been published in Danieli, Y. (2009) "Massive trauma and the healing role of reparative justice", in C. Ferstman, M. Goetz and A. Stephens (eds) *Reparations for Victims of Genocide, Crimes against Humanity and War Crimes: Systems in place and systems in the making*, The Hague: Martinus Nijhoff, 41–78.

2 Held in Kigali on April 5, 2010.

References

American Psychiatric Association (1980) *Diagnostic and Statistical Manual of Mental Disorders*, 3rd edn, Washington, DC: American Psychiatric Association.

Danieli, Y. (1982) "Therapists' Difficulties in Treating Survivors of the Nazi Holocaust and Their Children", unpublished thesis, New York University.

Danieli, Y. (1985) "The Treatment and Prevention of Long-term Effects and Intergenerational Transmission of Victimization: A lesson from Holocaust survivors and their children", in C.R. Figley (ed.) *Trauma and its Wake*, New York: Brunner/Mazel, 295–13.

Danieli, Y. (1988) "Treating Survivors and Children of Survivors of the Nazi Holocaust", in F.M. Ochberg (ed.) *Post-traumatic Therapy and Victims of Violence*, New York: Brunner/Mazel, 278–94.

Danieli, Y. (1992) "Preliminary Reflections from a Psychological Perspective", in T.C. van Boven, C. Flinterman, F. Grunfeld and I. Westendorp (eds) *The Right to Restitution, Compensation and Rehabilitation for Victims of Gross Violations of Human Rights and Fundamental Freedoms Vol. 12*, Netherlands Institute of Human Rights, 196–213.

Danieli, Y. (1994) "Countertransference, Trauma and Training", in J.P. Wilson and J. Lindy (eds) *Countertransference in the Treatment of Post-Traumatic Stress Disorder*, New York: Guilford Press, 368–88.

Danieli, Y. (1998) *International Handbook of Multigenerational Legacies of Trauma*, New York: Kluwer Academic/Plenum Publishing Corporation.

Danieli, Y. (2002) *Sharing the Front Line and the Back Hills: International protectors and providers, peacekeepers, humanitarian aid workers and the media in the midst of crisis*, Amityville, NY: Baywood Publishing Company, Inc.

Danieli, Y. (2006) "Reappraising the Nuremberg Trials and their Legacy: The role of victims in international law", *Cardozo Law Review*, 27(4): 1633–49.

Danieli, Y. (2009a) "Massive Trauma and the Healing role of Reparative Justice", in C. Ferstman, M. Goetz and A. Stephens (eds) *Reparations for Victims of Genocide, Crimes against Humanity and War Crimes: Systems in place and systems in the making*, The Hague: Martinus Nijhoff, 41–78.

Danieli, Y. (2009b) "Massive Trauma and the Healing Role of Reparative Justice", *Journal of Traumatic Stress*, 22(5): 351–7.

Danieli, Y., Rodley, N.S. and Weisaeth, L. (1996) "Conclusion", in Y. Danieli, N.S. Rodley and L. Weisaeth (eds) *International Responses to Traumatic Stress: Humanitarian, human rights, justice, peace and development contributions, collaborative actions and future initiatives*, Amityville, NY: Baywood Publishing Company, 439–59.

Eissler, K.R. (1967) "Perverted Psychiatry?", *American Journal of Psychiatry*, 123: 1352–8.

Engdahl, B., Jaranson, J., Kastrup, M. and Danieli, Y. (1999) "Traumatic Human Rights Violations: Their psychological impact and treatment", in Y. Danieli, E. Stamatapoulou and C.J. Dias (eds) *The Universal Declaration of Human Rights Fifty Years and Beyond*, Amityville, NY: Baywood Publishing Company, 337–55.

Feinberg, K.R. (2005) *What is Life Worth? The unprecedented effect to compensate the victims of 9/11*, New York: Public Affairs.

Figley, C.R. (1995) *Compassion Fatigue: Coping with secondary traumatic stress disorder in those who treat the traumatized*, New York: Brunner/Mazel.

Hocking, F. (1965) "Human Reactions to Extreme Environmental Stress", *Medical Journal of Australia*, 2(12): 477–83.

Horowitz, M.J. (1976) *Stress Response Syndrome*, New York: Aronson, Inc.

Keilson, H. (1992) *Sequential Traumatization in Children*, Jerusalem: The Hebrew University, The Magnes Press.

Kestenberg, M. (1980) *Discriminatory Aspects of the German Restitution Law and Practice*, paper presented at the First World Congress of Victimology, Washington, DC, August 1980.

Klain, E. (1998) "Intergenerational Aspects of the Conflict in the Former Yugoslavia", in Y. Danieli (ed.) *International Handbook of Multigenerational Legacies of Trauma*, New York: Kluwer Academic/Plenum Publishing Corporation, 279–96.

Krystal, H. (1971) "Review of the Findings and Implications of this Symposium", in H. Krystal and W.G. Niederland (eds) *Psychic Traumatizations: Aftereffects in individuals and communities*, New York: Little Brown, 222.

Krystal, H. and Niederland, W.G. (1968) "Clinical Observations on the Survivor Syndrome", in H. Krystal (ed.) *Massive Psychic Trauma*, New York: International Universities Press, 341–8.

Leitner, I. (1985) *Saving the Fragments*, New York: New American Library.

Norris, F.H. (2002) "Psychological Consequences of Disasters", *PTSD Research Quarterly*, 13(2): 1–7.

Prigerson, H.G. and Jacobs, S.C. (2001) "Traumatic Grief as a Distinct Disorder: A rationale, consensus criteria, and a preliminary empirical test", in M.S. Stroebe, R.O. Hansson, W. Stroebe and H. Schut (eds) *Handbook of Bereavement Research: Consequences, coping, and care*, Washington, DC: American Psychological Association, 613–30.

Roht-Arriaza, N. (2004) "Reparations in the Aftermath of Repression and Mass Violence", in E. Stover and H.M. Weinstein (eds) *My Neighbor, My Enemy: Justice and community in the aftermath of mass atrocity*, Cambridge: Cambridge University Press, 121–40.

Shear, M.K., Frank, E., Foa, E., Cherry, C., Reynolds, C.F., Bilt, J.V. and Masters, S. (2001) "Traumatic Grief Treatment: A pilot study", *American Journal of Psychiatry*, 158: 1506–8.

Sirkin, S., Iacopino, V., Grodin, M. and Danieli, Y. (1999) "The Role of Health Professionals in Protecting and Promoting Human Rights: A paradigm for professional responsibility", in Y. Danieli, E. Stamatopoulou and C.J. Dias (eds) *The Universal Declaration of Human Rights: Fifty years and beyond*, Amityville, NY: Baywood Publishing Company, 357–69.

Stover, E. (2005) *The Witnesses: War crimes and the promise of justice in The Hague*, Philadelphia: University of Pennsylvania Press.

Symonds, M. (1980) "The Second Injury to Victims", *Evaluation and Change*, Special Issue: 36–8.

Tedeschi, R. and Calhoun, L.J. (1996) "The Post-traumatic Growth Inventory: Measuring the positive legacy of trauma", *Journal of Traumatic Stress*, 9: 455–71.

Van Boven, T. (1999) "The Perspective of the Victim", in Y. Danieli, E. Stamatopoulou and C.J. Dias (eds) *The Universal Declaration of Human Rights: Fifty years and beyond*, Amityville, NY: Baywood Publishing Company, 13–26.

Wiesel, E. (1985) "Listen to the Wind", in I. Abrahamson (ed.) *Against Silence: The voice and vision of Elie Wiesel*, New York: Holocaust Library, 156–8.

2 Reparation and recovery in the aftermath of widespread violence

Traditional justice, restorative justice and mental health

Christophe Herbert, Charlie Rioux and Jo-Anne M. Wemmers

Crimes against humanity are "particularly odious offenses in that they constitute a serious attack on human dignity or grave humiliation or a degradation of one or more human beings" (*Rome Statute* 1998). A distinguishing characteristic of crimes against humanity is that they are not isolated or sporadic events, but are either part of a government policy or a widespread practice of atrocities tolerated or condoned by a government or a de facto authority. The types of events a person or group of people might experience with respect to crimes against humanity include murder; extermination; torture; rape; political, racial or religious persecutions; and other inhumane acts (Horton 2005).

Victimization affects people in a multitude of ways, including financially, physically, socially and psychologically. This chapter focuses on the psychological effects of crime. It is important to bear in mind that victimization can affect not only the victim who directly experienced the crime, but also their family and friends. According to a report from the World Health Organization, one in four people will suffer from a mental health disorder during their life (World Health Organization 2001). Research suggests that approximately one in three victims of violent crime is at risk of developing mental health problems (Kilpatrick *et al.* 1987). The risk of developing mental health problems is even greater in cases of crimes against humanity, which are among the most severe form of trauma a human being can experience (Srinivasa Murthy and Lakshminarayana 2006). Some types of crimes against humanity (e.g. rape, torture) are known to be higher risk factors for developing severe and chronic mental health problems (Ullman and Filipas 2001). Certain characteristics of the victimization such as extreme violence and thinking that you are going to die also increase the risk of developing mental health problems (Kilpatrick *et al.* 1987). The widespread and systematic nature of crimes against humanity means that any one victim may experience multiple victimizations in a short time, and may witness the victimization of others and know people who have been victimized as well. Thus, individuals may accumulate victimizations and trauma.

In this chapter we will discuss mental health problems commonly associated with violent victimization in order to better understand how these issues might play out in the case of crimes against humanity. Among the most frequent reactive mental health disorders victims of violence can suffer from, the three main ones are post-traumatic stress disorder, complicated grief and depression. Based on research on victims of violence, we consider how these three mental health conditions can affect victims' ability to participate in criminal justice and restorative justice procedures. Utilizing the wealth of clinical research available with victims of violence, we consider the possible parallels in the case of widespread violence. The chapter closes with a discussion of the implications for authorities' reactions to crime.

Common mental health problems in the aftermath of violent victimization

Since the 1960s psychiatrists and clinical psychologists have conducted a number of studies on the impact of traumatic events, such as criminal victimization, on individuals (Maguire 1991). Three common mental health problems following violent victimization such as murder (of a loved one), attempted murder, rape or violent assault are acute stress disorder and the related post-traumatic stress disorder; complicated grief; and major depression. These disorders may appear following any violent victimization. The only difference between conventional crimes and crimes against humanity is that these reactive disorders are likely to be more prevalent within the population following widespread and systematic violence.

Acute stress disorder and post-traumatic stress disorder

Acute stress disorder (ASD) and post-traumatic stress disorder (PTSD) are psychological reactions that can develop after a traumatic event. An event is considered traumatic if the person experienced, witnessed, or was confronted with one or a series of event(s) that involved actual or threatened death, serious injury, or threat to the physical integrity of self or others (American Psychiatric Association 1994, 2013). It seems clear that the nature of crimes against humanity satisfies this definition.

Following victimization, it is completely normal that the individual experience shock. In most cases the symptoms resolve rapidly. Only when the victim continues to suffer symptoms two days after the event can there be a diagnosis of ASD. The main difference between ASD and PTSD is the duration of symptoms. In the case of ASD, the symptoms last from two days to less than one month. If symptoms last one month or more, it is considered to be PTSD (American Psychiatric Association 1994).

ASD/PTSD symptoms fall into three main categories: 1) intrusion, 2) avoidance and 3) hyperarousal symptoms (American Psychiatric Association 1994). Suffering from ASD/PTSD can significantly limit the functioning of the individual. The intrusion symptoms consist of continually reliving the traumatic event day and night through intrusive memories, flashback episodes, and nightmares about the traumatic event. The avoidance symptoms consist of avoiding any reminder of the traumatic event. Victims may go to great lengths and develop elaborate strategies in an effort to avoid thinking about the traumatic event (despite the intrusion symptoms cited above), speaking about the event or being with people and objects that can awaken traumatic memories. This avoidance can be close to phobic avoidance. Finally, the hyperarousal symptoms means that victims experiences physical (muscular) and emotional tension. For example, they may be constantly on guard even in the absence of any imminent risk. Victims can also suffer from sleep disorders, irritability and concentration difficulties as a result of hyperarousal.

As a result of the symptoms of ASD/PTSD, victims have difficulty functioning. "The disturbance causes clinically significant distress or impairment in social, occupational, or other important areas of functioning or in the individual's ability to pursue some necessary task, such as obtaining necessary assistance" (American Psychiatric Association 1994, pp. 424–9). If the person is unable to work or study because of the effects of the trauma, victimization can have important consequences for their financial wellbeing. Moreover, the illness itself impedes the victim from actively seeking help, which can make recovery all the more difficult.

In Canada, the lifetime prevalence rate of PTSD is 9 percent and the current prevalence rate is 2 percent (van Ameringen *et al.* 2008). However, in countries that have experienced violent conflict the prevalence of PTSD is much higher. For example, research in Rwanda following the genocide found that 24.8 percent of adults still suffered from PTSD eight years after the event (Pham et al. 2004). Also, 30 percent to 44 percent of Rwandan orphans still suffered from PTSD 11 years following the genocide (Schaal et al. 2009). Finally, in a group of 850 women who were raped during the Rwanda genocide, 58 percent to 66 percent suffered from PTSD 11 years after the event (Cohen et al. 2009). It is estimated that around 150,000 to 250,000 women were raped during the Rwanda Genocide (Dyregrov *et al.* 2000). Hence, up to 155,000 female survivors of rape in Rwanda may suffer PTSD. Together these studies show that following mass victimization a large portion of the population suffers PTSD and that the effects can continue to be felt long after the events.

Complicated grief

The type of crime included in crimes against humanity, such as widespread and systematic murder and torture, means that many victims will have lost several relatives or even all of their family. They may have witnessed their execution or been forced to do the killing. These victims may suffer from complicated grief.

Complicated grief is a clinically significant grief reaction that occurs following the death of a loved one. While grief is a normal, healthy reaction to death, complicated grief obstructs the normal grieving process. The principal symptom of complicated grief is that the normal process is not occurring and the bereaved person is "stuck" in the grieving process. People who suffer from complicated grief can have depression, severe anxiety, disbelief, longing, anger, guilt, withdrawal, avoidance and preoccupation with the deceased (Bolton *et al.* 2011).

Complicated grief can be diagnosed when these symptoms persist for 6 months or more after a loss (Shear *et al.* 2011). These symptoms can cause substantial distress for the individual and have been associated with impaired quality of life, social isolation, maladaptive thoughts and behaviors, and increased suicide rates (Young *et al.* 2012). Unable to move on with their life, the person may be unable to work or to function socially, which may add to their distress and their isolation.

This disorder affects 10 percent to 20 percent of people suffering from the loss of a loved one (Jacobs 1993; Middleton *et al.* 1996) in the USA. This means that approximately one million Americans are suffering from complicated grief. The prevalence rate increases in the case of traumatic deaths such as rapes, torture, etc. (Filanosky and Field 2009). Therefore, we can expect the prevalence rate to be higher in the case of crimes against humanity. For example, according to the United Nations Human Rights Commission, we know that during the Rwanda genocide, approximately one million people out of a total population of 7.5 million were killed in a traumatic way (Dyregrov *et al.* 2000).

Major depression

People who have been victims of crimes against humanity can also suffer from depression. Depression is well known to be a comorbid mental health disorder that can occur simultaneously with ASD/PTSD and complicated grief.

Depression symptoms include fatigue or loss of energy almost every day and feelings of worthlessness or guilt almost every day. People who suffer from depression also present impaired concentration and indecisiveness and they suffer from insomnia or hypersomnia (excessive sleeping) almost every day. There is a marked reduction in interest or pleasure in almost all activities nearly every day. People feel restless or slowed down and there is a significant weight loss or gain. Most of the time, they suffer from recurring thoughts of death or suicide (American Psychiatric Association 1994).

According to an epidemiological study, the prevalence rate of depression is 6.7 percent of the adult population in the United States (Kessler *et al.* 2005). Approximately 30.4 percent of people (2 percent of the US population) who suffer from major depression present severe symptoms (Kessler *et al.* 2005). Research shows that the prevalence rate is higher following widespread violence. For example, five years after the genocide in Rwanda, the prevalence rate of depression among a sample of 368 Rwandans was approximately 15.5 percent (Bolton *et al.* 2002). However, depression was much more prevalent among a group of 850 women who had been raped during the genocide in Rwanda: between 65 percent and 81 percent of the women continued to suffer from depression 11 years after the genocide (Cohen *et al.* 2009).

Mental health in the aftermath of crimes against humanity

Widespread and systematic violent victimization, such as crimes against humanity or war crimes, generate a very high prevalence of specific mental health disorders within a population (Srinivasa Murthy and Lakshminarayana 2006). Thus hundreds, thousands or even millions of people within the same territory may simultaneously suffer severe mental health problems in reaction to the violence. These problems significantly reduce their functioning and can become chronic. Effectively, a large group of people within the population will be dysfunctional and these problems can continue for years after the events.

It is important to bear in mind, however, that crimes against humanity often leave the society in shambles with insufficient resources to provide victims with the support they need. When the violence is over, these disorders require a response in terms of public health. However, the number of people suffering from such disorders in this context can exceed the capacity of local organizations distributing mental health care services, thus leaving victims without adequate access to resources.

In addition, when victimization pervades a community, local health care providers may have been victims themselves; on the other hand they may have been perpetrators or, in the case of ethnic conflicts, they may simply be from the same ethnic group as the perpetrators. This can significantly limit the number of therapists that can provide care. Victims may mistrust therapists, whom they see as members of the "other" group. These questions always arise after widespread violence: What side was he for? What did he do? Can I trust him? Therapists may themselves be traumatized and not be neutral – or others may view them as not neutral. This constitutes a major obstacle for treatment, as it is imperative in the therapeutic process that the therapist exercise caring neutrality.

Moreover, after widespread victimization, a society will often be faced with many challenges and will need to set priorities. Basic physiological needs such as food and shelter are more urgent than mental health needs (Wemmers and De Brouwer 2011). Sometimes the mental health needs of victims are underestimated and neglected. Thus, following mass victimization, there may be insufficient resources to adequately address all of victims' needs and victims will not have access to the support that they need. How does a society react to crimes against humanity?

Justice after the conflict

Healing involves a long and painful journey, addressing the pain and suffering of victims, understanding the motivations of offenders, bringing together divided communities, trying to find a path to justice and ultimately peace (Tutu 2003). According to victims, justice is a necessary precondition for peace following mass violence (Wemmers 2010; Raymond 2010). However, justice has many faces and can take on many forms (see Wemmers in this volume). In the following we will examine the role of victims in three different mechanisms of transitional justice: amnesty, criminal prosecution and restorative justice. In particular, we will consider how victims who suffer from reactional mental health problems following victimization are able to function in their roles.

Amnesty

Faced with other priorities, governments may ignore the mental health problems within the population and participate in a form of denial. Amnesty or "pardon" means that the existing authorities want to collectively turn the page and make peace with the past without confronting it or holding offenders accountable for their crimes (Ahmed and Quayle 2009). New governments will sometimes chose amnesty following violent conflict as a way to make peace with former enemies and maintain an otherwise fragile power base.

Mental health problems may be viewed as inconvenient and authorities may encourage people to forget what happened and move on. It would be a mistake to think that amnesty does not require anything from victims. Much like the family members of victims of crimes or other traumatic events such as car accidents, who to tell the victim to stop dwelling on their victimization and to "move on", there is considerable pressure on the victim to forget. But when a person is suffering from ASD/PTSD, complicated grief or depression, this is clearly impossible. As much as victims may want to forget (i.e. avoidance), they may be haunted by intrusive thoughts about the event. While amnesty does not require victims to testify about their victimization and confront their offender, it does require that victims forget about what happened. Not talking about it cannot cure a mental health disorder. Avoidance may in fact make things worse. Silence can augment suffering and contribute to victims' feeling of isolation. Danieli (1988; see also Danieli in this volume) refers to the *conspiracy of silence* wherein the victim's healing is hindered by societal reactions of indifference, avoidance, repression and denial. Without proper support, victims will continue to suffer and the problem will not get better. Hence, mental health problems may persist years after the violence has ended.

Impunity has been shown to augment trauma (Westermeyer and Williams 1998) among refugees. Victims' groups such as the Madres de Plaza de Mayo work tirelessly demanding that justice be done for their missing children. The creation of the International Criminal Court (ICC) by the United Nations is an excellent example of how hard victims' rights groups have worked in order to put an end to impunity for crimes against humanity. While amnesty seems to be used to avoid the past, avoidance does not reduce victims' suffering.

Criminal prosecution

Justice is often thought of in terms of criminal prosecution or retributive justice. For example, the ICC was created in order to end impunity for crimes against humanity and to prosecute those responsible. Criminal prosecution depends largely on victims speaking out and making a complaint to authorities. However, this can be extremely difficult for victims and may require both bravery and tenacity. But speaking out is even more difficult when the victim suffers from depression or ASD/PTSD. The symptoms commonly associated with ASD and PTSD can prevent victims from filing a complaint because they avoid talking about the event and everything that reminds them of it (American Psychiatric Association 1994). Recalling their victimization in detail to authorities may therefore be particularly problematic for anyone suffering from ASD/PTSD. This is further complicated by negative attitudes towards justice. A study based on 2074 people from Rwanda who experienced the genocide demonstrated that PTSD is associated with less positive attitudes towards justice (Pham *et al.* 2004). Hence, victims of crimes against humanity may be reluctant to report their victimization to authorities.

Moreover, once they get up the courage to report their victimization, authorities may not respond well to victims' complaints. The political nature of crimes against humanity can complicate how states react to reports by victims. Preferring amnesty to prosecution, they may blame the victim, not take them seriously, create obstacles discouraging them from reporting, and encourage them to turn the page and forget (Huyse 2003; see also Manirabona and Wemmers in this volume). When this happens victims will not feel validated (Herman 2003). They may perceive this as denial of their victimization, which in turn can augment their suffering (Lemarchand 2011).

Should criminal justice authorities hear their complaint, victims may have difficulty fully understanding the logic of the justice system and how it works. Criminal law is complex and does not follow the lay logic of crime victims. For example, victims are not considered parties in the common law tradition of criminal law. Victims often have great difficulty understanding that they are only considered as witnesses and that they have no status in the trial (Shapland *et al.* 1985; Wemmers and Cyr 2004; Hall 2009). With little knowledge of the law and how it works, victims may not understand or may misinterpret what is going on (Wemmers 2008). Victims may be frustrated by the rules of the court of law and by their personal difficulty in functioning and defending themselves. Victims' expectations concerning the trial may also be unrealistic, which may lead to their disappointment. This incomprehension of the justice system is a major source of dissatisfaction for victims (Shapland 1985; Shapland *et al.* 1985; Kelly and Erez 1999).

The criminal justice system proceeds at its own pace. After having the courage and strength to file a complaint, victims may have to face a long wait before knowing whether or not the case will go to trial. It is especially difficult for a person suffering from ASD/PTSD to be patient, and the resulting incomprehension and anxiety can increase as weeks, months and sometimes years pass before the trial takes place. Long delays can discourage victims, making them feel as though their victimization is not taken seriously while they continue to suffer from the consequences of crime.

Common features of the criminal justice system can lead to a secondary victimization, and the trial is often a source of stress and anxiety for victims (Herman 2003; Parsons and Bergin 2010). Researchers have found that facing the perpetrator in court, remembering details of the crime, and confronting others who were present at the time of the offence can all trigger secondary responses to the initial trauma and increase the intensity and frequency of PTSD symptoms (Rothbaum *et al.* 1992; Campbell and Raja 1999; Herman 2003). Testifying and cross-examination are particularly challenging phases in the criminal justice process for anyone, especially for someone who is already traumatized (Herman 2003).

Judges, prosecutors and lawyers must also take into consideration that victims suffering from a mental health disorder due to victimization are not fully functional. Unfortunately, criminal justice authorities often lack the training to recognize and deal with mental health disorders such as PTSD (Parsons and Bergin 2010). Many difficulties may occur because of such mental health disorders. For example, people suffering from depression may have difficulties reading texts, speaking, or responding to questions because of symptoms they suffer from, and this can seriously hinder their participation in the court (Herman 2003). People suffering from ASD/PTSD may feel guilty for no reason, be confused by the facts (concentration and memory problems due to the hyperarousal symptoms) or be angry (symptom of irritability). Other people may view this as an antipathetic personality whereas it is only the manifestation of a symptom (American Psychiatric Association 2013). Furthermore, the victims may feel ashamed (e.g. in cases of group rape) (American Psychiatric Association 2013), or have a fear of retaliation, fear of not being believed, etc. (Avina and O'Donohue 2002). It is difficult for people who suffer from PTSD to face the perpetrator, to describe exactly what happened and to be questioned about their credibility and reliability (Rothbaum *et al.* 1992; Orth 2002; Herman 2003; Bell 2007).

How authorities treat victims can impact their recovery from crime (Wemmers 2013). There is some evidence that treating victims with respect and providing support to victims throughout the criminal justice process can reduce the risk of secondary victimization (Wemmers 1996; Orth 2002; Parsons and Bergin 2010). One study found that when criminal justice authorities treated victims fairly, informing them and consulting with them throughout the criminal justice process, victims' PTSD symptoms actually diminished (Wemmers 2013). A number of programs use victim advocates to provide social support throughout the trial, to explain the criminal justice process, to provide referrals to the social services, and sometimes to accompany victims to court (Parsons and Bergin 2010; Herman 2003).

In criminal justice there is, however, no guarantee that the trial will end favorably for the victim or that a conviction will end the victim's suffering. If the perpetrator is found not guilty, victims may feel fear for their life and worry about retaliation. They may think the society denies what happened and distrust the justice system. Even when the offender is found guilty by a court of law, it may not necessarily lessen the victim's psychological trauma (Damiani and Vaillant 2003). Indeed, recognition may take place, as well as condemnation, but the symptoms remain and the victim continues to live with the event (intrusive thoughts, etc.). According to Donaldson (2010), one of the priorities of victims is to experience psychological restoration, but this is rarely achieved through criminal prosecution. The first goal of the criminal justice system is not to help victims recover but to punish offenders. This can sometimes result in a misunderstanding between the victims and the justice system.

Thus, while victims may want offenders to be held accountable for their crimes, the criminal justice process is often difficult for victims. For victims with mental health conditions, such as PTSD, it can be anti-therapeutic, augmenting their suffering post-victimization. While these problems apply to criminal courts in general, they can be particularly important for courts dealing with crimes against humanity, such as the ICC, because of the high prevalence of mental health problems following widespread violence.

Restorative justice

Justice can also be restorative. Restorative justice is an attempt to create a non-adversarial dialogue among victims, offenders, and other affected individuals (Parsons and Bergin 2010). Individual measures of restorative justice, such as victim–offender mediation, enable victims to receive apologies, ask questions and explain the true impact of the crime against them. Collective measures of restorative justice include truth commissions and other forms of justice aimed at disclosing the truth regarding the events that transpired and acknowledging the harm done to victims (Huyse 2003; Cunneen 2008). Restorative justice focuses on reducing harm, and as such it recognizes the victim's suffering (Fattah 2001; Zehr 2002).

Like criminal justice, before the restorative justice process can begin, someone, usually the victim, will report the crime. As mentioned earlier, speaking out is not necessarily easy for victims, especially when they are trying to avoid recalling the traumatic event. However, unlike criminal justice, which focuses on proving the offender's guilt beyond a reasonable doubt, restorative justice starts from the premise that the offender committed the crime. If the offender contests his guilt and does not take responsibility for the act, there can be no mediation and the case must go to a criminal court (Zehr 2002; Walgrave 2008; Wemmers and Cyr 2004; Van Camp 2011). This is an important distinction because it means that the victim is never doubted and right from the start the victim is validated. However, it is also an important limitation because the accused has the right to contest the accusations made against them and, therefore, it will never be possible to apply restorative justice in all cases.

When there is recognition by the offender, restorative justice programs such as mediation bring victims and offenders together in a constructive dialogue. However, some authors fear that meeting with the offender may be too stressful (Marshall and Merry 1990; Wemmers and Canuto 2002). As a result, restorative justice programs have been strongly criticized by those working with victims. For example, in Quebec a survey among victim support workers showed that they thought that just mentioning mediation to victims could risk increasing the severity of their PTSD (Côté and Laroche 2002). Similarly, Reeves and Mulley (2000) warn that victims may not be ready to meet their offender. According to these authors, restorative justice instrumentalizes the victim for the offender's benefit (i.e. rehabilitation) much as the criminal justice system uses the victim for the benefit of society. This critique has led some authors to make a distinction between restorative justice, which focuses on the rehabilitation of the offender, and *reparative justice*, which is victim-centered (see Goetz in this volume).

Some studies have examined the impact of restorative justice programs on victims' mental health (Levine 2000). Wemmers and Cyr (2005) found that victims who participated in mediation generally said that they felt better after mediation and that it reduced their fear. Similarly, Umbreit and Coates (1993) found that mediation reduced victims' fear. Strang (2002) found that restorative justice reduced victims' anger and anxiety, increased their self-confidence, and permitted forgiveness. However, a minority of victims in these studies reported more fear, anxiety or depression (Launey 1987; Smith *et al.* 1988; Strang 2002) and felt worse after participating in mediation (Morris *et al.* 1993; Wemmers and Cyr 2005). Close examination of these cases reveals that they should never have gone to mediation in the first place because the offender never accepted responsibility for their behavior (Strang 2002; Wemmers and Cyr 2005).

However, these studies did not include measures of PTSD, complicated grief or depression. One study did look specifically at PTSD and restorative justice (Angel 2005). This study presents interesting results, but the sample is composed of victims whose PTSD is considered subclinical, which means that their symptoms are not strong enough to be considered diagnostic of PTSD. Hence, as in the other studies, these victims were generally healthy.

Victims suffering from reactional mental health problems following victimization may find it very difficult to participate in restorative justice. The presence of mental health problems is considered by professional mediators to be a counter-indicator for mediation (Kustec 2012). This applies both to victims and offenders. Victims suffering from ASD/PTSD might exhibit symptoms such as avoidance and hyperarousal, which would make it very difficult for them to participate in a face-to-face meeting with their offender either in mediation or in a criminal court. It would imply a direct and massive exposure, which is not recommended in cognitive behavioral therapy. Psychologists recommend exposing victims gradually over a number of sessions in accordance with a specific methodology (Kar 2011). Stressful events are considered a risk factor of chronicization of PTSD (Brewin *et al.* 2000). Therefore, when conducted improperly, with disregard for victims' mental health, restorative justice can be anti-therapeutic.

There is evidence, however, that restorative justice can be integrated in victims' therapy. Specifically, a meeting with the offender can be built into the therapy as part of gradual exposure of the victim to stressors. For example, therapists at the Center for the Prevention and Intervention for Victims of Sexual Assault in Laval, Quebec, will refer victims to mediation if they think that the victim is ready for it and it will be helpful for their recovery (Van Camp 2011; Amellal 2006). Because victims' access to mediation is managed by a mental health professional who is working with the victim, there is less risk that the victim will enter into something before they are ready and be shocked, scared or intimidated by the idea of meeting with their offender. This approach is victim-centered because mediation is only initiated when it is in the interest of the victim. Research suggests that when mediation is built into the victim's therapy, this can have positive impact on victims' self-esteem. Victims view it as an accomplishment and are very proud to learn that their therapist thinks that they are ready to confront their aggressor (Van Camp 2011). If for whatever reason the offender is not available for mediation, other techniques that incorporate dialogue can be integrated in the therapy such as writing a letter to their offender (which may or may not ever be sent) or meeting a surrogate offender (Wemmers and Canuto 2002). As Wemmers and Canuto (2002) point out, there are many different restorative justice programs and one of the key characteristics of restorative justice is its flexibility. One can adapt the program to meet the specific needs of the victim.

Restorative justice is often presented as an alternative to retributive justice (Fattah 2001; Cavadino and Dignan 1997). However, this approach has been strongly criticized as being insensitive to victims as it views crime as "conflict" rather than recognizing it as law-breaking behavior (Wemmers and Canuto 2002; Wemmers 2009). Research with victims of serious crimes suggests that victims view restorative justice as complimentary to retributive justice without replacing it (Van Camp 2011). The two serve different purposes and meet different needs. Restorative justice can provide psychological restoration that criminal prosecution is not always able to provide (Donaldson 2010). Criminal justice recognizes the crime committed, while restorative justice recognizes the harm suffered by the victim (Van Camp 2011). Thus, restorative justice programs for victims of serious crimes cannot and should not be used as an alternative for criminal justice.

As mentioned earlier, victims heal at their own pace and these things cannot be rushed. This is no different when it comes to crimes against humanity. Unlike the criminal justice system, where victims are ordered to testify, restorative justice does not order victims to participate. Their participation in restorative justice programs is voluntary and, therefore, victims should have the freedom to not participate or to participate at a later time. Victim participation in collective measures such as truth commissions is also voluntary; however, they can put added pressure on victims to participate. Hamber (2009) reports that victims in South Africa sometimes felt that they, personally, were not yet ready to move on even though they knew that as a nation they had to move forward. While such mechanisms of transitional justice are aimed at the collective level (i.e. to achieve peace), they have implications at the individual level (i.e. for the victims) as well.

Conclusion

Victims of crime can suffer severe mental health problems such as PTSD, complicated grief and depression as a result of violent victimization. When severe violence is widespread, as is the case with crimes against humanity, prevalence rates for reactive mental health problems are high, and may affect as much as 80 percent of victims. Moreover, in the aftermath of systematic violence, victims may not have access to proper mental health care due to high demand and a lack of resources. Without the proper care, these problems may become chronic.

How a society reacts to widespread violence and abuse of power, as it transitions towards a state of peace and stability, is important for the individual and the community. In this chapter we considered three mechanisms of transitional justice: amnesty, criminal justice and restorative justice. We conclude that all three mechanisms have consequences for victims and can augment victims' suffering, thus constituting a form of secondary victimization. However, under the right conditions, retributive and restorative justice can also positively impact victims' recovery from crime.

Victims want justice to be done, and amnesty denies them this and can augment the victims' trauma (Westermeijer and Williams 1998). Accountability is a key aspect of justice (Parmentier and Weitekamp 2007; see also Manirabona and Wemmers in this volume). Victims want to see offenders held to account for their behavior. However, this comes at a cost and requires victims to act as witnesses in the criminal justice process. Without evidence, which often comes from victim-witnesses, there cannot be a conviction.

Besides retributive justice, there is also restorative justice. Restorative justice recognizes the harm suffered by victims and starts from the premise that the offender accepts responsibility for his acts. It has been found to promote victims' wellbeing. While this is not a panacea, victim-centered programs that integrate reparative measures in victims' therapy seem to be quite successful (Amellal 2006). However, victims see restorative and retributive justice as complimentary forms of justice and not as alternatives (Van Camp 2011). Hence, restorative justice will never fully replace criminal justice.

It is not the role of the criminal justice system to help people with a mental health disorder caused by a traumatic event. But symptoms like avoidance, hyperarousal and lack of concentration can make participation in the criminal justice system difficult for victims suffering from such disorders. It is impossible to imagine that we could eliminate victim involvement in the criminal justice process, and there is considerable research suggesting that victims do not want to be shut out of the process but want to be included in it (Shapland *et al.* 1985; Davis and Mulford 2008). What we can do is to educate authorities about the impact of crime on victims' mental health and how common reactive mental health problems such as PTSD, complicated grief and depression might affect their behavior. In addition, we can provide services throughout the criminal justice process in order to make the process easier for victims.

References

Ahmed, A. and Quayle, M. (2009) "Can Genocide, Crimes against Humanity, and War Crimes be Pardoned or Amnestied?" *Amicus Curiae*, 79: 15–20.

Amellal, D. (2006) "VISA: Une école de la dignité", *Entre Nous*, 29(3): 2–5.

American Psychiatric Association (1994) *Diagnostic and Statistical Manual of Mental Disorders*, 4th edn, Washington, DC: American Psychiatric Association.

American Psychiatric Association (2013) *Diagnostic and Statistical Manual of Mental Disorders*, 5th edn, Washington, DC: American Psychiatric Association.

Angel, C. (2005) *Crime Victims Meet their Offenders: Testing the impact of restorative justice conferences on victims' post-traumatic stress symptoms*, unpublished doctoral dissertation, University of Pennsylvania.

Avina, C. and O'Donohue, W. (2002) "Sexual Harassment and PTSD: Is Sexual Harassment Diagnosable Trauma?" *Journal of Traumatic Stress*, 15(1): 69–75.

Bell, M.E. (2007) "Empowerment and Disempowerment for Victims of Intimate Partner Violence: An overview of the effects of criminal justice system practices", in K.A. Kendall-Tackett and S. Giacomoni (eds) *Intimate Partner Violence*, Kingston, NJ: Civic Research Institute.

Bolton, J., Skritskaya, N., Mancini, A.D. and Keshaviah, A. (2011) "Complicated Grief and Related Bereavement Issues for DSM-5", *Depression and Anxiety*, 28(2): 103–17.

Bolton, P., Neugebauer, R. and Ndogoni, L. (2002) "Prevalence of Depression in Rural Rwanda based on Symptom and Functional Criteria", *Journal of Nervous and Mental Disease*, 190: 631–7.

Brewin, C.R., Andrews, B. and Valentine, J.D. (2000) "Meta-analysis of Risk Factors for Posttraumatic Stress Disorder in Trauma-exposed Adults", *Journal of Consulting and Clinical Psychology*, 68(5): 748–66.

Campbell, R. and Raja, S. (1999) "Secondary Victimization of Rape Victims: Insights from mental health professionals who treat survivors of violence", *Violence and Victims*, 14: 261–75.

Cavadino, M. and Dignan J. (1997) "Reparation, Retribution and Rights", *International Review of Victimology*, 4: 153–82.

Cohen, M.H., Fabri, M., Cai, X., Shi, Q., Hoover, D.R., Binagwaho, A., Culhane, M.A., Mukanyonga, H., Karegeya, D.K. and Anastos, K. (2009) "Prevalence and Predictors of Posttraumatic Stress Disorder and Depression in HIV-infected and At-risk Rwandan Women", *Journal of Women's Health*, 18(11): 1783–91.

Côté, M.C. and Laroche, N. (2002) "Le réseau des CAVAC du Québec et la justice réparatrice", in J. Wemmers and K. Cyr (eds) *La justice réparatrice et les victimes d'actes criminels* (*Les cahiers de recherche criminologiques* no. 37). Montréal: Université de Montréal, Centre international de la criminologie comparée.

Cunneen, C. (2008) "Exploring the Relationship between Reparations, the Gross Violation of Human Rights and Restorative Justice", in D. Sullivan and L. Tift (eds) *Handbook of Restorative Justice: A Global Perspective*, New York: Routledge, 355–68.

Damiani, C. and Vaillant, C. (2003) *Être victime, aides et recours*, Paris: Vuibert.

Danieli, Y. (1988) "Treating Survivors and Children of Survivors of the Nazi Holocaust", in F.M. Ochberg (ed.) *Post-traumatic Therapy and Victims of Violence*, New York: Brunner/Mazel, 278–94.

Davis, R. and Mulford, C. (2008) "Victims' Rights and New Remedies: Finally getting victims their due", *Journal of Contemporary Criminal Justice*, 24: 198–208.

Donaldson, C. (2010) "Restorative Justice: Linking the Law and Health", *Perspectives in Public Health*, 130: 254–5.

Dyregrov, A., Gupta, L., Gjestad, R. and Mukanoheli, E. (2000) "Trauma Exposure and Psychological Reactions to Genocide Among Rwandan Children", *Journal of Traumatic Stress*, 13(1): 3–21.

Fattah, E.A. (2001) "Victims' Rights: Past, present and future – a global view", in R. Cario and D. Salas (eds) *Œuvre de Justice et Victimes*, vol. 1, Paris: L'Harmattan Sciences Criminelles.

Filanosky, C. and Field, N.P. (2009) "Continuing Bonds, Risk Factors for Complicated Grief, and Adjustment to Bereavement", *Death Studies*, 34(1): 1–29.

Hall, M. (2009) *Victims of Crime: Policy and practice in criminal justice*, London: Routledge.

Hamber, B. (2009) *Transforming Societies after Political Violence*, Dordrecht: Springer.

Herman, J.L. (2003) "The Mental Health of Crime Victims: Impact of legal intervention", *Crime and Delinquency*, 33: 468–78.

Horton, G. (2005) "Dying Alive: A legal assessment of human rights violations in Burma", available at: www.ibiblio.org/obl/docs3/Horton-2005.pdf (accessed August 15, 2013.

Huyse, L. (2003) "Justice", in D. Bloomfield, T. Barnes and L. Huyse (eds) *Reconciliation After Violent Conflict: A handbook*, Stockholm: International Institute for Democracy and Electoral Assistance, 97–115.

Jacobs, S.C. (1993) *Pathologic Grief: Maladaptation to loss*, Washington, DC: American Psychiatric Press.

Kar, N. (2011) "Cognitive Behavioral Therapy for the Treatment of Post-traumatic Stress Disorder: A review", *Neuropsychiatric Disorder and Treatment*m, 7: 167–81.

Kelly, D.P. and Erez, E. (1999) "Victim Participation in the Criminal Justice System", in R.C. Davis, A. Lurigio and W. Skogan (eds) *Victims of Crime*, 2nd edn, Thousand Oaks, CA: Sage, 231–44.

Kessler, R.C., Chiu, W.T., Demler, O. and Walters, E.E. (2005) "Prevalence, Severity, and Comorbidity of Twelve-month DSM-IV Disorders in the National Comorbidity Survey Replication (NCS-R)", *Archives of General Psychiatry*, 62(6): 617–27.

Kilpatrick, D.G., Saunders, B., Veronen, L.J., Best, C.L. and Von, J.M. (1987) "Criminal Victimization: Lifetime prevalence, reporting to police and psychological impact", *Crime and Delinquency*, 33(4): 479–89.

Kustec, V. (2012) *Le point de vue des intervenants travaillant avec les jeunes contrevenants sur le recours à la médiation dans les cas de crimes graves*, Masters thesis, University of Montreal.

Launey, G. (1987) "Victim-Offender Conciliation", in B. McGurk, D.M. Thorton and M.Williams (eds) *Applying Psychology to Imprisonment: Theory and Practice*, London: Her Majesty's Stationery Office, 274–300.

Lemarchand, R. (2011) *Forgotten Genocides: Oblivion, denial and memory*, Philadelphia: University of Pennsylvania Press.

Levine, M. (2000) "The Family Group Conference in the New Zealand Children, Young Persons, and Their Families Act of 1989 (CYPandF): Review and evaluation", *Behavioral Sciences and the Law*, 18: 517–556.

Maguire, M. (1991) "The Needs and Rights of Victims of Crime", in M. Tonry (ed.) *Crime and Justice: A review of the research*, Chicago: University of Chicago Press, 363–433.

Marshall, T. and Merry, S. (1990) *Crime and Accountability: Victim/Offender Mediation in Practice*, London: Her Majesty's Stationery Office.

Middleton, W., Burnett, P., Raphael, B. and Martinek, N. (1996) "The Bereavement Response: A cluster analysis", *British Journal of Psychiatry*, 169: 167–71.

Morris, A., Maxwell, G.M. and Robertson, J.P. (1993) "Giving Victims a Voice: A New Zealand experiment", *Howard Journal of Criminal Justice*, 32(4): 301–21.

Orth, U. (2002) "Secondary Victimization of Crime Victims by Criminal Proceedings", *Social Justice Research*, 15: 313–25.

Parmentier, S. and Weitekamp, E. (2007) "Political Crimes and Serious Violations of Human Rights: Towards a criminology of international crimes", in S. Parmentier and E. Weitekamp (eds) *Crime and Human Rights*, vol. 9 of *Sociology of Crime, Law and Deviance*, Amsterdam: Elsevier, 109–44.

Parsons, J. and Bergin, T. (2010) "The Impact of Criminal Justice Involvement on Victims' Mental Health", *Journal of Traumatic Stress*, 23(2): 182–8.

Pham, P.N., Weinstein, H.M. and Longman, T. (2004) "Trauma and ASD/PTSD in Rwanda", *Journal of the American Medical Association*, 292: 602–12.

Raymond, E. (2010) *L'expérience de la justice pour les victimes des crimes contre humanité*, Montreal: University of Montreal.

Reeves, H. and Mulley K. (2000) "The New Status of Victims in the UK: Opportunities and threats", in A. Crawford and J. Goodey (eds) *Integrating a Victim Perspective Within Criminal Justice*, Aldershot: Darmouth Publishing, 125–46.

Rome Statute of the International Criminal Court (1998), Article 7, available at: http://untreaty.un.org/cod/icc/index.html (accessed August 15, 2013).

Rothbaum, B.O., Foa, E.B., Riggs, D.S., Murdock, T. and Walsh, W. (1992) "A Prospective Examination of Posttraumatic Stress Disorder in Rape Victims", *Journal of Traumatic Stress*, 5: 455–75.

Schaal, S., Elbert, T. and Neuner, F. (2009) "Narrative Exposure Therapy versus Interpersonal Psychotherapy: A pilot randomized controlled trial with Rwandan genocide orphans", *Psychotherapy and Psychosomatics*, 78(5): 298–306.

Shapland, J. (1985) "The Criminal Justice System and the Victim", *Victimology: An International Journal*, 10: 585–99.

Shapland, J., Wilmore, J. and Duff, P. (1985) *Victims in the Criminal Justice System*, Aldershot: Glower Publishing.

Shear, M.K., Simon, N., Wall, M., Zisook, S., Neimeyer, R., Duan, N., Reynolds, C., Lebowitz, B., Sung, S., Ghesquiere, A., Gorscak, B., Clayton, P., Ito, M., Nakajima, S., Konishi, T., Melhem, N., Meert, K., Schiff, M., O'Connor, M.F., First, M. and Sareen, J., (2011) "Complicated Grief and Related Bereavement Issues for DSM-5", *Depression and Anxiety*, 28(2): 103–17.

Smith, D., Blagg, H. and Derricourt, N. (1988) "Mediation in the Shadow of the Law: The South Shore experience", in R. Matthews (ed.) *Informal Justice?*, London: Sage Publications, 123–50.

Srinivasa Murthy, R. and Lakshminarayana, R. (2006) "Mental Health Consequences of War: A brief review of research findings", *World Psychiatry*, 5(1): 25–30.

Strang, H. (2002) *Repair or Revenge: Victims and restorative justice*, Oxford: Clarendon Press.

Tutu, D. (2003) "Foreword", in D. Bloomfield, T. Barnes and L. Huyse (ed.) *Reconciliation After Violent Conflict: A handbook*, Stockholm: International Institute for Democracy and Electoral Assistance, 4.

Ullman, S.E. and Filipas, H.H. (2001) "Predictors of ASD/PTSD Symptom Severity and Social Reactions in Sexual Assault Victims", *Journal of Traumatic Stress*, 14(2): 369–89.

Umbreit, M.S. and R.B. Coates (1993) "Cross-Site Analysis of Victim Offender Mediation in Four States", *Crime and Delinquency*, 39(4): 565–85.

Van Ameringen, M., Mancini, C., Patterson, B. and Boyle, M.H. (2008) "PostTraumatic Stress Disorder in Canada", *CNS Neuroscience Therapy*, 14(3): 171–81.

Van Camp, T. (2011) *Meeting Victims' Needs: The interplay between victim and restorative justice policies and victims' needs*, doctoral thesis, University of Montreal.

Walgrave, L. (2008) "Restorative Justice: An alternative for responding to crime", in G. Shoham, O. Beck and M. Kett (eds) *International Handbook of Penology and Criminal Justice*, Boca Raton, FL: CRC Press, 25–50.

Wemmers, J.M. (1996) *Victims in the Criminal Justice System*, Amsterdam: Kugler.

Wemmers, J.M. (2008) "Victim Participation and Therapeutic Jurisprudence", *Victims and Offenders*, 3: 165–91.

Wemmers, J.M. (2010) "The Meaning of Fairness for Victims", in P. Knepper and S. Shoham (eds) *International Handbook of Victimology*, Boca Raton, FL: Taylor & Francis Group, 27–43.

Wemmers, J.M. (2013) "Victims' Experiences in the Criminal Justice System and Their Recovery from Crime", *International Review of Victimology*, 19(3): 221–33; published online before print, July 15, 2013, doi: 10.1177/0269758013492755.

Wemmers, J.M. and Canuto, M. (2002) "Expériences, attentes et perceptions des victimes à l'égard de la justice réparatrice: Analyse documentaire critique", Ottawa: Ministère de la Justice.

Wemmers, J.M. and Cyr, K. (2004) "Victims' Perspectives on Restorative Justice: How much involvement are victims looking for?" *International Review of Victimology*, 11(2–3): 259–74.

Wemmers, J.M. and Cyr, K. (2005) "Can Mediation Be Therapeutic for Crime Victims? An evaluation of victims' experiences in mediation with young offenders", *Canadian Journal of Criminology*, 47(3): 527–44.

Wemmers, J.M. and De Brouwer, A.M. (2011) "Globalization and Victims' Rights at the International Criminal Court", in J.J.M. Van Dijk and R. Letschert (eds) *The New Faces of Victimhood: Globalization, transnational crimes and victim rights*, Dordrecht: Springer, 279–302.

Westermeyer, J.M. and Williams, M. (1998) "Three Categories of Victimization Among Refugees in a Psychiatric Clinic", in J.M. Jaranason and M. Popkin (eds) *Caring for Victims of Torture* (pp. 61–87), Washington, DC: American Psychiatric Association.

World Health Organization (2001) "Mental Disorders Affect One in Four People: The world health report", available at: www.who.int/whr/2001/media_centre/press_release/en/index.html (accessed August 15, 2013).

Young, I.T., Iglewicz, A., Glorioso, D., Lanouette, N. Seay, K., Ilapakurti, M. and Zisook, S. (2012) "Suicide, Bereavement and Complicated Grief", *Dialogues in Clinical Neuroscience*, 14(2): 177–86.

Zehr, H. (2002) *The Little Book of Restorative Justice*, Intercourse, PA: Good Books.

3 Restoring justice for victims of crimes against humanity

Jo-Anne M. Wemmers

The creation of the International Criminal Court (ICC) following the adoption of the *Rome Statute* in 1998 was seen by many as a huge step forward for victims of crimes against humanity. Not only would the ICC address impunity, which throughout history countless tyrants had enjoyed, but it also included procedural rights for victims. Hence, many experts praised the ICC because of the hope that it held for victims. Indeed, the ability of the ICC to provide justice to victims was viewed by some experts in and around the court as the key to its success. In other words, if the court is unable to provide justice to victims, it will be considered a failure.

If the ICC is to provide justice to victims, then we need to ask ourselves, what is justice according to victims and why is it important? People's perceptions of fairness are the central object of study in organizational justice theory, an area of social psychology. It has been used in a wide variety of settings including civil litigation (Thibaut and Walker 1975; Lind and Tyler 1988), people's contacts with police (Tyler 1990), and more recently victims' contacts with the criminal justice system (Wemmers 1996; Strang 2002; Orth 2002).

In this chapter we will examine the concept of justice and what it means to victims of crimes against humanity. In particular, the chapter addresses the different elements of justice that are available to the ICC with respect to the reparation of victims. This analysis reveals the opportunities and limitations of the ICC for restoring justice to victims.

What is the function of fairness information?

Research suggests that fairness information helps us to manage uncertainty (Van den Bos and Lind 2002). Victimization is a source of tremendous uncertainty. It can shatter one's view of the world and cause one to question his or her fundamental beliefs. Things we thought we could expect – such as trustworthiness in others – suddenly don't apply anymore. Following victimization, victims often need to reorganize or restructure their view of the world (Wemmers 2003; Hill 2004). Fairness information provides victims with an order that they can understand as they rebuild their view of the world. The need for certainty becomes all the more important in the context of war, where the entire society is plunged into chaos. Daily routines, such as children going to school or families going to the local market, are no longer possible. What we thought was an organized and structured world becomes unpredictable and frightening.

Trust between social groups is important for social harmony, and society's desire to rebuild social trust following widespread violations of human rights is a driving force behind transitional justice. Transitional justice is justice associated with political change (Roht-Arriaza 2006). It refers to the range of approaches that states may use to address past human rights violations and includes both judicial measures, such as the International Criminal Court, and non-judicial measures. How a state deals with its legacy of violence and violations of human rights is crucial in determining how the society recovers. Regardless of the approach followed, a key notion is that of justice and, in particular, restoring justice. Hence, justice information can play a vital role in the recovery of the individual as well as society.

Concern for the healing or therapeutic effects of judicial measures is central to therapeutic jurisprudence. Therapeutic jurisprudence looks at various aspects of the law to determine whether or the extent to which substantive rules of law, legal procedures, and the roles or actions of legal actors are therapeutic. Conversely, it considers how the same processes can be non-therapeutic, or even anti-therapeutic. This approach draws attention to the emotional and psychological side of the law and the legal process. It envisages the law as an instrument of healing and rehabilitation and suggests that the law's anti-therapeutic effects should be minimized when such minimalization is consistent with other justice values such as equality and proportionality. In other words, victim healing should never trump the rights of the accused; however, whenever possible, we should consider victim healing as well as other legal values such as due process.

While the term "therapeutic jurisprudence" is relatively new in victimology, the idea that victims are affected by their experiences in the criminal justice sytem is not at all new. Victimologists have used the term "secondary victimization" to refer to the anti-therapeutic effects of insensitive reactions by others, including criminal justice officials. Lawmakers and those who apply the law need to be aware of how their actions affect the mental health of victims.

Fair procedures have been found to be therapeutic because of their ability to reduce uncertainty and restore a sense of order (Wemmers 2011; Van Camp 2011). In victims of crime, the perception of fairness is associated with well-being. Victims who feel that they have been treated fairly exhibit lesser trauma symptoms (Byrne *et al.* 1996; Wemmers and Cyr 2005, 2006; Wemmers 2011).

For example, research on victims' trauma symptoms and their justice judgments – that is, the judgments that victims form on whether justice has been accomplished – shows that victims who feel that they were treated fairly by authorities exhibit less trauma symptoms than victims who feel that they were treated unfairly. And while both groups get better over time, those who feel they were treated fairly appear to heal faster. In other words, when victims feel that they have been treated fairly, this seems to help their recovery from their victimization. Research with victims of crimes against humanity suggests that justice not only contributes to reconciliation, it is often viewed as a prerequisite for it (Van der Merwe 2008; Raymond 2010). In the context of crimes against humanity, justice information may not only help individual healing but also facilitate social transformation.

The meaning of fairness

What is fairness, and when do victims feel that justice has been restored? Fairness is a multidimensional concept. Originally, social psychologists focused on distributive justice or outcomes as a determinant of fairness judgments. Distributive justice refers to the fair distribution of outcomes or resources. For example, equity theory (Walster *et al.* 1973) posits that fairness is achieved in social relationships when people feel that they are getting back what they are putting into a relationship. Applying this to crime victims, for example, we might consider the proportionality between the victims' suffering and the offenders' punishment (see Jones *et al.* in this volume). This is just one example of fair distribution. Other criteria also exist, such as need-based distribution and distribution based on equality.

Since the 1970s justice theorists have argued that how outcomes are reached also affects people's fairness judgments. Thibaut and Walker (1975) were the first to identify procedural justice as a key determinant of people's justice judgments. In their view, procedures matter because they ensure fair outcomes. They were a means to an end. However, in order to maximize outcomes, people want to maintain control over the decision and control over the process. Decision control essentially means being able to accept or reject an outcome or decision. Process control refers to having a voice or input into the process, for instance, the ability to present evidence. Process control is also referred to as "voice" in the justice literature (Folger 1977). The importance of voice is a well-established finding in justice research (Van den Bos 1996). People consistently judge procedures as fairer when they are given an opportunity to express themselves in the decision-making process. Of the two types of control, Thibaut and Walker argued that process control was more important to people, because in a crisis situation (where a decision needed to be made quickly), they were willing to forfeit decision control to a third party (i.e. a judge) but always wished to maintain process control (1975).

Later, Lind and Tyler (1988; Tyler and Lind 1992) presented the relational or group-value model of procedural justice. In their view, procedural justice is not instrumental, or a means to an end, but rather normative. Procedural justice, they argue, sends a message to group members about their value or worth to the group. Their notion of procedural justice is rooted in social identity theory, which posits that part of people's identity is defined as a shared identity derived from membership with social groups (Tajfel and Turner 1979). People want to belong to valued groups and to feel that they are worthy group members. Hence, a key determinant of procedural justice is being treated with dignity and respect. When victims feel that they are treated with respect or "standing", this sends the message that they are valued members of society (Wemmers 1996).

The importance of standing is reflected in the *cushion of support* that fair procedures provide authorities. Repeatedly, research has shown that fair procedures make unfavorable outcomes more palatable (Lind and Tyler 1988; Laxminarayan 2012). Victims will maintain their confidence in criminal justice authorities, despite their inability to catch and punish offenders, provided the procedures followed are thought to be fair (Wemmers 1996). Unable to guarantee favorable outcomes, the authorities must guarantee fair procedures in order to maintain people's confidence and support. Otherwise they risk losing public support and, with it, their power base (Tyler 1990).

More recently, justice theorists have argued that we need to separate justice that stems from interpersonal interactions with authorities from the perceived fairness of formal rules and procedures. Authors like Colquitt (2001) argue that procedural justice refers to the formal rules and procedures. For example, procedural justice would refer to victims' legal right to participate in procedures before the court, or their right to request reparation. They reserve the term *interactional justice* for the quality of the treatment or the interpersonal interactions between individuals. Interactional justice could describe victims' interactions with the police or, in the case of the ICC, it could refer to victims' interactions with representatives of the court, with their legal representative or with representatives of non-governmental organizations working with victims.

Another source of justice is informational justice, referring to the quality of the information and explanations that are shared with those subject to the procedure. Essentially, it refers to the communication or outreach activities that aim to inform victims about the activities of the court.

While justice theory recognizes the importance of the group, it essentially focuses on the individual. This may be sufficient when we are studying victims of conventional crimes, where our focus is often the direct victim of crime. But what about mass victimization, where there is a need to restore justice at the level of society as well as at the individual level? Do the same dimensions of justice apply? In their work on justice judgments and collective victimization, Lillie and Janoff-Bulman (2007) distinguish "macro" justice, focusing on the needs of group, from "micro" justice, focusing on the needs of individual. They find that the justice literature focuses largely on individual justice judgments and does not readily lend itself to macro-level justice. In the context of crimes against humanity, both levels of justice may be relevant for victims. In his research with victims and the South African Truth and Reconciliation Commission, Brandon Hamber (2009) notes that victims spoke of these two levels of justice and the possible conflict between the two. For example, some of the victims in his study saw quite clearly that South African society needed to move forward but that they themselves did not feel ready yet; they commented on how they would sometimes have to temporarily put aside their needs for the good of the group.

Justice in the context of the ICC

What might this mean in the context of the ICC and justice for victims? Does the court have several different kinds of justice available to it? If so, what kinds of justice does the court have available in order to provide justice for victims? In the following, we will examine the research on the different elements of justice in relation to victims in order to get a better understanding of the possible implications for the ICC.

The ICC was established in order to put an end to impunity. In so far as the court can arrest, try and punish offenders, the court may be a source of distributive justice for victims. Up until now, however, it has proven to be very difficult for the court to catch and punish offenders. Since first opening its doors in 2002, the ICC has condemned only one person, Thomas Lubanga Dyilo. Moreover, Dyilo was only tried and condemned for his recruitment of child soldiers. Efforts to widen the charges against Dyilo in order to include sex crimes were unsuccessful. Many of the accused persons for which the court has issued a warrant are still at large and have so far successfully evaded justice. In addition, in at least two cases, the accused has been released following failure by the pre-trial chamber to confirm the charges.[1]

Clearly, principles of justice must prevail and the court must not condemn someone in the absence of evidence. However, the slow progress of the court regarding the conviction of offenders is indicative of the difficulties it faces and its limited ability to provide distributive justice to victims.

Besides punishment, the court can also provide reparation for victims. Reparation is a key feature of the ICC and one that distinguishes it from its predecessors. Recently, Trial Chamber 1 emphasized the importance of reparation for the court when it reiterated a statement made previously by Pre-Trial Chamber 1 that "the court's success is, to some extent, linked to the success of its reparation system" (*The Prosecutor v. Dyilo* 2012 ICC 01/04–01/06, par. 178.7). What is the court's reparation system? Specifically, Article 75 (2) of the *Rome Statute* states that "the Court may make an order directly against a convicted person specifying appropriate reparations to, or in respect of victims, including restitution, compensation and rehabilitation". Hence, reparation by the court is contingent upon conviction. This means that distributive justice, in terms of reparation by the offender, will be no more frequent than there are convictions. It may even be less frequent than convictions if offenders are insolvent.

Given the limitations on the court's ability to provide distributive justice, what other possibilities does the court have to restore justice for victims? Can the court still provide justice to victims, even when is unable to punish offenders? Or is the dream of universal justice for victims an illusion?

Victim reparation

While outcomes are important, victims seeking reparation do not care only about outcomes; the procedure can be more important than the outcome. A study by

Bruce Feldthusen and colleagues (2000) with victims of organized sexual violence found that for many victims the reparation process was more important than the actual outcome. They found that victims enter the reparation process with therapeutic goals. These include obtaining recognition of their victimization and of the accountability of the offender. In particular, victims placed great value on being treated with dignity and respect throughout the decision-making process. Victims knew that full financial reparation would not always be possible and often this was not their primary goal (Van Hecke and Wemmers 1992).

Traditionally in criminal law, reparation has focused on financial compensation for losses. However, today, thanks in part to research with victims, reparation has come to mean much more than compensation, including symbolic and future-oriented forms of reparation. These include rehabilitation, which means providing victims with medical, psychological, legal and social services aimed at promoting their healing; and guarantees of non-repetition, or crime prevention measures, aimed at preventing such crimes from happening again.

On August 7, 2012, Trial Chamber 1 of the ICC published the court's first decision pertaining to reparation. Interestingly, the offender in this case, Thomas Lubanga Dyilo, was insolvent; yet rather than forgo the possibility of ordering reparation, the Chamber ordered that the ICC's own Trust Fund's resources be used to provide reparation to victims. The Chamber did not specify the exact reparation to be made to each victim. Instead, it outlined a general framework.

According to the Chamber, reparations are to be applied in a broad and flexible manner (Art. 180) and, in view of this, should not be limited to victims who participated in the case (Art. 187). This broad approach implies possible recognition of a large number of victims despite the limited opportunities to obtain offender accountability through the court. From a therapeutic perspective, the opportunity for a large number of victims to obtain recognition through reparation and hence to regain a sense of justice is very important, both for individual healing and for the recovery of society as a whole.

The Chamber endorsed a five-step implementation plan through which victims will obtain reparations. Specifically, the ICC's Trust Fund, together with the Registry and the Office of Public Counsel for Victims in consultation with a group of experts are expected to follow these steps:

1. Identify localities which ought to be involved in the reparations process. In this respect, any localities mentioned in the judgment would be of particular importance.
2. Launch a consultation process in the identified localities to enable victims to express their propositions and priorities regarding reparations.
3. Assess the harm suffered by victims (the assessment conducted by a team of experts).
4. Carry out public debates in each locality in order to explain the reparations principles and procedures and to address victims' expectations.
5. Collect proposals for collective reparation measures that are to be developed in each locality.

Following this consultation process, the Trust Fund will present selected proposals to the Chamber for approval. Once these are approved by the Chamber they can be implemented.

What is interesting about the framework for reparation endorsed by Trial Chamber 1 is its attention to procedural and informational justice. To begin with, the Chamber outlines procedural rules for the decision-making process, which include victims at various stages of the process. In terms of procedural justice, the formal rules set out by the Chamber are a possible source of fairness. The Chamber has ordered that consultations take place in the affected areas. Research with victims of crime indicates that fair procedures are those in which victims are given an opportunity to participate: where they can speak and be heard. Authors such as Doak (2011) argue that victims should have the opportunity to give a free narrative account. The inclusion of a consultation process in order to enable victims to directly express their views has the potential to enhance the perceived fairness of the reparations process.

In addition to the formal procedures, the quality of victims' interactions with authorities can be a source of justice. Sanders *et al.* (2000) argue that interpersonal interactions between victims and criminal justice officials are more important for victims than procedural rights that permit only indirect participation. For example, research with victims of crime has found that when victims are treated equally poorly in terms of respect for their rights, they will judge their treatment more favorably when they had personal contact with authorities than when there was only indirect contact (Wemmers 1996; Wemmers and Cyr 2006). Victims are more likely to feel that they were treated fairly when they have been able to actually meet with criminal justice authorities, because interpersonal contact allows victims to express themselves to authorities and to be heard. Hence interactional justice is very important and sometimes more important than other types of justice.

With whom will victims before the ICC be interacting? The Chamber's decision indicates that representatives of the court, namely the Trust Fund together with the Registry and the Office of Public Counsel for Victims, will be responsible for the consultations and that they will take place in the affected areas. Holding consultations in the affected areas encourages victim participation. Victims who engaged in the consultation process will know that their views were heard. But is it feasible to think that these representatives will be able to meet with all victims? One needs to keep in mind that the situations currently before the court involve countless victims. For example, the war in the Democratic Republic of Congo (DRC), which is just one of the eight situations currently before the court, has been qualified by human rights organizations as the deadliest war since World War II (Shah 2010). Some 5.4 million people are believed to have died since the outbreak of fighting in 1998, and it is estimated that another 45,000 people die each month that the conflict continues (International Rescue Committee 2008). Moreover, the pre-existing economic, social and institutional weaknesses in this African country amplify the profound impact of wartime victimization (Stevens *et al.* 2007). Concretely, this means that in just this one situation millions of victims are affected.

Given the large number of victims touched by these crimes, is it more realistic for authorities to meet with non-governmental organizations (NGOs) working with victims in the affected areas than with the victims themselves? Thus victims' participation in the consultation process would be indirect, namely via NGOs. This offers victims the advantage of protection, as they would not have to speak out publicly about their victimization. However, it also means that victims would lose process control in the decision-making process. This control would effectively be transferred to others acting on their behalf. How would this affect victims' justice judgments? Is consultation with an NGO sufficient, or do victims necessarily want to express their views to the court?

Similarly, victim participation at the court is indirect: the ICC's rules and procedures indicate that victims will be represented at the court by a lawyer (their legal representative). This has the advantage that one legal representative can represent many victims. Also, speaking via their legal representative has as an advantage that victims do not have to testify before the court. Research shows that testifying can be a stressful experience for victims (Herman 2003). Having their representative speak on their behalf may allow victims' voices to be heard without the added stress of testifying (Wemmers 2010).

The disadvantage of legal representation is that the victims will not directly have a voice in procedures. Their legal representatives are their voice. Hence, their experience with the court will be largely determined by their interpersonal contact with their legal representative. Moreover, while the first cases before the ICC involved a relatively small number of victims, sometimes with their own legal representative (e.g. Luc Walleyn represented one victim in the Dyilo case), later cases have included many more victims and by extension a legal representative sometimes represents hundreds of victims. In these cases, victims will interact with non-governmental organizations (NGOs) in the field, which then relay information about victims to legal representatives, who in turn represent groups of victims before the court. Thus, victims' evaluations regarding interactional justice will largely be determined by actors outside of the court.

In addition, the inclusion of public debates in each locality in order to explain the process may positively affect informational justice judgments. While such debates cannot guarantee that each victim will receive all of the information that they need, it is a step in the right direction. It shows that the Chamber values information and recognizes its importance for victims. Informational justice is characterized by accurate, candid, comprehensive and timely information. Research with victims shows that information has a positive impact on their justice judgments. Victims who are informed of the developments in their case, even if the news may not always be good, still maintain positive justice judgments. In contrast, victims who are not kept informed feel that they were treated unfairly (Wemmers and Raymond 2011). Information is key to maintaining support in the face of unfavorable outcomes. These findings illustrate the therapeutic value of information for victims. Information reduces uncertainty and as such, it can help reduce anxiety, restore trust or confidence in authorities and provide victims with a sense of justice. Importantly, it is not about giving victims good news, but about being honest and candid with them.

The court's outreach activities can also contribute to victims' assessments of informational justice. In this way, the court has a key role to play in informing victims about its activities and explaining decisions. Outreach workers can use various media such as the radio but also meetings with community members in order to inform victims. There have been attempts to move the trials "on location", which have not been successful due to security concerns. While the court has been active in its outreach activities, posting live video of trials on the internet, we assume that victims, for example in villages in the DRC, have been on the internet and viewed the trial. This is where victims' legal representatives and the NGOs play a vital role. In addition, for security reasons, it will at times be better for the court to not contact victims directly and instead to communicate through their representative or an NGO. Other challenges such as illiteracy and language barriers can also justify that a NGO assists the victim in order to facilitate communication.

When considering victims' justice judgments, it is important to bear in mind that reparation does not take place in a vacuum. Research with fairness judgments shows that people can substitute one type of fairness information for another. For example, if victims do not have information about the outcome but do have information about the procedure, then they will base their fairness judgments on the available information. When new fairness information becomes available, they will modify their justice judgments accordingly. Research shows that what comes first matters (Van den Bos and Lind 2002). In other words, if a person has information about the process before they have information about the outcome, then their overall justice judgment will be more strongly affected by procedural justice than if they were to know the outcome first. Likewise, if victims have outcome information before they have process information, then their fairness judgments will be more strongly influenced by distributive justice. Hence, when considering victims' justice judgments and the court, it is important to bear in mind victims' experiences with the court prior to any possible reparations.

Challenges

Possible problems may arise with the Chamber's five-step plan for reparations, however, when any localities or groups are excluded. While the Chamber has emphasized the need to be inclusive, it is possible that groups not included in the judgment may be shut out of the consultation process. Failing to recognize a group, the court effectively sends a message to victims that their group is not important, which may result in secondary victimization.

In addition, while the Chamber makes it clear that the process should be transparent, it does not specifically address the final decision-making process: which proposals will be selected and which will be approved? Assuming that choices will have to be made, there is a potential for conflict as groups compete for recognition. However, fair procedures can make an unfavorable outcome more palatable. Hence, if the consultation and information for victims described in the Chamber's plan provides victims' with a sense of procedural fairness, this may make it easier for victims to accept it when they do not receive reparation.

However, the Chamber's decision of August 7, 2012 was not yet final. On August 13, the defense moved to appeal their decision and on August 29, appeal was granted. Even though the Chamber had not ordered the offender to pay reparation and any reparation would made using the Trust Fund's resources, which come largely from donations from member states, the defense appealed the decision. They claimed that the Chamber's approach to reparation was too broad. For example, the Chamber explicitly included victims of sexual violence in their decision; however, Thomas Lubanga Dyilo was not formally accused of sex crimes. The Chambers broad approach was good news for victims of sex crimes who failed in their attempts to have sex crimes included in the charges. It offered the hope of recognition for these victims after they had been shut out of the trial.

Even victims appealed the decision. The legal teams of two victims, known as V01 and V02, in the Lubanga case claimed that the Chamber made an error when it rejected individual requests for reparation. This reflects the competition between victims for scarce resources. While the Chamber emphasized collective reparations, in order to get the most out of the court's limited resources, victims of the case focused on their individual interests. This highlights the difference between justice at the macro or group level and justice at the micro level. Despite efforts by Chamber 1 to shift the focus away from individual needs to the collective need, these two victims were apparently reluctant to forfeit their individual interests for the collective needs of the group. This stresses how important it is that the court establishes just procedures in order to ensure the fair distribution of reparation.

Procedural justice in terms of formal rules and procedures of the court is a main source of justice over which the court has control. While other types of justice are partially or completely out of its control, it has considerable control over the court's procedures. However, victims' rights may be vehemently contested within the court. For example, if we consider victim participation at the court, to date some 700 decisions relating to victim participation have been made by the various Chambers of the court (Hérbert-Dolbec 2012). This is a major problem from a procedural justice perspective because the different decisions have sometimes been conflicting. This creates inconsistencies in the treatment of victims across cases.

However, the disagreement surrounding victims' rights applies not only to victim participation but equally to victim reparation. While I was at the ICC, I studied attitudes within the court towards reparation and found that while everyone agrees that there should be clear rules, there is no agreement as to what those rules should be and who should make them (Wemmers 2011). The *Rome Statute* states that the court will establish principles of reparation (Art. 75.1). For some people at the court, this means creating general principles, which would guide Chambers in their decisions. For others, general principles would result from legal decisions. The principles established by Chamber 1 were a first attempt at establishing some sort of general principles on reparations. As is the case with victim participation, the court might make multiple and even contradictory decisions regarding reparation. Any inconsistencies in the decisions across Chambers could undermine victims' procedural justice judgments. When people see like cases being treated differently, they tend to judge the treatment as unfair (Leventhal 1980).

Conclusion

The ability of the ICC to provide justice to victims is not limited to its ability to provide favorable outcomes to victims, which is a good thing considering that so far, with only one conviction in ten years, the court has provided very little to victims in terms of outcomes. Reparation by the offender is contingent upon a conviction, and so it too offers little in way of distributive justice.

Besides distributive justice, there exist many other forms of justice including procedural justice, interpersonal justice and informational justice. However, not all of these types of justice are completely within the power of the court. Given the large number of victims involved in the cases before the court, the ICC can offer little in terms of interactional justice. Victims' primary source of interactional justice will be with those outside of the court such as their legal representative and NGOs working on their behalf.

Unable to guarantee fair outcomes, the court needs to make use of other forms of justice, especially procedural and informational justice, over which it has control. The evaluation plan proposed by Trial Chamber 1 is a step in the right direction. Its inclusive approach and special attention for victims is to be applauded. However, we will have to see how much of it remains intact following decisions by other Chambers including the Appeals Chambers. Procedural justice lies squarely in the hands of the court. Consequently, those working within the court need to think about the therapeutic and anti-therapeutic effects of their decisions.

The success of the ICC depends on its ability to provide justice to victims. If the court is not seen to be a source of justice, it will lose the support of the victims for whom it was created in the first place. The power of the court as an instrument for transitional justice lies in its ability to restore justice, and with it, restore a sense of order or certainty to victims of crimes against humanity. If the court can restore justice to victims, it promises to be a powerful tool for transitional justice, helping to heal both victims and the society in which they live.

Note

1 Bahar Idriss Abu Garda in the Sudan situation or Callixte Mbarushimana in the Congo.

References

Byrne, C., Kilpatrick, D., Beaty, D. and Howley, S. (1996) "Has Victims' Rights Legislation Improved CJS Treatment of Crime Victims?", paper presented at the Annual Meeting of the International Society for Traumatic Stress Studies, San Francisco, November.

Colquitt, J.A. (2001) "On the Dimensionality of Organizational Justice: A construct validation of a measure", *Journal of Applied Psychology*, 86(1): 386–400.

Doak, J. (2011) "The Therapeutic Dimension of Transitional Justice: Emotional repair and victim satisfaction in international trials and truth commissions", *International Criminal Law Review*, 11(2): 263–98.

Folger, R. (1977) "Distributive and Procedural Justice: Combined impact of 'voice' and improvement of experienced inequity", *Journal of Personality and Social Psychology*, 35: 108–19.

Lind, E.A., MacCoun, R.J., Ebener, P.A., Felstiner, W.L.F., Hensler, D.R., Resnik, J. and Tyler, T.R. (1989) *The Perception of Justice: Tort litigants' views of trial, court-annexed arbitration, and judicial settlement conference*, Santa Monica, CA: Rand, The Institute for Civil Justice.

Hamber, B. (2009) *Transforming Societies after Political Violence*, Dordrecht: Springer.

Herman, J.L. (2003) "The Mental Health of Crime Victims: Impact of legal intervention", *Journal of Traumatic Stress*, 16(2): 159–66.

Hérbert-Dolbec, M.L. (2012) "Victimes et l'impunité dans le droit des conflits armés", paper presented at the Student Circle of the Quebec Society of International Law, Montreal, March.

International Rescue Committee (2008) "Mortality in the Democratic Republic of Congo: An ongoing crisis", available at: www.rescue.org/sites/default/files/resource-file/200–7_congoMortalitySurvey.pdf (accessed December 1, 2011).

Laxminarayan, M. (2012) *The Heterogeneity of Crime Victims: Variations in legal preferences*, Nijmegen: Wolf Legal Publishers.

Leventhal, G.S. (1980) "What Should Be Done with Equity Theory?" in K.J. Gergen, M.S. Greenberg and R.H. Willis (eds) *Social Exchange: Advances in theory and research*, New York: Plenum Press, 27–55.

Lillie, C. and Janoff-Bulman, R. (2007) "Macro versus Micro Justice and Perceived Fairness of Truth and Reconciliation Commissions", *Peace and Conflict: Journal of Peace Psychology*, 13(2): 221–36.

Lind, E.A. and Tyler, T. (1988) *The Social Psychology of Procedural Justice*, New York: Plenum Press.

Orth, U. (2002) "Secondary Victimization of Crime Victims by Criminal Proceedings", *Social Justice Research*, 15(4): 313–25.

Raymond, E. (2010) *Justice pour les crimes contre l'humanité et génocides : Point de vue et attentes des victimes*, Masters thesis, University of Montreal, Canada.

Roht-Arriza, N. (2006) "The New Landscape of Transitional Justice", in N. Roht-Arriza and J. Mariezcurrena (eds) *Transitional Justice in the 21st Century: Beyond truth and justice*, Cambridge: Cambridge University Press, 1–16.

Sanders, A., Hoyle, C., Morgan, R. and Cape, E. (2001) "Victim Impact Statements: Don't work, can't work", *Criminal Law Review*, 6: 447–58.

Shah, A. (2010) "The Democratic Republic of Congo, Global Issues", available at: www.globalissues.org/article/87/the-democratic-republic-of-congo (accessed December 1, 2011).

Stevens, G. and Raphael, B. (2007) "Public Effects of Disasters and Mass Violence", in *Encyclopaedia of Stress*, Amsterdam: Elsevier Academic Press, 814–15.

Strang, H. (2002) *Repair or Revenge: Victims and restorative justice*, Oxford: Clarendon Press.

Tajfel, H. and Turner, J.C. (1979) "An Integrative Theory of Intergroup Conflict", in W.G. Austin and S. Worchel (eds) *The Social Psychology of Intergroup Relations*, Monterey: Brooks/Cole, 33–47.

The Prosecutor v. Dyilo (2012) ICC 01/04–01/06.

Thibaut, J. and L. Walker. (1975) *Procedural Justice: A psychological analysis*, Hillsdale: Wiley.

Tyler, T. (1990) *Why People Obey the Law*, New Haven: Yale University.

Tyler, T. and Lind, E.A. (1992) "A Relational Model of Authority in Groups", in M.P. Zanna (ed.) *Advances in Experimental Social Psychology*, vol. 25, San Diego: Academic Press, 115–91.

Van Camp, T. (2011) Is *there More to Restorative Justice than Mere Compliance to Procedural Justice? A qualitative reflection from the victims' point of view*, Doctoral thesis, University of Montreal.

Van den Bos, K. (1996) "Procedural Justice and Conflict", unpublished thesis, Leiden University.

Van den Bos, K. and Lind, E.A. (2002) "Uncertainty Mangement By Means of Fairness Judgments", Advances in Experimental Social Psychology, 34: 1–59.

Van der Merwe, H. (2008) "What Survivors Say About Justice: An analysis of the TRC victim hearings", in A. Chapman and H. Van der Merwe (eds) *Truth and Reconciliation in South Africa*, Philadelphia: University of Pennsylvania Press, 23–44.

Van Hecke, T. and Wemmers, J. (1992) *Schadebemiddelingsproject Middelburg*, Wetenschappelijk Onderzoek- en Documentatiecentrum, 116, Arnhem: Gouda Quint bv.

Walster, E., Walster, G.W. and Berscheid, E. (1973) "New Directions in Equity Research", *Journal of Personality and Social Psychology*, 25(2): 151–76.

Wemmers, J.M. (1996) *Victims in the Criminal Justice System*, Amsterdam: Kugler Publications.

Wemmers, J.M. (2003) *Introduction à la Victimologie*, Montreal: Les Presses de l'Université de Montréal.

Wemmers, J. (2010) "Victims' Rights and the International Criminal Court: Perceptions within the court regarding victims' right to participate", *Leiden Journal of International Law*, 23(3): 629–43.

Wemmers, J.M. (2011) "Victims in the Criminal Justice System and Therapeutic Jurisprudence", in E. Erez, M. Kilchling and J. Wemmers (eds) *Victim Participation in Justice and Therapeutic Jurisprudence: A comparative analysis*, Durham: Carolina Academic Press, 67–85.

Wemmers, J.M. and Cyr, K. (2005) "Can Mediation be Therapeutic for Crime Victims? An evaluation of victims' experiences in mediation with young offenders", *Canadian Journal of Criminology and Criminal Justice*, 47(3): 527–44.

Wemmers, J.M. and Cyr, K. (2006) *Victims' Needs Within the Context of the Criminal Justice System*, Montreal: International Centre for Comparative Criminology.

Wemmers, J. and Raymond, E. (2011) "La justice et les victimes: L'importance de l'information", *Criminologie*, 44(2): 157–70.

Part II

Victims and the law

4 Reparative justice at the International Criminal Court

Best practice or tokenism?

Mariana Goetz

Traditionally governments have regarded justice for victims as "a complication, an inconvenience and a marginal phenomenon" (Van Boven 1993: 53). In this light, the establishment of the International Criminal Court's (ICC's) *sui generis* regime that enables victims to participate in proceedings and to claim reparation has been a significant achievement (*Rome Statute of the International Criminal Court* 1998). The ICC Statute establishes a groundbreaking mandate, which brings victims of genocide, war crimes and crimes against humanity to the forefront of the criminal justice process in a manner designed to protect their physical and psychological wellbeing as well as their dignity and privacy (Art. 68.1). The ICC Statute provides a full range of justiciable rights to an effective remedy and reparation, in support of these norms. Its legal framework sets out that victims in general have the right to be informed of decisions that concern them (R. 92.3). Where their interests are affected, they may participate in the justice process by presenting their views and concerns at appropriate stages of proceedings; this is to a certain extent modeled on the civil law notion of *partie civile*, where civil parties can be enjoined into criminal proceedings with a view to claiming damages (Art. 68.3, Rr. 89–91). They are entitled to protection and support in relation to their appearance before the court (Art. 43.6). In addition, they can be granted legal aid to ensure their legal representation in proceedings through a court-appointed common legal representative (R. 16.1.(b)). Finally, the ICC enables individual victims to claim reparation for harm suffered, which may be awarded on an individual or collective basis (Rr. 94 and 97). A Trust Fund for Victims has been established for the purpose of implementing reparations, having both the function of implementing reparations awards ordered by the court, and providing assistance to victims outside the scope of reparation (Arts. 75; 79).

While the ICC's reparative mandate is enabling and groundbreaking on paper, this chapter questions its effect in practice, considering what reparative justice means and what it should mean in the context of crimes against humanity. To what extent is the ICC's judicial process able to deliver justice to victims that is "reparative" in practice? On paper, the ICC legal framework not only meets international best-practice standards on victims' rights, such as those encapsulated in the UN *Basic Principles and Guidelines on the Right to a Remedy and*

Reparation, it is an example of international best practice in its own right. Nonetheless, it is argued here that without developing an institution-wide understanding of key values that underpin how justice can be reparative for victims in practice, both procedurally and substantively, the court is unlikely to successfully fulfill its mandate in relation to victims. In this regard it is useful to first unpack the notion of reparative justice as well as what is implied by a "victim-centered approach".

Reparative justice

The concept of reparative justice developed here is distinct from the better-known notion of *restorative justice*, which seeks to promote dialogue between the victim and the offender in order to collectively resolve the aftermath of the offence (Marshall 1999: 5, Braithwaite 2002: 11). The notion of *reparative justice* presented here is singularly concerned with victims' experience of the justice process in terms of how far it repairs the specific harm suffered.

In order to define reparative justice, I have broken the concept down into three components. The first relates to the notion of reparation, as developed from its classic definition under international law. This encompasses the substantive scope and content of an outcome or award aimed at redressing specific harm. The second relates to the significance of procedural rights that facilitate and enable victims to effectively seek and obtain an appropriate final outcome. This includes practical rights, such as victims' rights to information about proceedings, victims' ability to access proceedings, including their degree of voice and control over them, and rights to protection and support, including legal assistance. Finally, the third component of reparative justice relates to more subtle and nuanced aspects of victims' experiences of the justice process. These include perceptions of fairness, trust and interactional justice, as well as notions drawn from trauma theory such as solidarity, empathy and empowerment that go to the core of restoring victims' dignity.

For most international law and international human rights scholars, the starting point in understanding the notion of reparation is the often-cited Chorzów Factory case, which held that "reparation must, as far as possible, wipe-out all the consequences of the illegal act and re-establish the situation which would in all probability have existed if that act had not been committed" (*Germany v. Poland* 1928: 49). This founding judgment gives a clear indication of the need to consider a range of consequences that result from the violation in order to redress the specific harms endured. There is an inherent recognition that in order to "wipe-out all the consequences", a range of measures may be needed in addressing the multifaceted aspects of victims' suffering in a holistic manner (Danieli 2009: 75). Beyond this, the Chorzow case provides us with limited insights in relation to victims' experiences of reparation awards in terms of their scope, content and delivery, given that the case relates to reparation between states *inter se*.

Turning to international human rights jurisprudence, the United Nations Human Rights Committee has developed a body of jurisprudence setting out the scope of adequate and effective remedies as well as appropriate reparation. In *Bautista de Arellana v. Colombia*, the Committee stated that "administrative remedies cannot be deemed to constitute adequate and effective remedies ... in the event of particularly serious violations of human rights" (*Bautista de Arellana v. Colombia* 2005: par. 82), and in *Albert Wilson v. the Philippines*, the Committee stated that "although compensation may differ from country to country, adequate compensation excludes purely "symbolic" amounts of compensation" (2003: 17). In *Bozize v. Central African Republic* (1994), the Committee referred to the duty to provide "appropriate" compensation. By this, the Committee indicates that token amounts of compensation or merely symbolic gestures are not satisfactory in the face of serious human rights violations.

Similarly, the Committee Against Torture, in *Ali Ben Salem v. Tunisia* (2005), made it clear that "[r]edress should cover all the harm suffered by the victim, including restitution, compensation, rehabilitation of the victim and measures to guarantee that there is no recurrence of the violations". In the case of *Kepa Urra Guridi v. Spain* (2002) the Committee indicated that monetary compensation was insufficient. Thus, in terms of the scope and extent of the substantive award of reparation, among the established criteria, reparation should be appropriate and comprehensive, including restitution, compensation, rehabilitation, satisfaction, and guarantees of non-repetition. It should also be non-tokenistic and address the specific harm suffered.

Gender-specific criteria and best-practice standards have also developed: for instance demonstrating an increased recognition of the victimization suffered by family members, and designing reparations intended to empower women and girls rather than placing them back into situations of subordination or discrimination that normalizes violence against women (Coalition for the Rights of Women and Girls 2008).

Developments at domestic as well as international levels have, over time, established similar criteria in terms of the multifaceted elements relevant to individual experiences of justice from a procedural point of view. The UN *Declaration of Basic Principles of Justice for Victims of Crime and Abuse of Power* (United Nations 1985) and the UN *Basic Principles and Guidelines on Victims' Right to a Remedy and Reparation* (United Nations 2005), which encapsulate international best-practice standards at domestic and regional levels, recognize that victims have both procedural and substantive rights to justice.

Victims' rights to information, protection, support and effective access to justice constitute procedural rights to the remedy, while the reference to adequate, effective and prompt reparation refer to the substantive or material outcome. However, the procedural and substantive rights to a remedy and reparation are intrinsically linked, reflecting victims' multifaceted needs for information, knowledge and truth about what transpired, as well as seeing perpetrators investigated and held to account, followed by adequate consideration of the specific harm suffered and appropriate reparation to redress it. In some instances the procedural remedy, fulfilled by an investigation, trial or conviction, may in and of itself constitute full or partial reparation (*Tibi v. Ecuador* 2004 and others), in that the outcome is sufficient to repair the harm, in and of itself. However, the very serious violations that are the subject of the ICC's jurisdiction will generally involve large numbers of people, and will often involve significant and multidimensional needs relating to the victims' past, present and future realities (Danieli 2009). Thus, reparative justice encapsulates both process and end result, both of which become enmeshed in the victims' continuing reality.

International human rights jurisprudence, reflected for instance in the 2005 UN Principles, set out qualitative standards that correspond to both procedural and substantive rights. The 2005 Principles outline victims' rights to remedies for gross violations of international human rights law and serious violations of international humanitarian law, namely, the kinds of violations over which the ICC has jurisdiction. The 2005 Principles set out the following process-related rights:

- equal and effective access to justice;
- adequate, effective and prompt reparation for harm suffered;
- access to relevant information concerning violations and reparation mechanisms (United Nations 2005: Principle IX).

In addition, the *Nairobi Principles on Women and Girls' Right to a Remedy and Reparation* have set out process rights of importance to women. These recognize the need to guarantee the full participation of women and girls in every stage of the reparation process, including design, implementation, evaluation and decision-making, as well as the need for procedures that are sensitive to gender, age, cultural diversity and human rights and that take into account women's and girls' specific circumstances and their dignity, privacy and safety (Coalition for the Rights of Women and Girls 2008).

The jurisprudence of the Inter-American Court has gone further, and in ensuring victims' voices are represented and heard in open court as claimants, it has incorporated their views in its judgments: for instance, detailing how reparations are to be put in place, or imposing on the violating states precise directives on how the judgment should be published domestically or what rate of interest to apply to compensation schemes. For instance, in *Gonzales y Otras v. Mexico* (2009), the Inter-American Court handed down 37 pages of detailed determinations on the scope and modalities of reparations to be meted out by the Mexican government in favor of the victims, holistically considering the multifaceted consequences and specific aspects of the harm suffered, and including public acts of acknowledgment; measures to ensure non-repetition; compensation; rehabilitation; material harm; emotional (moral) harm; and modalities of payment.

The Inter-American Commission's human rights model is able to provide a favorable qualitative experience for victims (though it is by no means perfect: for example, there are significant delays). In particular, the relationship that victims can develop with the Inter-American Commission includes some positive aspects. Given the American Convention on Human Rights' mandate in relation to reparation (Art. 63), a space has been created wherein victims, as claimants, are actively able to express the consequences of the violations in personal terms, and make specific request for reparation to address a range of issues that may deal with the past, present or future. In this manner they are actively engaged in the process and can shape the awards and the modalities of their implementation.

A number of fundamental concepts are at play here, which are highlighted in research relating to participants' experiences of procedural justice in terms of the level of voice and control individuals have over a justice process (Lind *et al.* 1990). This research demonstrated that individuals who were given a voice before a decision was taken indicated a higher score for procedural fairness than individuals who had only post-decision voice or none at all. Providing relevant information also increased the perceived fairness of the process. In this respect, victims' ability to make themselves known and to voice their views and concerns can empower them, providing necessary recognition at a number of levels, which is a key element in victims' healing (Danieli 2009).

As noted by Wemmers, "[v]ictimological research has shown that how Courts proceed and in particular, how they treat victims, is important to victims' sense of justice" (2009: 214). Wemmers points to research of Tyler and Lind (1992), who argue that procedural justice is composed of trust and standing. With respect to trust, a significant aspect in management models considered by Tyler and Lind relates to levels of transparency in decision-making at the workplace, and its impact on trust. In this regard, transparency and open access to information is a relevant factor in building trust. Wemmers also points to Colquitt (2011), who refers to the interaction between victims and judicial authorities as "interactional justice". Related to exploring victims' experiences of justice, Wemmers, like Blader and Tyler (2003), considers the quality of the procedures and the quality of the decision as being central.

These qualitative nuances, which all have a bearing on how and to what extent a justice process can be reparative, are clearly encapsulated in a recent General Comment issued by the Committee Against Torture (CAT 2012) that aims to clarify the concept of "redress" and a "victim-centered" approach to justice seeking. The Committee explained that a victim-centered or a reparative justice approach must satisfy victims' procedural rights to a remedy, including the right to complain, the right to an investigation and, where there is sufficient evidence, the right to a fair and independent judicial process. Furthermore, the Committee emphasized that the ultimate aim of these combined rights is the restoration of the victims' dignity.

Trauma theories' contribution to reparative justice

Trauma theories provide a number of fundamental insights into how victims might experience the justice process. Trauma implies a notion of tearing, rupture or structural breakdown, and can only be defined and understood with reference to a specific context. The work of Keilson (1992, discussed in Becker 2004: 5) has influenced the way in which one understands trauma. Instead of being identified as an experience that has consequences, trauma is considered as an open-ended process, in which the "description of the changing traumatic situation is the framework that organizes our understanding of trauma" (Becker 2004: 5). These insights are invaluable in understanding why trauma continues after events have stopped and why victims might not show symptoms until many years later, which could coincide with a justice process. Also key in Keilson's approach is that there is no "post" in trauma but only a continuing traumatic process, whereby those who assist victims will also become part of the traumatic situation and cannot operate outside of it.

In response to the ruptures and structural breakdowns that occur in a traumatic situation or sequence, recovery relies on recognition of harm and a process of reintegrating fragmented experiences at a number of levels. In cases of extreme traumatization, characterized by systematic torture or brutal conflict, collective aspects of trauma become significant. Victims in such extreme contexts need to deal with the individual intra-psychic process, while at the same time dealing with society. Because of the disorientation that ruptures and fragmentation generate, the relationship aspect of healing is always more powerful and important than the aspect referring to the content (Becker 2004). Trauma workers in Chile explained the solidarity and "bonds of commitment" that needed to develop between victims of the dictatorship and those working with them as part of a lively relationship, reconfirming the life of the patients. As explained by Becker, "in this sense, to cure means not so much to repair destruction, rather it emphasizes a willingness to share it" (Becker 2004:5). Becker expressed the potential limitations of psychotherapy and considers moving "beyond the framework of therapy", emphasizing the "importance of truth, justice, respect and empathy" (2004: 9–13) in order to "reaffirm the life" of the survivors. In this respect, the UN Basic Principles as well as the ICC *Rome Statute* (Art 68.1) are mindful of the treatment of victims, reinforcing the notion that justice is a holistic experience that rests on respect of dignity.

Thus, in addition to satisfying victims' substantive and procedural rights to adequate reparation so as to redress the consequences of specific harms suffered, the notion of reparative justice encompasses a number of other key values that collectively aim at restoring victims' dignity. These include voice, control, fairness, respect, truth, trust, empathy, solidarity and empowerment. These relational aspects are particularly relevant to vulnerable groups, such as women who may have specific difficulties in restoring their relationships and place in society. In the absence of specific attention to these subtle but fundamental postures, the justice process might fail to restore victims' dignity and instead could further reinforce ongoing traumatic experiences of social exclusion, isolation and stigma. In the same way, failures to consider involving victims, particularly women, in the design of adequate reparation may result in the further entrenchment of discrimination and inequalities that perpetuate violence against women in conflict.

The ICC's reparations mandate in practice

In the case of *The Prosecutor v. Thomas Lubanga Dyilo*, both the case's scope and its procedural challenges affected victims' perceptions of the court and the relevance of its proceedings. In terms of the challenges affecting victims, there was some surprise at the fact that Thomas Lubanga was the first to be indicted and transferred to The Hague on March 16, 2006, as he was perceived as a relatively small fish. There was also incomprehension at the narrow charges. When discussing the fact that the only crime being prosecuted in the court's first case was the crime of conscripting, enlisting and actively using children under the age of 15 in hostilities (*The Prosecutor v. Thomas Lubanga Dyilo* 2006), victims of the killings, rapes and lootings perpetrated by the United Patriotic Front (UPC, Thomas Lubanga's militia) were astounded, responding with "ah bon?" and expecting some kind of logic to follow. When local human rights workers on the ground explained the implications, in that essentially the victims of killings, rapes and lootings would have no redress, they indicated that the ICC was "practically irrelevant" (REDRESS 2007).

There has also been considerable cynicism about the lack of implication of Uganda or its armed forces in the conflict, although it is widely accepted that Uganda funded and supported the UPC (*Democratic Republic of Congo v Uganda* 2005), and a belief has therefore arisen that the court was biased against the Democratic Republic of Congo (DRC) in favor of Uganda. For many in Ituri, the court's apparent favoring of the Hema tribe that had links to Uganda, confirmed existing narratives about the conflict, whereby those from outside, or those with connections with the West, would end up stealing scarce resources. Even international NGOs were seen as predators pillaging all that was left: the victims' stories of suffering (REDRESS 2007). As the case progressed, there were numerous delays, including two lengthy stays of proceedings, the first of which took place before the trial was scheduled to begin, with the Trial Chamber ordering the immediate release of the accused due to lack of evidence. In its *Decision on the consequences of non-disclosure of exculpatory materials covered by Article 54(3)(e) agreements and the application to stay the prosecution of the accused, together with certain other issues raised at the Status Conference on 10 June 2008*, the Trial Chamber found that the prosecutor had misused a provision that allows the prosecutor to exceptionally obtain information on a confidential basis, as lead information to assist with further investigations. While Lubanga was ultimately not released, the trial did not commence until January 26, 2009, with the conviction being handed down on March 14, 2012, six years after his transfer, in a case concerning a single war crime, recruitment of child soldiers who were under 15 years old in 2002–3 and were now in their early twenties.

Another area of contention concerns the failed attempts to include charges of gender violence in the case, in spite of ample evidence revealed during testimony. This resulted in the specific harm committed against girl child soldiers being excluded from the case. Civil society groups made several attempts to intervene on this issue, and in 2009 the representatives of the victims participating in the case filed a motion to his effect. While initially successful, the Appeals Chamber in its *Judgment on the appeals of Mr Thomas Dyilo and the Prosecutor against the Decision of Trial Chamber I of 14 July 2009*, dated December 8, 2009, reversed the Trial Chamber's decision that had enabled inclusion of these charges.

There was also a degree of mistrust and confusion on the ground regarding the Trust Fund for Victims' assistance and reparations mandates. The Trust Fund for Victims, established pursuant to Article 79 of the *Rome Statute*, has a dual mandate to undertake assistance projects on the one hand, and to implement reparations awards on the other. As regards its assistance mandate, it is able to use the voluntary contributions that it raises to fund projects to assist victims where there is material, physical or psychosocial necessity (Reg. 50(a)(ii) of the Regulations of the Trust Fund). According to best-practice standards, victims should be supported in their quest for justice, including legal or material support. Such assistance aims to respond to victims' immediate needs for medical, psychosocial or other material imperatives pending the outcome of justice processes, in order to enable victims' enjoyment of their rights. This function is quite separate from the Trust Fund's mandate to implement reparations awarded by the Chambers of the court, though the two could easily be confused in the absence of adequate explanation at grass-roots level. Indeed, civil society groups on the ground in Democratic Republic of Congo thought they had been excluded or had missed the opportunity to claim reparation, in the belief that the Trust Fund for Victims' assistance projects were in fact the court's reparations – a confusion that is not surprising given that the assistance was being implemented by the Trust Fund for Victims, which is also mandated to implement reparations (REDRESS 2011a).

When a second case was announced, namely, *The Prosecutor v. Germain Katanga and Mathieu Ngudjolo* (2013), who were from opposing factions to the UPC made up mainly from the Lendu community, significant issues became apparent in terms of the perception of fairness regarding who had been defined as the "victims" of the conflict in the two cases. Thomas Lubanga's UPC, drawn from the Hema community, had ethnic ties with Uganda and committed widespread rapes, pillaging and killings against the opposing Lendu community in particular. However, Lendu civilians did not feature significantly among the victims in Lubanga's case, because the only victims considered in the Lubanga case were child soldiers, who were largely drawn from the Hema's own community. Lubanga had called on his supporters to send a child or a cow in support of the war effort – many children referred to their time in the militia as "military service" (REDRESS 2007).

In contrast, the second case, against Katanga and Ngudjolo of the FNI (Front des nationalistes et intégrationnistes) and FPRI (Force de résistance patriotique en Ituri), armed groups were drawn from the Lendu and related Ngiri communities. This second case contains a broader list of charges including rape, sexual slavery, killings, destruction of property and pillaging committed against the Hema. Thus, the victimized Hema civilian population is well represented in the second case. However, because of the narrow choice of crimes pursued in the first case, and the fact that the only victims in that case are child soldiers, many of whom are Hema, the Hema community have been favored as the victims in both cases. To add to this, the UPC (Hema) are seen as being supported by Uganda, which in turn is seen as responsible (among others states) for fuelling the conflict and benefiting from natural resources, while reinforcing local cleavages and histories of exclusion, divisions and injustice. Needless to say, perceptions of bias and injustice arose instantly, confirming existing geopolitical constructs.

Finally, there are also significant backlogs in processing applications, with victims who had applied to participate (particularly those whose cases did not fit into the narrow charges) never being told either way what had happened to their applications (REDRESS 2012: 24). Some victims, who had applied during the course of the trial, were left in limbo without any determination ever being made on their application; thus they were denied the right to be informed or to exercise voice or control over the process. For many victims, being informed of the number that the Registry assigns to each applicant has a symbolic value – that of being recognized by somebody somewhere (REDRESS 2013). In many instances, victims' legal representatives were unable to meet with their clients because the court's security protocols did not allow counsel to travel to certain areas determined at times to be insecure, and this reinforced victims' sense of isolation and lack of solidarity.

Thus, while on paper victims have the right to information, the right to participate by presenting their views and concerns, and the right to legal representation, in practice victims' exercise of these rights has often not been effective in terms of enabling a sense of empowerment or restoration of dignity. Equally, the exercise of these rights has not played (as yet) a significant part in facilitating victims' abilities to obtain full, prompt and adequate outcomes. As will be seen in relation to the ICC's first reparations decision discussed below, victims' participation may not have any bearing at all on the form or implementation of reparations.

Procedural successes involving victims?

While there were many challenges in the first case, from a purely legal and procedural point of view there were some successes involving victims too. Victims were represented by two legal teams as well as by the ICC's internal Office of Public Counsel for Victims, which provided support to the two teams as well as representing unrepresented victims. In all, 123 victims were represented, who were either child soldiers or indirect victims of child recruitment (such as parents or teachers). Through their legal representatives, the victims played a crucial role in raising awareness of the lack of gender perspectives in the prosecutor's case as well as the narrow charges that failed to recognize other egregious harms inflicted on the children themselves, such as sexual slavery and torture (*The Prosecutor v. Thomas Lubanga Dyilo* 2009a). Victims' representatives provided useful input into the trial, for instance on the issue of names and identity in the

DRC (*The Prosecutor v. Thomas Lubanga Dyilo* 2009a). Victims were enabled to appear in The Hague in person to present their views and concerns, setting a historic precedent. Three victims travelled to the court and appeared in their capacity as victim-participants in the case, presenting their individual stories orally and situating the locations from where they were recruited on the trial record as potential sites for reparation. In addition, in the Trial Chamber also invited them to testify, as witnesses of the court, independently from the prosecution or defense witnesses (Wakabi 2010).

Some of the key areas for stock-taking on victim participation include late intervention on the ground, lack of systematic mapping done to reach relevant victims in a coherent or proactive manner, insufficient and irregular outreach (particularly in the first two or three years leading to the start of the trial), insufficient communication and contact between victims and their lawyers, and an over-reliance on intermediaries who were in turn insufficiently trained, supported, protected or remunerated. Perhaps the most fundamental difficulty, from the point of view of how the process is able to support the restoration of victims' dignity even in a modest manner, was the lack of any regular or consistent interlocutor able to listen to the victims over the duration of the process (REDRESS 2009b), as well as the lack of consideration given to the quality of contact the victims actually had either with officials of the court or with their lawyers.

The ICC's first reparations decision

Trial Chamber I issued its first decision relating to reparations in its *Decision establishing the principles and procedures to be applied to reparations*. This decision is somewhat procedural and to a certain extent only sets out a framework for reparations to be determined and implemented by the Trust Fund for Victims, rather than actually making an award based on an assessment of claims or victims' harm. Nonetheless, the Appeals Chamber determined that the reparations decision constituted a reparations order under Article 75 of the ICC Statute in its *Decision on the admissibility of the appeals against Trial Chamber I's "Decision establishing the principles and procedures to be applied to reparations" and directions on the further conduct of proceedings*.

The decision of August 7, 2012 establishes reparation principles applicable to the Lubanga case alone. Though Article 75 of the *Rome Statute* indicates that the court will set out reparations principles, which one assumes would be applied across all cases, no such principles were drawn up due to lack of agreement among the plenary of judges. Instead, a case-specific approach has been taken, with the three judges of Trial Chamber I establishing principles "not intended to affect the rights of victims to reparations in other cases" (par. 181). This approach creates uncertainty as regards future reparations decisions. For instance, while the August 7 decision affirms that "the right to reparations is a well-established and basic human right" (par. 185), this recognition may not apply in future cases. This renders it more difficult for the court's Victims' Participation and Reparation Section and its Outreach Unit to communicate the court's reparations mandate to victims' communities in the DRC and in other situations. Moreover, when assessing the decision against the three components of reparative justice set out above, significant issues arise at every level.

In relation to substantive aspects of the award, the decision recognizes as a matter of principle that "the right to reparation is well established", but it does not make a determination as to whether it is actually a justiciable individual right, or whether indirect victims hold rights in the specific case at hand. This lack of determination generates significant uncertainty for potential beneficiaries. While the decision considers the potential scope (who can benefit) and potential extent (content of awards) of reparations, these are couched in permissive terms, delegating the responsibility of identifying victims and awarding reparation to the Trust Fund for Victims. The Chamber indicated that reparations *may* be granted to direct and indirect victims, including the family members of direct victims or individuals who intervened to help the victims or to prevent the commission of these crimes, as well as to legal entities such as schools or hospitals. It has also indicated that reparations funded through the Trust Fund *would tend to be* collective in nature (par. 274).

The Chamber gave some broad indications to the Trust Fund identifying who may be considered a victim. It found that it would be inappropriate to limit reparations to the group of victims that participated in the trial and those who applied for reparations. Instead, the Chamber noted that pursuant to Rule 85, reparations may be granted to direct victims who suffered harm as a result of being enlisted, conscripted and actively used in hostilities under the age of 15 (in Ituri, DRC, from September 1, 2002 to August 13, 2003), which goes beyond the children recruited and used by Thomas Lubanga's UPC and could potentially apply to all children recruited by any faction during that period.

In addition, the "damage, loss and injury" to be repaired could, if appeals against this ruling are upheld, be granted to a wider class of victims, including indirect victims beyond child soldiers, if it can be shown that the harm would not have been inflicted but for the recruitment. This proximate cause criteria regarding the chain of causation, if upheld on appeal and applied by the Trust Fund, could include the victims of the child soldiers – i.e. the civilian population that suffered pillaging, rapes and killings. The standard of proof that the Chamber indicates would be appropriate, again only as a suggestion, is a "wholly flexible" standard of balance of probabilities, which the defense, in the *Decision on the defense request for leave to appeal the decision establishing the principles and procedures to be applied to reparations* (2012), deems to be too vague to be applied by a non-judicial organ.

From a victims' perspective, the potentially broader reach of the decision is helpful; so is the inclusion of other forms of harm such as sexual violence not prosecuted at trial, as this alleviates the lack of recognition of specific harms suffered by the children, particularly the sexual violence suffered by girls, that were mentioned during the trial. However, the scope may also be so wide as to lose any connection to the conviction and to the justice process, and may, when administered collectively, end up looking quite indistinguishable from other forms of assistance being provided by humanitarian organizations on the ground, or indeed through the assistance mandate of the Trust Fund itself. In this regard it is important, from a reparative justice perspective, not to lose the link with the specificity of harm that is being repaired so that the assistance continues to be integral to the remedy and reparation that together aim to provide redress and justice.

All these issues are controversial and remain on appeal more than a year after the initial decision, including the issue of whether the Chamber can delegate responsibility for the implementation and oversight of the reparations proceedings. The Victims' Team 01 has questioned in its *Appeal of the 7 August decision* (September 3, 2013) whether the Trial Chamber erred in law by not considering individual applications for reparation (contrary to Art. 75–1), and whether the Chamber could defer the determination of reparations to the Trust Fund for Victims, without itself remaining seized. Furthermore, Victims' Team 01 asserted that all reparations awards are pronounced against the convicted person and that the Trial Chamber erred in law by dispensing the convicted person from any responsibility relating to reparation other than voluntarily presenting his excuses.

As the Chamber has found Lubanga to be impecunious, it absolved him of any liability in relation to the victims, and merely left it open to him to volunteer an apology on a public or confidential basis. However, the fact that the Chamber failed to find him liable to make reparation has, in the author's view, been confused with his ability to pay. The Chamber should have found him liable for reparation as a matter of victims' entitlement, and separately found him unable, at least for the present, to comply with the order. In divesting itself from the task of identifying the victims, or a class of victims, and quantifying the harm to be repaired (and attributing the appropriate proportion to Lubanga), the Chamber has to a certain degree disconnected the justice outcome from the reparations that it is hoped will follow. The Chamber foreclosed the possibility of Lubanga making reparation, even if his financial circumstances were to change, though this position may yet be overturned on appeal. Setting out his liability in the event that assets were identified would create a stronger basis for such potential assets to be pursued vigorously by states as a matter of cooperation.

As regards the forms of reparation that might be implemented, the decision of August 7 sets out a series of principles relating to rehabilitation, restitution, compensation and symbolic forms of reparation. The principles set out hold that the needs of all the victims should be taken into account, particularly children, the elderly, those with disabilities, and victims of sexual or gender violence, and that "[t]he right of victims to rehabilitation is to be implemented on the basis of principles of non discrimination and shall include a gender-inclusive approach that encompasses males and females of all ages" (par. 232).

As regards procedural considerations that affect victims' ability to exercise their views and concerns or voice and control over the process, including the ability to influence the design of the process and substantive awards to follow, the decision not to consider the individual applications for reparations filed by victims is problematic, as is the decision not to hold hearings as part of a reparations phase of proceedings. At the time of completion the reparations applications were some 17 pages long and required significant efforts, for both victims and civil society, to complete and forward to the court, all the while raising expectations of potential pecuniary damages (REDRESS 2011a). Many of the confusing messages that the victims have had to face could have been avoided had the court established its reparation principles in advance, as intended by Article 75 of the Statute.

In terms of implementation, the Chamber recommended that the Trust Fund for Victims appoint a multidisciplinary team of experts to assist in preparing and implementing a reparations plan as foreseen under the Trust Fund's regulations. The Chamber endorsed the Trust Fund's five-point plan, whereby it is to identify the localities which ought to be involved in the reparations process; undertake a consultation process in the localities identified, enabling victims to express their proposals and priorities; assess the harm suffered by the victims; carry out public debates in each locality in order to explain the reparations principles and procedures and to address the victims' expectations; and collect proposals for collective reparations measures, developed in each locality.

The decision raises the importance of so-called "managing expectations", a term that has gained currency in ICC circles. While it is important that the victims are not given false hope and that their expectations are not harmfully raised, they are from a legal point of view entitled to justice and the ICC legal framework gives them a right to claim reparation. Giving victims unrealistic hope would be harmful; however, this needs to be carefully balanced with their right to be informed and the need for them to be empowered to claim legitimate entitlements, once again reinforcing the rationale that reparations principles should have been identified in advance and should provide a higher degree of certainty about both the process and outcomes.

The decision addresses the need to reintegrate child soldiers, "reintegrating them into society in order to end the successive cycles of violence" (par. 216). While most of the language used in the decision is respectful of victims' dignity, this statement implies that it is the child soldiers who need reintegrating as a means to an end, rather than presenting their wellbeing as an end itself in order to restore their healthy integration into their communities. Moreover, the statement is somewhat gender biased: it seems misplaced when applied to girls who were recruited into Lubanga's militia and used as "wives" to leaders, and who, after the conflict, ended up begging with their babies in the market place – their families having moved away due to the stigma. While by this time numerous children had applied to participate in ICC proceedings, these girls continued to be invisible – some local activists explained that "they were already lost" and seemed to think that this needed no further explanation (REDRESS 2007). In this scenario, it is not just the girls that need "reintegrating", it is the community and society who need to work at accepting and supporting young mothers as dignified and respected members of the community.

Challenges for the Trust Fund for Victims

The breadth and indeterminate nature of the decision presents numerous challenges for the Trust Fund for Victims, not least how to apply the broad notion of proximate cause in order to determine who the beneficiaries of reparations should be. It puts the Trust Fund in a delicate position: without a clear delimitation of the class, the Fund will have to define and limit the scope of who will be considered eligible for the purpose of reparations in this case. This first step will be necessary before it can contemplate implementing its five-point plan, wherein it will need to communicate the scope of reparation order to identify the appropriate communities to involve and engage with as part of the process. The limitation of who will be considered a victim is likely to appear arbitrary to affected communities, and it would facilitate the work of the Trust Fund if this decision were taken judicially by the court, making its reasoning publicly available and communicating it in an accessible statement addressed to those affected. In this respect, as indicated in the various appeals against the reparations decision, it will be helpful to consider that reparations are in the first place ordered against the convicted person. Framing the scope of beneficiaries in a manner that is linked to the convicted persons' liability, while accounting for the reasonably foreseeable gender consequences, would be an appropriate means of maintaining a link with the justice process.

How to ensure that reparations are perceived as such raises significant challenges for the Trust Fund for Victims. Acknowledging the specificity of harm and communicating that the programs and services, which may in practice be quite similar to the assistance projects that the Trust Fund for Victims is already funding, are in fact the end result of a justice process, will be a challenge for a number of reasons. First, visibly linking the Trust Fund's projects or services to the court may put the beneficiaries at risk on the ground, given the scarcity of resources and ethnic tensions. Second, singling out some victims over others may further deepen local cleavages while also stigmatizing or singling out children formerly associated with armed groups. When considering reparation for child victims, it is critical to consider the best interests of the child in the first place (REDRESS 2006). Anecdotal evidence from projects aimed at the reintegration of child soldiers run in other contexts, such as Northern Uganda, have shown that while initially aimed exclusively at the former child soldiers, it was found that such exclusive rehabilitation singled them out from their peers, creating resentment in the communities where other children were not allowed to benefit from targeted programs. Thus, projects benefiting children more holistically within a community or locality was seen as more favorable to the former child soldiers as they were not singled out or stigmatized and their reintegration was thereby aided (REDRESS 2006).

Best practice or tokenism?

There is much to suggest that the first prosecutor's approach may have been somewhat opportunistic, identifying the simplest and narrowest case where evidence appeared to be easiest to obtain, without much foresight into local patterns of victimization and how the cases might in fact be regarded on the ground.

In prosecuting these crimes, investigators and prosecutors have a responsibility towards victims, just as the police do at domestic level. As explained by Becker (2004), the necessary engagement of investigators and prosecutors will become part of the ongoing traumatic experience of victims. Thus, consideration of investigators' and prosecutors' roles and relationships with victims should be informed by an understanding of reparative justice and their inevitable role within it. Mapping, research and consultations should inform both investigators' and prosecutors' communications strategies, detailing approaches to be taken at different levels – from the individual victim, to communities, to nationwide communications. Questions regarding adequate training and appropriate attitudes of all those involved should become instinctive.

There are positive indications that the court's second prosecutor may be taking these issues to heart. Fatou Bensuouda, formerly the Deputy Prosecutor, took up office in June 2012. In March 2013, she dismissed charges against the co-accused in the case against the Kenyan elected President Kenyatta. However, in her *Statement on the Notice to Withdraw Charges against Mr. Muthaura*, March 2013, she chose to address the people of Kenya in a direct, transparent and respectful manner, updating them on her actions and explaining these as follows:

> I wish to inform you, that today I filed a notice to the Judges to withdraw charges against Mr. Francis Kirimi Muthaura. I have done so after carefully considering all the evidence available to me at this time. It is my duty to proceed only when I believe that there is a reasonable prospect of conviction at trial. If not, then it is my responsibility as Prosecutor to take the decision to withdraw the charges.
>
> (Bensuouda 2013)

The fact that the prosecutor has chosen to communicate with those affected in a manner that might demonstrate a sense of obligation to do so may be a first step towards building strategies into the court's work that provide a mindful approach to victims' dignity, with an emphasis on consistent, regular and direct communication with victims. Incorporating trauma theory into the court's understanding of its reparative justice mandate will be critical if it is to be a success in the eyes of those most affected by its work. In this regard, the court will need to integrate Becker's notion that the "relationship aspect is always more powerful and important than the aspect referring to the content" (2004: 5) into every way that it relates to victims, from public information to the design of its new courtroom facilities in The Hague.

In exploring the notion of reparative justice and the ICC's ability to deliver qualitative elements that underpin this concept, it becomes clear that the court has embarked on a novel experiment, and that there is a dearth of victims' voices or interests represented in theoretical discussions about international criminal law goals and objectives. In this regard, feminist perspectives in international justice discourse provide one of the few relevant viewpoints that inform a broader victims' perspective. For instance, feminist writers have questioned women's absence in forums designing justice processes, or the lack of gender-specific case strategies in seeking accountability for mass criminality. Bell and O'Rourke argue that feminist writing in the area of transitional justice should focus more on how justice debates can help obtain material gains for women (Bell and O'Rourke 2007).

In this light, it is perhaps significant to note the lack of acknowledgment that mass victimizations such as genocide, war crimes and crimes against humanity tend to overwhelmingly affect populations vulnerable to the scourge of conflict, namely marginalized groups or those living close to subsistence, who are inherently voiceless and under-represented in decision-making (Chambers 2006). Given their disempowerment and absence of voice in international justice discourse, this key stakeholder group is habitually far removed from the decision-making process that designs justice mechanisms that will affect them. This results in numerous key aspects about the process being potentially unsuited to their reality, needs and concerns. Ensuring that they are sensitively engaged in the design of reparations facilitated by the Trust Fund for Victims will be critical with respect to the overall success of the reparative justice process. In addition, enabling victims to engage in transitional justice debates at domestic level, voicing and engaging in the design of such processes on the basis of a victim-centered approach, would go a long way to providing a measure of reparative justice that may be sustainable and well adapted to victims' local realities. In this respect, there is a need for reparative justice to be examined as a subject of both theoretical and empirical research relating to international justice.

References

Albert Wilson v. The Philippines (2003) Communication No.868/1999, UN HCR Views.

Ali Ben Salem v. Tunisia (2005) AHRLR 54.

Bautista de Arellana v. Colombia (2005) Communication No. 563/1993, UN HRC Views.

Becker, D. (2004) *Dealing with the Consequences of Organised Violence in Trauma Work*, Berlin: Berghof Research Centre for Constructive Conflict Management.

Bell, C. and O'Rourke, C. (2007) "Does Feminism Need a Theory of Transitional Justice? An introductory essay", *International Journal of Transitional Justice*, 1: 23–44.

Bensouda, F. (2013) "Statement of the Prosecutor of the International Criminal Court, Fatou Bensouda, on the Notice to withdraw charges against Mr Muthaura", ICC Prosecutor's Statement, 11 March.

Blader, S. and Tyler, T. (2003) "A Four-component Model of Procedural Justice: Defining the meaning of 'fair' process", *Personality and Social Psychology Bulletin*, 29(6): 747–58.

Braithwaite, J. (2002) *Restorative Justice and Responsive Regulation*, New York: Oxford University Press.

Bozize v. Central African Republic (1994) CCPR/C/50/D/428/1990.

CAT (Committee Against Torture) (2012) *General Comment No. 3, Implementation of Article 14 by States Parties*, CAT/C/GC/3.

Chambers, R. (2006) "Vulnerability, Coping and Policy", *IDS Bulletin*, 37(4).

Coalition for the Rights of Women and Girls in Armed Conflict and Others (2008) *Nairobi Principles on Women and Girls' Right to a Remedy and Reparation*, Nairobi.

Colquitt, J.A. (2001) "On the Dimensionality of Organizational Justice: A construct validation of a measure", *Journal of Applied Psychology*, 86(3): 386–400.

Danieli, Y. (2009) "Massive Trauma and the Healing Role of Reparative Justice", in C. Ferstman, M. Goetz and A. Stephan (eds) *Reparations for Victims of Genocide, War Crimes and Crimes against Humanity: Systems in place and systems in the making*, Leiden and Boston: Martinus Nijhoff.

Democratic Republic of Congo v Uganda (2005) ICC 116.

Germany v. Poland (1928) PCIJ 17: 29, 49.

Gonzales y Otras v. Mexico (2009), Inter-Am Ct. H.R. 205.

Keilson, H. (1992) *Sequential Traumatization in Children*, Jerusalem: Magnes Press, The Hebrew University of Jerusalem.

Kepa Urra Guridi v. Spain (2002) CAT/C/34/D/212/2002.

Lind, E.R, Kanfer, R. and Earley, C.P. (1990) "Voice, Control, and Procedural Justice: Instrumental and non-instrumental concerns in fairness judgments", *Journal of Personality and Social Psychology* 59: 952–9.

Marshall, T.F. (1999), *Restorative Justice: An Overview*, London: Home Office.

REDRESS (2006) *Victims, Perpetrators or Heroes? Child soldiers before the International Criminal Court*, London: REDRESS.

REDRESS (2007) *Field Mission to Rural Districts of Ituri* (interview by REDRESS), February 8, 2007.

REDRESS (2009) *Victims' Central Role in Fulfilling the ICC's Mandate*, paper presented at the 8th assembly of State Parties, The Hague, November 2009.

REDRESS (2011a) *Justice for Victims: The ICC's reparations mandate*, London: REDRESS.

REDRESS (2011b) *Thomas Lubanga Trial: Timeline of Victims' engagement in the case*, Press Briefing, 25 August 2011, London.

REDRESS (2012) *The Participation of Victims Before the International Criminal Court: A review of the practice and consideration of options for the future*, London: REDRESS.

REDRESS (2013) *Feedback from Outreach Meeting in Rural Districts of Ituri* (interview by REDRESS), June 27, 2013.

Rome Statute of the International Criminal Court (1998) UNTS 2187.

The Prosecutor v. Germain Katanga and Mathieu Ngudjolo (2013) ICC-01/04–01/07.

The Prosecutor v. Thomas Lubanga Dyilo (2008) ICC-01/04–01/06–1401.

The Prosecutor v. Thomas Lubanga Dyilo (2009a) ICC-01/04–01/06–1891.

The Prosecutor v. Thomas Lubanga Dyilo (2009b) ICC-01/04–01/06–2205.

The Prosecutor v. Thomas Lubanga Dyilo (2012a) ICC-01/04–01/06–2904.

The Prosecutor v. Thomas Lubanga Dyilo (2012b) ICC-01/04–01/06–2953.

Tibi v. Ecuador (2004) Inter-Am Ct. H.R 243.

Tyler, R. and Lind, E.A. (1992) "A Relational Model of Authority in Groups", in M.P. Zanna (ed.) *Advances in Experimental Social Psychology*, vol. 25, San Diego: Academic Press.

United Nations (1985) *Declaration of Basic Principles of Justice for Victims of Crime and Abuse of Power*, available at: www.un.org/documents/ga/res/40/a40r034.htm (accessed July 31, 2013).

United Nations (1993) *Resolution 48/153 Situation of Human Rights in the Territory of the Former Yugoslavia: Violation of human rights in the Republic of Bosnia and Herzegovina, the Republic of Croatia and the Federal Republic of Yugoslavia (Serbia and Montenegro)*, available at: www.un.org/documents/ga/res/48/a48r153 (accessed July 31, 2013).

United Nations (1993) *Resolution 96/149 Situation of Human Rights in the Territory of the Former Yugoslavia: Violation of human rights in the Republic of Bosnia and Herzegovina, the Republic of Croatia and the Federal Republic of Yugoslavia (Serbia and Montenegro)*.

United Nations. (2005) *Basic Principles and Guidelines on the Right to a Remedy and Reparation for Victims of Gross Violations of International Human Rights Law and Serious Violations of International Humanitarian Law*, available at: www.refworld.org/docid/4721cb942.html (accessed July 31, 2013).

Van Boven, T. (1993) *Study Concerning the Right to Restitution, Compensation and Rehabilitation of Human Rights and Fundamental Freedoms*, Geneva: Sub-commission on Prevention of Discrimination and Protection of Minorities of the United Nations.

Wakabi, W. (2010) "Three Victims to Testify This Week", *The Lubanga Trial at the International Criminal Court*, January 11, available at: www.lubangatrial.org/2010/01/11/three-victims-to-testify-this-week/ (accessed July 31, 2013).

Wemmers, J.M. (2009) "Victims and the International Criminal Court: Evaluating the success of the ICC with respect to victims", *International Review of Victimology*, 16(2): 211–27.

World Bank (2011) *World Development Report on Conflict, Security and Development*. Washington, DC: World Bank.

5 It doesn't go away with time

Victims' need for reparation following crimes against humanity

Amissi M. Manirabona and
Jo-Anne M. Wemmers

Crimes against humanity are committed as part of a widespread or systematic attack against a civilian population. They include murder, imprisonment, torture, the enforced disappearance of people, and political persecution. These crimes often have a political dimension; because of this it can take years before victims are acknowledged, and sometimes they never are fully recognized, as new governments may prefer amnesty to prosecution. Yet victims often continue to ask for reparation long after the occurrence of crimes. For example, it took more than 40 years to see the adoption of the Civil Liberties Act of 1988 providing an apology and reparations to Japanese Americans for the US internment policy during World War II. Similarly, over 60 years after the end of World War II, Holocaust survivors and their descendents continue to ask for reparation including restitution of stolen property (Project Heart 2013). Even though slavery was abolished in the United States in 1865, in recent years there have been attempts by African Americans, descendants of victims of slavery, to obtain reparation from companies and individuals involved in slavery-related victimizations (Hylton 2004). These examples show that victims continue to ask for reparation long after the actual crimes have occurred and that reparation can take on many different forms, from an apology to restitution. The International Criminal Court (ICC), whose mandate includes provisions for reparation for victims of crimes against humanity, is currently struggling with how to give form to this right. In this chapter we will examine what constitutes reparation for victims of crimes against humanity and, in particular, what victims seek in terms of reparation many years after victimization.

The systematic and widespread nature of crimes against humanity means that by definition they involve mass victimization. It is important to bear in mind that when victimization is widespread, entire communities are victimized in addition to individual victims. Within a community, any one person may have experienced multiple victimizations directly as well as have family, friends and neighbors who experienced multiple victimizations. According to the *Basic Principles and Guidelines on the Right to a Remedy and Reparation for Victims of Gross Violations of International Human Rights Law and Serious Violations of International Humanitarian Law*, which were adopted by the General Assembly of the United Nations in 2006,

> Victims are people who individually or collectively suffered harm, including physical or mental injury, emotional suffering, economic loss or substantial impairment of their fundamental rights, through acts or omissions that constitute gross violations of international human rights law, or serious violations of international humanitarian law.... The term "victim" also includes the immediate family or dependants of the direct victim and persons who have suffered harm in intervening to assist victims in distress or to prevent victimization.
>
> (Art. 8)

Thus the victims of crimes against humanity include the direct victim, their families and their communities.

Reparation is a very important tool for the healing and recovery of the individual victim and of the society afflicted with crimes against humanity. Although reparation can never bring back the dead nor adequately compensate victims for all pain and suffering, it can facilitate reconciliation and can help victims recover from victimization and therefore improve their quality of life (*TRC Final Report* 1998; Hárdi and Kroó 2011). As Hárdi and Kroó note, "reparation represents the moral victory of the survivor, in contrast to the threats of the aggressors: It demonstrates that the promised horrors will not be fulfilled; that the survivor can experience self-worth, recognition, respect, and empowerment" (2011: 138). From a psychosocial perspective, reparation can aid an individual to come to terms with a traumatic event and help attribute responsibility by redirecting blame "toward those truly responsible and relieve the guilt that survivors themselves often feel" (Hamber 2000: 218). The granting of reparation awards to victims of gross violations of human rights enables the survivors to experience in a concrete way the state's acknowledgement of wrongs done to victims and survivors, family members, communities and the nation at large (*TRC Final Report* 1998). The reparation process has to take into account the whole degree of suffering of victims so that the community can pull through those particularly traumatic episodes with a sense of justice (Mégret 2009). Reparation adds value to the reconciliation process by restoring the survivors' dignity, and by affirming the values, interests, aspirations and rights advanced by those who suffered (*TRC Final Report* 1998: 312). Finally, reparation enables victims to regain trust in the legal order, which is often lost following a crime (Malsch 2002). Crimes against humanity jeopardize peace, security and social cohesion. The reconstruction of a new, peaceful and healthy society depends on reparation (Parmentier and Weitekamp 2007; Raymond 2010).

In legal terms, the right to reparation for wrongdoings has been well established at both the national and international level. It is entrenched in core international instruments dealing with the protection of basic human rights. For example, Article 9 (5) of the *International Covenant on Civil and Political Rights* (1966) clearly reaffirms that "[a]nyone who has been the victim of unlawful arrest or detention shall have an enforceable right to compensation". Article 2(3) (a) adds that

> each State Party to the present Covenant undertakes [to] ensure that any person whose rights or freedoms as herein recognized are violated shall have an effective remedy, notwithstanding that the violation has been committed by persons acting in an official capacity.

According to the *Basic Principles and Guidelines* (2006) the aim of reparation is "to promote justice by redressing gross violations of international human rights law or serious violations of international humanitarian law" (Art. 15).

Although reparation is important for victims, little is known about what constitutes fair and just reparation. The International Criminal Court has recently been tackling the prickly question of reparation for the victims of the first offender to be convicted by the court, Thomas Lubanga Dyilo. In its decision on August 7, 2012 regarding reparations, the court established that reparation of the harm caused to victims is designed to relieve the suffering caused by the occurrence of the crimes; to afford justice to the victims by alleviating the consequences of the wrongful acts; to deter future violations; and to contribute to the effective reintegration of offenders (*The Prosecutor v. Thomas Lubanga Dyilo* 2012). The court also held that reparations can assist in promoting reconciliation between the offender, the victims and the affected communities (*The Prosecutor v. Thomas Lubanga Dyilo* 2012). However, the court stopped short of ordering reparation for victims.

In this chapter we examine a study involving victims' need for reparation some 30 years after victimization. Our aim is to explore the meaning of reparation for victims of crimes against humanity long after their victimization. First, we will briefly describe the situation of Haitian victims of crimes against humanity. Next, literature on reparation is presented. This is followed by a description of the study and our findings. The chapter closes with a discussion of the findings and their implications.

Crimes against humanity: the case of Jean-Claude Duvalier

Jean-Claude Duvalier, "Baby Doc", was the head of state of Haiti from 1971 to 1986. He came to power at age 19 following the death of his father, François "Papa Doc" Duvalier, who ran Haiti from 1957 to 1971. Like his father, Jean-Claude Duvalier ran Haiti with an iron fist and with total disregard for fundamental human rights. Widespread crimes were committed "against his challengers and critics – opposition party members, trade unionists, independent journalists, university professors, and human rights activists" in acts characterized by "an absence of fundamental freedoms and human rights violations" (Human Rights Watch 2011: 12). In 1986, Duvalier and his wife fled for exile in France as the level of economic disparity and political corruption rendered Haiti an ungovernable state.

Under Baby Doc's rule, hundreds of political prisoners held in a network of prisons known as the "triangle of death" died from mistreatment or were victims of extrajudicial killings (Human Rights Watch 2011). The Duvalier regime plunged Haiti into a reign of terror where every real or imagined opponent was murdered or "disappeared" by the Tonton Macoutes, the president's private death squads. Independent newspapers and radio stations were closed and the journalists working at them were beaten, in some cases tortured, jailed, and forced to leave the country (Human Rights Watch 2011). Fort Dimanche most often served as the detention facility for long-term political prisoners, and was infamous for its inhuman conditions (Lemoine 1996). According to Amnesty International (2011), it is estimated that over 40 thousand Haitians lost their lives due to extrajudicial executions, torture, forced disappearances, forced exile, mis-treatment and deaths in custody. Today, these grave human rights abuses still remain shrouded in absolute impunity (Amnesty International 2011).

In addition to crimes against humanity, Jean-Claude Duvalier is alleged to have stolen almost 800 million dollars from Haitian foreign aid and taxes and deposited the money into personal accounts in Haiti and Switzerland (Vlasic and Cooper 2011). Vlasic and Cooper (2011) note that Duvalier was ranked at number six on a list of the world's most corrupt political leaders of the past two decades, surpassing presidents Ferdinand Marcos of the Philippines and Sani Abacha of Nigeria in terms of stolen money as a percentage of GDP. All in all, Duvalier is reported to have stolen the equivalent of approximately 1.7 to 4.5 percent of Haiti's entire GDP for every year he was in power (Vlasic and Cooper 2011).

Surprisingly, on January 17, 2011 Jean-Claude Duvalier returned to Haiti where he continues to enjoy total impunity and freedom. Since his return to Haiti, victims and human rights organizations have filed complaints in an effort to ensure that Duvalier be tried for crimes against humanity that he allegedly committed during his term as President. Duvalier's return to Haiti was also closely followed by Haitians living abroad, who demanded that he be held accountable for the crimes he committed. In Montreal, for example, former victims of the Duvalier regime joined forces, creating the Committee Against Impunity and For Justice in Haiti.[1]

Although Duvalier is not in custody, he is under indictments of corruption and other financial crimes. The charges of crimes against humanity were dropped on January 27, 2012 by an investigating judge in Port-au-Prince. However, since then an appeal has been lodged. As a result, the Court of Appeals summoned Duvalier to testify at a hearing scheduled on February 7, 2013 but, as usual, he failed to appear. Afterwards, a warrant was issued ordering him to appear before the court on February 28, 2013. He appeared before the court and for the first time pleaded not guilty to charges of corruption and human rights abuses. Victims were very encouraged to see Duvalier appear before the court. On February 20th 2014, the Court of Appeals ordered further investigation into the allegations, a decision that paves the way for Duvalier to stand trial for human rights violations. Despite many postponements, victims and their representatives remain hopeful that justice will be done one day (Tremblay 2013).

Forms of reparation

The UN's *Basic Principles and Guidelines* state that victims should, "as appropriate and proportional to the gravity of the violation and the circumstances of each case, be provided with full and effective reparation (Art. 15) ... which include the following forms: restitution, compensation, rehabilitation, satisfaction and guarantees of non-repetition (Art. 18)". This multifaceted approach to reparation is confirmed by the current trend in international criminal justice, which emphasizes the "need to go beyond the notion of punitive justice, towards a solution which is more inclusive, encourages participation and recognizes the need to provide effective remedies for victims" (*The Prosecutor v. Thomas Lubanga Dyilo* 2012: 64).

Restitution consists of measures designed to return victims, whenever possible, to the situation that existed prior to their victimization. According to Henzelin *et al.*, "restitution seeks to restore the victim to the situation – financial, personal or legal – that prevailed prior to the offence" (2006: 331). Restitution may take the form of return of property or reimbursement of expenses incurred as a result of the offence. For a long time, restitution was the main form of reparation both in general international law and in domestic law (Mégret 2009). However, the recent practice of international criminal tribunals suggests that restitution is rarely available and, as such, is often a complicated remedy to administer. Therefore, in practice international law is now focusing its attention on other forms of reparation.

Compensation is a sort of redress that is designed to reimburse, in monetary form, the equivalent of what has been lost by victims as a result of the crime. Its purpose is to make good in monetary terms "any economically assessable damage suffered by the victim, or victim's family" (Henzelin *et al.* 2006: 332). It is a form of economic relief that is aimed at addressing the harm that has been inflicted (*The Prosecutor v. Thomas Lubanga Dyilo* 2012: 76). In its recent decision on reparation, the ICC held that compensation

> should be considered when i) the economic harm is sufficiently quantifiable; an award of this kind would be appropriate and proportionate (bearing in mind the gravity of the crime and the circumstances of the case); and ii) the available funds mean this result is feasible.
>
> (*The Prosecutor v. Thomas Lubanga Dyilo* 2012: 76)

The court seems to prefer collective reparations, which address the harm the victims suffered on an individual and collective basis. Clearly, in many cases of crimes against humanity, it would be very difficult to determine the amount of compensation to be paid. Loss of life, torture, rape or unlawful imprisonment is not easy to quantify. In addition to the extensive material damages suffered by victims, one would need to calculate the moral damages and lost opportunities as a result of the victimization and this would be impossible. Thus, to some extent, any kind of compensation is symbolic reparation.

The aim of rehabilitation is to empower the victim to resume as full a life as possible. Rebuilding the life of someone whose dignity has been destroyed takes time, and long-term material, medical, psychological and social support is needed. Rehabilitation often consists of "remedies intended to assist victims in reintegrating in the society under the best possible conditions by providing, for instance, medical, psychological, legal or social services" (Henzelin *et al.* 2006: 332). In addition to medical and psychological care for individual victims, rehabilitation may also include the fulfillment of significant community needs. The widespread and systematic nature of crimes against humanity means that they may target one or more specific communities. When a community is affected it is important to consider both the rehabilitation of the group as a whole and that of its individual members as both the individual and the group begin the process of working through a violent past (*TRC Final Report* 1998; Hamber 2000). The work of the ICC's Trust Fund for Victims shows that rehabilitation may be complementary to peace-building or socioeconomic or humanitarian programs designed to enhance recovery from the crisis in which crimes against humanity occurred. The Trust Fund for Victims is in part designed to fulfill the humanitarian functions of the court, which contribute to peace-building and socioeconomic recovery (Wemmers 2009).

Satisfaction consists of measures designed to reinstate the dignity of victims, both by putting an end to the violations and by acknowledging the harm suffered by the victims. In international law, satisfaction is considered a third form of reparation that can be pertinent when restitution or compensation cannot provide full reparation (Khan 2007). However, given the adverse and widespread effects of crimes against humanity on the physical, emotional and socioeconomic conditions of victims, the current trend in international criminal justice is to put satisfaction at the forefront of reparation and healing process (Mégret 2009). According to the *Basic Principles and Guidelines* (Art. 22), satisfaction is about recognition by the offender or the state and includes an official declaration, acknowledgement or apology for the harm done, with the aim of restoring the dignity, the reputation and the rights of the victim and of persons closely connected with the victim. It also includes criminal prosecution and sanctions against persons liable for the crimes. Through what is known as reparative justice, which includes the establishment of Truth Commissions, public apologies and the acknowledgement of responsibility and the acceptance of facts, justice is thought to repair both individual victims (direct and indirect) and their communities. Therefore, rather than being an alternative, this kind of reparation is a necessary and complementary component of the whole reparation process.

Finally, guarantees of non-repetition are a commitment made by the state to never again engage in or tolerate practices similar to those that led to the gross violations of human rights, backed by a number of reforms and restructuring initiatives to make good that promise (Mégret 2009). This includes legislative and administrative measures that contribute to the maintenance of a stable society, rule of law, and the prevention of recurrences of human rights violations (*TRC Final Report* 1998).

Reparation and time: some contrasting arguments

Political arguments

Crimes against humanity often occur in a context of political violence and abuse of power by authorities. Following a period of gross violations of human rights, governments may actively encourage citizens to turn the page and forget past wrongdoings as they move forward. When this occurs, victims may experience what Danieli (2009) refers to as the conspiracy of silence: a strong social pressure to not talk about past victimizations. The most frequent source of impunity is amnesty legislation, which is an officially declared and imposed forgiving and forgetting (Huyse 2003). Outgoing elites unilaterally pardon their leaders, introducing amnesty legislation prior to leaving office. For example, in 1983 the military junta in Argentina passed the so-called Law on National Pacification one month before holding democratic elections. This law granted amnesty for all political and related crimes by its officials and military (Huyse 2003). Amnesty legislation creates an obstacle to prosecution and hence provides impunity for offenders.

In Haiti the current head of state, Michel Martelly, has already said that he prefers to grant amnesty to Jean-Claude Duvalier (Ives 2011). Hence, although amnesty legislation has not been passed in Haiti, the political will to prosecute Duvalier is absent. The main reason behind formal or implied amnesty may be the fear of the possible destabilization of the new government by supporters of the previous repressive regime should its leaders be brought to justice (Lutz 1989). These supporters may continue to wield considerable power in the new government. There may also be concern about the costs of prosecution and a possible compensation program and the heavy financial burden that this would place on the national economy (Lutz 1989).

In current practice, despite some criticisms, nothing in international law seems to restrain states from granting amnesty to criminals. But it is an approach that remains very unpopular with victims. In general, people are willing to grant of amnesty after acknowledgment and recognition of victimization through a formal process where wrongdoers publicly and honestly present their apology (Hamber 2000).

Legal arguments

Most crimes are subject to a statute of limitations. That is to say that after a given period of time, the offender can no longer be prosecuted. Particularly serious crimes, however, are exceptions to this rule. According to international law, crimes against humanity do not have a statute of limitations. In 1968, the United Nations adopted the international *Convention on the Non-Applicability of Statutory Limitations to War Crimes and Crimes against Humanity*. The principle that there is no period of limitation for war crimes and crimes against humanity has gained universal application in international law, at least in relation to criminal justice. This acceptance acknowledges that the need to prosecute crimes against humanity does not go away with time.

In relation to other forms of reparation such as compensation, there remains some uncertainty as to whether statutory limitations have really been suppressed by the *Convention*. A strong argument can be made that no time limit is acceptable for victims of crimes against humanity. To begin with, the *Basic Principles and Guidelines* specify that there should be no statute of limitations and that even in civil matters, such limitations should not be "unduly restrictive" (Art. 7).

Moreover, in countries with a civil legal tradition, for example, a claim for compensation is made following the opening of criminal prosecution. Thus, whenever prosecutions are initiated, claims for reparation are receivable in jurisdictions with a civil legal tradition. In common law systems, criminal proceedings are separate from civil proceedings. However, times have changed and many common law jurisdictions have adopted laws that enable victims of international crimes to receive compensation irrespective of when the offence has been committed. In Canada, for example, the *Crimes against Humanity and War Crimes Act* established the creation of a Crimes against Humanity Fund. Although this fund has yet to receive any money, the idea is that the money in the fund can go to victims and the families of victims of offences under this Act (CAHWCA 2000: s. 30).

Morally speaking, one cannot impose a statute of limitations on a claim for reparation "when the defendant impaired the plaintiff's ability to pursue it sooner or when the institution that must approve the claim would not previously have recognized the claim's legitimacy" (Forde-Mazrui 2004: 741). If, for example, victims of crimes against humanity under the Baby Doc regime were prevented from filing a claim, then one could argue that they were unable to exercise their right and that any statute of limitations should not apply.

Nevertheless, we often see limitations imposed on other forms of reparation such as compensation in civil matters. Governments may chose to impose time constraints on opportunities for obtaining reparation after grave human rights violations (Lutz 1989). Such statutory limitations introduce a legal barrier that prevents the victims from seeking reparation. There are many arguments for such legal barriers. To begin with, there is the problem of identifying victims. With the passage of time, it may be hard to determine the true identity of victims. A second problem is related to causation and the difficulty in proving a causal link between the victim's current situation and their victimization. The causal link between the plaintiff's injury claim and the defendant's breach of the legal standard is a very important requirement in reparation. Yet it is not easy to prove that a particular plaintiff's situation today is the direct result of a wrong committed many decades ago or that the damage suffered was a foreseeable consequence of the defendant's conduct (Malveaux 2005; Hylton 2004). For example, the Indian Residential School Settlement Agreement in Canada provides compensation to former residential school students for each year that an individual spent at a residential school. While many scholars attribute the current social problems found in many First Nations communities to their loss of culture, community and family, which was the direct result of the residential school policy (see Woolford in this volume), the settlement agreement does not acknowledge this because it limits reparation to the direct victims of the residential schools (Reagan 2010). Even if a causal link can be established, when many decades have passed between the initial injury and compensation, proof of the amount of economic loss suffered by the victims is "generally speculative and an exercise in imagination" (Massey 2004: 164). Thus victims may find themselves confronted with limitations that exclude them or severely limit their access to reparation.

Thus international law recognizes that for crimes against humanity, time does not remove the need for reparation and, in principle, statutes of limitations cannot bar reparation claims by victims. The difficulty is how to ensure that authorities recognize a given offense as a crime against humanity. Fortunately, however, in the case of Haiti there are reports from international organizations that substantiate the international significance of crimes committed under the Duvalier regime. For example, the Inter-American Commission on Human Rights has pointed out that human rights violations committed during Duvalier's regime are crimes against humanity that are subject neither to a statute of limitations nor to any amnesty (Inter-American Commission on Human Rights 2011). Human Rights Watch agreed and added that even if the statute of limitations were accepted, in all cases of forced disappearances it would not begin to run until the whereabouts of the victims had been clarified (Human Rights Watch 2011). In the aftermath of Duvalier's return to Haiti, Amnesty International published the testimonies and other evidence it had gathered on abuses between 1971 and 1986 that demonstrate that human rights violations during that time were widespread and systematic, amounting to crimes against humanity (Amnesty International 2011).

Victimological arguments

Some authors argue that time does not affect victims' need for reparation. Van Boven (1993) contends that for many torture survivors, the passage of time does not lessen the suffering. The interest of many survivors (and their relatives) in reparation persists over long periods of time. While victims' needs may change over time, the need for reparation does not diminish and victims may require assistance and support over a long period (Van Boven 1993). According to Cohen (1995), no amount of time can be long enough to eliminate the need for truth and accountability. Hamber mentions that "many years after the violations the calls for justice do not disappear" and that "the demands for justice do not fade with the passage of time" (2000: 221). Likewise, the need for reparation does not disappear even after the main offenders have been sanctioned. For example, even as recently as 1992, nearly 50 years after Nuremberg Tribunal, the announcement of a new accord aroused the expectations of many Holocaust survivors who "packed the shabby waiting room … jammed its telephone lines, and mailed in tens of thousands of requests for applications" in the hope of obtaining compensation (REDRESS 2001: 64).

Indeed, other authors have argued that the need for reparation grows over time. Cunningham and Silove (1993) argue that survivors suffer a series of traumas, and that their priorities vary substantially over time. Public indifference to the wrongs suffered may lead to increased feelings of injustice and may fuel claims for redress at a later point (REDRESS 2001). According to Lutz (1995), normal psychological responses to severe human rights abuses may actually prevent a victim from seeking redress for a long time. Survivors are initially concerned with rebuilding their lives and meeting their more basic needs such as food and shelter. According to REDRESS, "in the earliest stages following the experience of torture, reparation is simply not a priority, not even an issue, for victims" (REDRESS 2001: 64). Their main, immediate and desperate request is for their release from the dangerous situation and none of them will express the desire to receive compensation or any other kind of reparation before they are safe. It may then take a considerable period of time before making a claim for any kind of reparation (REDRESS 2001: 64). This idea supports the contention that victims of crimes against humanity have to reach a point of "readiness" before the desire for reparation emerges, or indeed before it can have any beneficial effect for them (REDRESS 2001). According to Hamber (1998), victims will be left feeling dissatisfied when reparations are granted before the survivor is psychologically ready.

Thus while authorities may wish to limit the possibilities for reparation for political or legal reasons, there is no indication from the research with victims of crimes against humanity that the need for reparation dissipates over time. On the contrary, there is some evidence that victims' need for reparation grows over time, especially when it has been ignored. Research on the long-term needs of victims of crimes against humanity is rare. What kinds of reparation do victims of crimes against humanity prefer? In the following sections of this chapter, we will present a study with Haitian victims of crimes against humanity. The categories of reparation described in the UN's *Basic Principles and Guidelines* will be used to analyze interviews with victims. In evaluating this study, we aim to understand what reparation means to victims some 30 years after victimization.

Method

This research is based on interviews conducted with victims of crimes against humanity that were committed during the Duvalier regime in Haiti. The interviews were carried out within the framework of a joint project between the Institute for Justice and Democracy in Haiti, the Bureau des Avocats Internationaux, the Canadian Centre for International Justice, the International Centre for Comparative Criminology and the Committee Against Impunity and for Justice in Haiti. The project was approved by the Ethics Committee of the Faculty of Arts and Sciences of the University of Montreal. The project had two purposes: 1) to obtain victims' testimonies regarding the gross violations of human rights committed under the Duvalier regime, and 2) to study victims' attitudes and perceptions regarding reparation. The present chapter is only concerned with the latter objective.

Respondents were recruited with the help of the Haitian community in Montreal. The project was launched with a press conference, which generated publicity for the project. In addition, announcements were made in various local media including the local Haitian radio station.

Participants were invited to contact the researchers for an interview. The interviews began in April 2011 and continued through the summer. The interviews lasted from 30 minutes to two hours. Interviews were conducted in French and were taped with the permission of the respondent. The tapes of the interviews were later transcribed prior to analysis.

The participants were members of Haitian diaspora living in Montreal. In total, ten interviews were conducted. The respondents were seven men and three women. Their ages ranges from 29 to 93 years. All but one of respondents had lived in Montreal for more than ten years. Nine of the participants were direct victims and one was an indirect victim. Many of the direct victims were also indirect victims, as they had family members who had also been victimized. The victimizations described by the respondents occurred 26 to 36 years before the interviews took place.

All of the respondents experienced, either directly or indirectly, acts of torture, illegal and arbitrary arrest and detention, cruel treatment, forced deportation, inhuman and degrading acts, and other forms of ill treatment. One of the respondents reported the loss of consciousness following a round of torture. The seemingly endless physical suffering from torture also caused emotional distress and trauma. Many victims thought they might die or that they would lose the use of their body parts. Many witnessed extra-legal executions and other scenes of torture and ill treatment, which led them to believe that soldiers and police officers might kill them at any time. Respondents were physically and mentally tortured, humiliated and forced into exile with their families, and these events continued to effect them years afterwards.

Furthermore, many respondents were victimized because of the nature of their employment. For example, journalists were often targeted because they were able to use the media to inform people about what was going on. Two respondents, who were journalists during the Duvalier regime, reported having been arrested at work without any notification of what they were accused of. They told the interviewer that they were falsely accused of attempting to organize a rebellion against the authority in power. In addition, many of respondents were victimized because of their political views and had been falsely accused of being communists.

The sample is small and not representative. However, the interviews are extremely rich and provide valuable insights into the perceptions of victims of crimes against humanity under the Duvalier regime.

Results

Consequences

In order to understand the needs of victims, we have to first understand the consequences of their victimization (Parmentier and Weitekamp 2007). The nine direct victims who participated in this study all reported having suffered physical injuries. Many of their injuries had long-term consequences on their physical health. One respondent mentioned permanent injuries that rendered him unable to sleep lying on a bed. To this day he was only able to sleep sitting up on a sofa due to the extreme pain that he experienced. Another respondent reported having caught diseases such as tuberculosis during their detention and that because of this, they suffered poor health today. One female participant reported to have suffered a miscarriage as a result of the ill treatment she received. She was very depressed and her depression was compounded when she learned that she would never be able to conceive again.

In addition, *all* of respondents reported to have suffered from trauma and psychological problems resulting from direct experience of forced exile and displacements, family dislocation, loss of property (houses, lands, cars, etc.), loss of jobs, loss of career opportunities and separation from loved ones and from their homeland. Emotional suffering was also caused by the loss of family, friends, neighbors and co-workers who were either murdered, "disappeared" or died in detention. Respondents were also upset when they learned about the ill treatment, illegal arrest and torture of their friends, family and co-workers.

Living in exile offered the victims safety; however, it also brought emotional pain and suffering, as it forced them to leave the people and things they loved behind them. Many left their jobs, their homes and their extended family behind. Moreover, when victims left their country they hoped that they would soon be able to return; however, exile lasted much longer than they had thought it would. Forced into exile, victims not only lose their self-esteem but lose control over their lives as well. Thus the respondents in this study continued to be affected by their victimizations many years later.

Reparation

The following sections provide insight into victims' points of view regarding reparation. TheUN's *Basic Principles and Guidelines* describes various types of reparation, which it breaks down into five categories: restitution; compensation; rehabilitation; satisfaction; and guarantees of non-repetition. Are they all equally important to the victims of crimes against humanity in this study, or are some of them more important than others?

Restitution

The majority of respondents interviewed did not speak of the restitution of property, although their lives had clearly been affected by their victimization. Only one respondent said that they wanted the government to take legal action and return all properties (especially lands and houses) occupied by Duvalier's supporters.

In terms of the restitution of rights, almost all of respondents wanted the restoration of liberty and legal rights for every one in Haiti as well as free movement and security for Haitians living overseas who wish to travel to Haiti. In addition, one young man born in exile outside of Haiti wished to be granted Haitian citizenship. He was very shocked and concerned to learn that he could not undertake any investments in Haiti as he was not considered a Haitian national.

Compensation

None of the victims interviewed expressed the desire to be financially compensated. Some of them were of the view that nothing could compensate for their sufferings, and others did not believe in compensation at all. Moreover, they did not see how a poor country like Haiti could get money to compensate thousands of victims when the basic needs of many Haitians are currently not being met. Respondents felt that, even if they suffered greatly and continue to suffer, many people living in Haiti suffer as well, especially following the 2010 earthquake. According to the respondents, in this context it would be wrong to make demands on the limited resources of Haiti when the people in Haiti badly need these resources. If money were available for reparation, they felt that it should be used to improve the socioeconomic conditions of all people in Haiti. This may also be interpreted as a communitarian view of reparation where people do not wish to receive individual advantages following an event that affected many victims in different ways.

Rehabilitation

Rehabilitation is about providing victims with what they need to resume a full life, and this can include material and monetary recovery as well as emotional restoration. None of the victims interviewed in this study directly mentioned the need for medical and psychological care or social and legal services. Even those who continued to suffer the long-term physical effects of their victimization did not spontaneously refer to the need for such services. Those victims with medical needs relied on public health services available in Quebec. The respondents had successfully integrated into Quebec society, finding employment and building a new life. Nevertheless, talking about their victimization was potentially difficult for victims; during the interviews, we referred participants to a local victim-support group specialized in helping torture victims,[2] but we had no way of knowing whether the victims actually sought help.

Satisfaction

This form of reparation was the one mentioned most often by respondents during the interviews. All of them focused on the necessity and urgency that perpetrators of human rights abuses be tried and punished. According to all of the participants, the trial of Duvalier and his accomplices is a *sine qua non* condition for justice and reconciliation in Haiti. Their first priority was the trial of Duvalier, after which the trial of his accomplices would follow. They felt that Duvalier, as head of state, should be held responsible for what occurred under his leadership. One of the respondents stressed that, even if Duvalier inherited a corrupt system from his father, he was the president and as such he carried responsibility. Respondents emphasized that regardless of the outcome of a possible trial, it was important that Duvalier be held accountable. Even if amnesty were ultimately granted to Duvalier, it was considered important that the state recognize the victims' suffering and prosecute Duvalier.

Some of the respondents wished to directly participate as witnesses if their personal security could be guaranteed in Haiti. However, most respondents expressed little confidence in the Haitian criminal justice system, which, they felt, had been long troubled by corruption and lack of transparency.[3] Some respondents thought that it would be better if Duvalier were to be tried by an international tribunal. In this respect, many expressed the hope that the international community and Canada in particular would help in a possible trial of Duvalier and his accomplices.

Besides holding Duvalier to account, many respondents also felt that a trial might provide them with answers to some of their questions. These respondents expressed the need to know why they had been persecuted, tortured and forced into exile.

Other victims wanted to see Duvalier himself acknowledging the crimes committed under his regime. Three respondents stressed that it was important that Duvalier publicly acknowledge the past. According to these respondents, recognition by the perpetrator of the wrong committed is very important for victims. They were quite clear that acknowledgement by an offender is distinct from a trial, which may or may not end in a conviction, and even if the accused is found guilty they may never acknowledge their responsibility.

Another form of recognition by the state is an apology. One of the respondents saw reparation in terms of an apology by the current president of Haiti, in which he would recognize the crimes committed in the past and apologize for them.

The victims in this study felt that the truth must be known about the oppression and mass victimizations committed in the past. In this respect, they wanted a public discussion about the crimes that occurred during the Duvalier regime. A public discussion was viewed as an important step towards justice and accountability. Besides the long-term effects in terms of creating a collective memory of past events, dialogue through truth-telling was considered by the victims in this study to be important in order to get answers to their questions about what really happened as well as to empower them through recognition. Victims complained about the unbearable silence. They viewed this as denial of the past but also, in particular, they worried that with time a new generation would forget what happened.

In addition to an open and public discussion about the past, many victims also wanted the current Haitian government to create a public record of the crimes, documenting deaths and disappearances. They felt that this was important in order to ensure that all Haitians, especially the youth, know what happened and why this happened. One of them went on to say that his children would like to know what happened, yet there is neither a history book about what happened in Haiti nor archives documenting the past. According to him, the time has come to do this so that people can remember. Respondents felt that if the memory of what happened were not preserved then the same errors would unavoidably happen again. The large number of young supporters of Duvalier exacerbated their concerns. In their view, the current supporters of Duvalier are mostly young people who do not fully know what he did.

Guarantees of non-repetition

It was clear that respondents were concerned that past abuses of power could be repeated and that they were eager to see change. Impunity showed offenders that they could get away with violating human rights. Respondents wanted to see measures put into place, including criminal prosecution, in order to ensure that the crimes committed in the past could not occur again. Ending impunity would be very important for future generations, as it would show that such crimes would no longer be tolerated. Moreover, the accountability of all criminals would strengthen the rule of law as well as democracy in Haiti, while the absence of accountability strengthens wrongdoers, revictimizes the victims and frustrates the whole society. To this end, one respondent felt that the international community could play an important role andcould facilitate the transformation of the Haitian criminal justice system. For example, he felt that they could send international experts to train local personnel.

Education was felt to be a key element in order to guarantee that past mistakes would not be repeated. According to two of the respondents, the Haitian government should undertake a national campaign of remembrance and education for youth and children in order to prevent future repetition of similar crimes.

The need for reparation for the victims of crimes against humanity in this study can be hierarchically classified as in Table 5.1.

Discussion

Before discussing the findings, it is important to bear in mind that the sample used in this study was small and not representative of all victims of crimes against humanity or even all Haitian victims of crimes against humanity. Caution must be used when interpreting the findings. It is possible that a different sample

Table 5.1 Hierarchy of victims' need for reparation 30 years post-victimization

Form of reparation	*Order of importance*
Satisfaction: accountability; prosecution	1
Satisfaction: truth; acknowledgement	2
Guarantees of non-repetition	3
Rehabiliation: community development	4
Restitution of rights	5
Compensation	6

would have given rise to different results. This study only explored victims' perceptions of reparation. Further research is needed.

The findings show that not all forms of reparation are equally important for the victims in this study; they were particularly interested in satisfaction. Still marked by the harm they suffered, these victims did not desire compensation or restitution of property. Only one of the victims mentioned the need for restitution in general and in particular the restitution of lands and houses illegally occupied. None of the victims referred to monetary compensation or rehabilitation. This is in sharp contrast with other groups of victims of crimes against humanity. For example, victims of the Holocaust around the world continue to seek restitution of property over 60 years after the war (Project Heart 2013). The Indian Residential School Settlement Agreement was largely based on the provision of financial compensation to former victims of Canada's Indian Residential Schools (Reagan 2010). The lack of interest in financial compensation is therefore not something that we see with all victims of crimes against humanity.

One may wonder why none of the respondents mentioned the need for monetary compensation. We have to consider the context in which these victims find themselves. To begin with, these victims living in Montreal consider themselves to be the lucky ones in comparison with millions of other Haitians who remain in their country. There is a sense of empathy for their compatriots living in Haiti among members of the Haitian diaspora living in wealthy countries such as Canada. Haiti is considered too poor to be able to afford to pay compensation. The devastating earthquake that struck Haiti on January 12, 2010 likely compounded this feeling of empathy. Haiti is a poor country. Victims may be more reluctant to request money from a poor country than from a rich one. According to Hamber (2000), it is when victims remain in a situation of extreme impoverishment that they are inclined to request material and financial reparations. Therefore, it is possible that the victims in this study did not favor financial reparation because, although they were living in exile, they were living in relative comfort in Canada rather than living in poverty in Haiti. The relative poverty of Haiti as a nation may explain why victims did not favor financial compensation for their suffering.

A second possible explanation, which is specific to this study, is the ideology or beliefs of the victims. Many of the victims who participated in this study were politically involved when they were victimized. Ideologically, their main concerns remain the struggle for justice and equality in Haiti. Hence, rather than tax Haitian society, they might focus on other means of reparation.

In addition, the desire to see that any available money is dedicated to national reconstruction displays a community vision of compensation not only because of empathy but also because of the attempt to collectivize possible blame in case the acceptance of compensation is perceived as an absolution of their victimizers' responsibility.

The victims in this study were largely concerned with ending impunity and holding Duvalier accountable. All of them felt very strongly about bringing him to justice so that they could heal from victimization. Edelman and her colleagues (1996) insist that a situation of impunity, where no sanctions are taken against the perpetrators, can have serious negative consequences for the individual survivor. It functions, they argue, as a second injury, which can cause additional anxiety. Impunity has been found to heighten post-traumatic stress symptoms in victims (Westermeyer and Williams 1998). Because no measures are taken against those who caused the injury, a life of repetition of the trauma is created (Edelman *et al.* 1996). According to Gurr and Quiroga:

> Impunity interrupts the normal process of healing of the survivor of repression, the grief of the families of disappeared victims, and the process of social reparation. Impunity prolongs the psychopathological consequences of repression, both in the individual and in the society.
>
> (2001: 27)

In short, impunity is devastating for the health of the survivor.

Although it is not unusual to find that victims of crimes against humanity value prosecution (REDRESS 2001; Wemmers 2006), it is possible that the sample was biased due to the nature of project. As was mentioned earlier, the aim of the project was twofold: to obtain testimonies regarding the gross violations of human rights committed under the Duvalier regime and to study victims attitudes and perceptions. Hence, it is possible that the victims who were drawn to this project were necessarily people who thought the prosecution of Duvalier was important.

At a social-political level, the main concern of all of participants was the persistence of political and economic conditions that allow the human rights violations to continuously take place. They sought guarantees of non-repetition. Impunity was interpreted as a sign that nothing had changed. They wanted the victimization to stop. Ending impunity was considered a sign of change that would show that new government had broken with the past. Our respondents were concerned that Haiti was still very far from being a stable and peaceful country that protects fundamental rights and freedoms.

Besides criminal prosecution, the victims in this study also favored other forms of public recognition and acknowledgement. These include a public apology by Duvalier himself or, in his absence, by the current president. An adequate and sincere apology facilitates the "rehumanization" of the survivor and the establishment of a sense of meaning (Jaranson *et al.* 2001). According Hárdi and Kroó (2011) the apology creates a "balance shift" between perpetrator and victim.

Other possible forms of public recognition include a public discussion of the past events and a public documentation of events. For many victims it is important that the past not be forgotten in order to ensure that it does not happen again. As mentioned above, the broader recognition of victims' suffering is, in itself, an important component of justice (Suzuki 2012). This includes teaching children about what happened and making it part of the group's collective history (Wemmers and Manirabona, forthcoming). For example, a study conducted by Stover (2005) found that among the victims of the war in the former Yugoslavia, "justice meant piercing the veil of the denial" about the past. Hárdi and Kroó (2011) mentioned that reparation is essential as it helps the victim create a survivor identity and restore her/his dignity, feeling of self-value, pride, confidence, and trust. According to these authors, the act of reparation is a key moment not only for the victimized individual, but also for the society as a whole: "without reparation, the reconstruction of a new, peaceful, and healthy society would be impossible" (Hárdi and Kroó 2011: 138).

The importance that the victims in this study place on public recognition suggests that the introduction of a truth commission in Haiti might be a worthwhile idea to pursue in the context of the country's transition towards a stable democracy. Truth commissions have been successfully used in countries such as Guatemala and South Africa to create a public record of past atrocities. Reparative justice mechanisms such as truth commissions or community healing meetings "can help to open the door for the possibility of the individual and the country to begin the process of working through a violent and conflicted history" (Hamber 2000: 215). These transitional justice mechanisms can facilitate healing and change at the level of society and would help the Haitian people to overcome their troubling past and rebuild their country on a new basis of justice, reconciliation and peace.

Conclusion

Based on the views of the victims in this study, a three-step plan for the transition of Haiti emerges. The first element is the criminal prosecution of Jean-Claude Duvalier for crimes against humanity. This process has currently been initiated, but it is not at all certain whether Duvalier will in fact be tried for crimes against humanity. If not, prosecution at the international level, such as the Inter-American Court, would be a possibility and one that would have the support of the victims in this study. Second, the current government should publicly recognize and apologize for the crimes committed under the old regime. This would provide validation and satisfaction to victims. Third, the current government should establish a truth commission in Haiti, which would gather testimonies and document the crimes against humanity that were committed under the old regime. This would stimulate a public discussion and provide a public record of the past injustices which would provide satisfaction to victims as well as educate the new generation about the crimes committed in the past. This process would be healing both for the individual victims involved and for Haitian society as a whole. By implementing these three actions, Haiti might redress past injustices and move towards a democratic and stable peace.

Notes

1 Comité contre l'Impunité et pour la Justice à Haïti.
2 RIVO (Réseau d'intervention auprès des personnes ayant subi la violence organisée) is a Montreal-based NGO specializing in providing psychological support to survivors of torture and other organized violence.
3 The concerns related to corruption within the Haitian justice system as well as the political influence of the executive on the judiciary have also been mentioned by Human Rights Watch in its recent world report; see Human Rights Watch (2013).

References

Amnesty International (2011) *Haiti: 'You Cannot Kill the Truth': The Case against Jean-Claude Duvalier*, available at: www.amnesty.org/en/library/info/AMR36/007/2011 (accessed July 31, 2013).

Cohen, S. (1995) "State Crimes of Previous Regimes: Knowledge, accountability, and the policing of the past", *Law and Social Inquiry*, 20: 7–50.

Crimes against Humanity and War Crimes Act 2000, ch. 24, Canada: S.C.

Cunningham, M. and Silove, D. (1992) "Principles of Treatment and Service Development for Torture and Trauma Survivors", in J.P. Wilson and B. Raphael (eds) *International Handbook of Traumatic Stress Syndromes*, New York: Plenum.

Danieli, Y. (2009) "Massive Trauma and the Healing Role of Reparative Justice", in C. Ferstman, M. Goetz and A. Stephens (eds.) *Reparations for Victims of Genocide, Crimes Against Humanity and War Crimes: Systems in place and systems in the making*, The Hague: Marinus Nijhoff, 41–78.

Edelman, L., Kordon, D. and Lagos, D. (1996) "La impunidad: Reactivacion del trauma psyquico", *Reflexion*, 24: 24–6

Forde-Mazrui, K. (2004) "Taking Conservatives Seriously: A moral justification for affirmative action and reparations", *California Law Review*, 92(3): 683.

Gurr, R. and Quiroga, J. (2001) "Approaches to Torture Rehabilitation: A desk study covering effects, cost-effectiveness, participation, and sustainability", *Torture*, 11(Supp. 1), 7–35.

Hamber, B. (1998) "Repairing the Irreparable: Dealing with double-binds of making reparations for crimes of the past", paper presented at "Dealing with the Past", The International Conflict Research Institute Conference, Belfast, June.

Hamber, B. (2000) "Repairing the Irreparable: Dealing with the double-binds of making reparation", *Ethnicity and Health*, 5: 215.

Hárdi, L. and Kroó, A. (2011) "The Trauma of Torture and the Rehabilitation of Torture Survivors", *Journal of Psychology*, 219: 133–42.

Henzelin, M., Heiskanen, V. and Mettraux, G. (2006) "Reparations to Victims before the International Criminal Court: Lessons from international mass claims processes", *Criminal Law Forum*, 17: 317.

Human Rights Watch (2001) *Haiti: Duvalier prosecution a "rendezvous with history"*, available at: www.hrw.org/news/2011/04/14/haiti-duvalier-prosecution-endezvous-history (accessed July 31, 2013).

Human Rights Watch (2011) *Haiti's Rendezvous with History: The case of Jean-Claude Duvalier*, New York: Human Rights Watch.

Human Rights Watch (2013) *World Report 2013: Haiti*, available at: http://www.hrw.org/world-report/2013/country-chapters/haiti.

Huyse, Luc (2003) "Justice", in D. Bloomfield, T. Barnes and L. Huyse (eds) *Reconciliation after Violent Conflict: A handbook*, Stokholm: IDEA, 97–121.

Hylton, K.A. (2004) "Framework for Reparations Claims", *Boston College Third World Law Journal*, 24: 31.

Inter-American Commission on Human Rights (2011) *Statement on the Duty of the Haitian State to Investigate the Gross Violations of Human rights Committed during the Regime of Jean-Claude Duvalier*, available at: www.oas.org/en/iachr/docs/other/Haiti2011.asp (accessed July 31, 2013).

Ives, K. (2011) *As Inauguration Nears: Martelly prepares Duvalier amnesty and political offensive*, available at: www.haiti-liberte.com/archives/volume4–40/As%20Inauguration%20Nears.asp (accessed July 20, 2013).

Jaranson, J.M., Kinzie, J.D., Friedman, M., Southwick, S., Kastrup, M. and Mollica, R. (2001) "Assessment, Diagnosis and Intervention", in E. Gerrity, T.M. Keane and F. Tuma (eds) *The Mental Health Consequences of Torture*, New York: Kluwer Academic/Plenum Press.

Khan, I. (2007) *Rights of the Victims: Reparation by International Criminal Court*, New Delhi: A.P.H. Publishing.

Lemoine, P. (2006) *Fort-Dimanche, Fort-la-Mort*, New York: Freeport.

Lutz, E.L. (1989) "After the Elections: Compensating victims of human rights abuses", in N.J. Kritz (ed.) *Transitional Justice: How emerging democracies reckon with former regimes*, vol. 1, Washington, DC: United States Institute of Peace Press.

Malsch, M. (2002) "Compensation of Non-Material Damage in Civil and Criminal Law in the Netherlands", *International Review of Victimology*, 9: 31–42.

Malveaux, S.M. (2005) "Statutes of Limitations: A policy analysis in the context of reparations litigation", *George Washington Law Review*, 74: 68–122.

Massey, C. (2004) "Some Thoughts on the Law and Politics of Reparations for Slavery", *Boston College Third World Law Journal*. 24(1): 161–6.

Mégret, F. (2009) "The International Criminal Court Statute and the Failure to Mention Symbolic Reparations", *International Review of Victimology*, 16: 127–47.

Parmentier, S. and Weitekamp, E. (2007) *Sociology of Crime Law and Deviance*, vol. 9: *Crime and Human Rights*, Bingley: Emerald Group Publishing.

Project Heart (2013) "Holocaust Era Asset Restitution Taskforce", available at: www.heartwebsite.org (accessed July 16, 2013).

Prosecutor v. Thomas Lubanga Dyilo (2012) ICC-01/04–01/06.

Raymond, E. (2010) *Justice pour les crimes contre l'humanité: Point de vue et attentes des victimes*, unpublished thesis, University of Montreal.

Regan, P. (2010) *Unsettling the Settler Within*, Vancouver: UBC Press.

REDRESS (2001) *Torture Survivors' Perceptions of Reparation: Preliminary survey*, available at: www.redress.org/downloads/publications/TSPR.pdf (accessed July 31, 2013).

Stover, E. (2005) *The Witnesses*, Philadelphia: University of Pennsylvania.

Suzuki, S. (2012) "Overcoming Past Wrongs Committed by States: Can non-state actors facilitate reconciliation?", *Social and Legal Studies*, 21: 201–13.

Tremblay, P. (2013) *Poursuivre Jean-Claude Duvalier en Haiti: Obstacles juridiques et procéduraux*, paper presented at the Conference on Transitional Justice in Haiti organized by the Canadian Centre for International Justice, June 26, University of Montreal.

Truth and Reconciliation Commission (1998) *Truth and Reconciliation Commission Report*, Vol 5.

United Nations (2005) *Basic Principles and Guidelines on the Right to a Remedy and Reparation for Victims of Gross Violations of International Human Rights Law and Serious Violations of International Humanitarian Law*, available at: www.refworld.org/docid/4721cb942.html (accessed July 31, 2013).

United Nations General Assembly (1966) *International Covenant on Civil and Political Rights*, available at: http://treaties.un.org/doc/Publication/UNTS/Volume%20999/volume-999-I-14668-English.pdf (accessed July 31, 2013).

United Nations General Assembly (1968) *Convention on the Non-Applicability of Statutory Limitations to War Crimes and Crimes against Humanity*, available at: http://www1.umn.edu/humanrts/instree/x4cnaslw.htm (accessed July 31, 2013).

Van Boven, T. (1993) *Study Concerning the Right to Restitution, Compensation and Rehabilitation of Human Rights and Fundamental Freedoms*, Geneva: Sub-Commission on Prevention of Discrimination and Protection of Minorities of the United Nations.

Vlasic, M.V. and Cooper, G. (2011) "Beyond the Duvalier Legacy: What new 'Arab Spring' governments can learn from Haiti and the benefits of stolen asset recovery", *Northwestern University Journal of International Human Rights*, 10: 19.

Wemmers, J. (2006) *Reparation and the International Criminal Court: Meeting the needs of victims*, available at: www.cicc.umontreal.ca/activites_publiques/conferences/joanne_wemmers/r apport_reparation.pdf (accessed July 31, 2013).

Wemmers, J. (2009) "Victims and the International Criminal Court: Evaluating the success of the ICC with respect to victims", *International Review of Victimology*, 16(2): 211–27.

Wemmers, J. and Manirabona, A. (2014) "Regaining Trust: The importance of justice for victims of crimes against humanity", *International Review of Victimology*, 20(1): 101–9.

Westermeyer, J. and Williams, M. (1998) "Three Categories of Victimization Among Refugees in a Psychiatric Clinic", in J.M. Jaranason and M. Popkin (eds) *Caring for Victims of Torture*, Washington, DC: American Psychiatric Association, 61–87.

6 The prosecute or expel dilemma in far-away lands

Alternative universal justice for victims of international crimes

Fannie Lafontaine[1]

The justification for the creation of international criminal institutions such as the International Criminal Court (ICC) is the traditional failure of states where a serious international crime has occurred, or of which the perpetrator is a national, to undertake investigations and prosecutions in respect of such crimes. International criminal courts are the incarnation of the international community's conviction that "the most serious crimes of concern to the international community as a whole must not go unpunished" as they "threaten the peace, security and well-being of the world" and "deeply shock the conscience of humanity" (*Rome Statute* 1998: 3).

The same rationale explains the development of the principle of universal jurisdiction. This legal doctrine provides that any state can exercise its criminal jurisdiction over the most serious international crimes even though, at the time of commission, the crime had no territorial or national link with the state in question. Universal jurisdiction is indeed based on the notion that some crimes – including genocide, crimes against humanity, war crimes, enforced disappearances and torture – are of such exceptional gravity that they affect the international community's fundamental interests as a whole. Every member of the international community therefore has a right – or an obligation, as we shall see – to ensure that these crimes do not go unpunished. Universal jurisdiction may well be, "together with the exercise of international criminal courts and tribunals", the "only alternative to the impunity resulting from insistence on jurisdiction by the territorial or national state" (Cassese 2006: 559).

Criminal justice for certain grave violations of international law is much founded on the idea of repression – of individual accountability for the commission of such violations. However, this initial focus on the perpetrator in the global "fight against impunity" gradually gave more space to victims, as this book amply discusses. The ICC and other international or internationalized courts now entitle victims to participate in their own right in the proceedings and the courts may also award reparation to them.[2] The ICC system as regards victims, including the Trust Fund for Victims,

> reflects the growing international consensus that justice for victims of the gravest human rights crimes cannot be achieved without their participation

in the judiciary process; and without their direct involvement in defining and implementing the most appropriate means of reparation and rehabilitation. Therefore, the *Rome Statute* established a unique system in which the elements of retributive and restorative justice aim to be reconciled.

(International Criminal Court n.d.)

At least implicitly, the *Rome Statute* recognizes that the international jurisdiction needs to palliate to a certain extent for the territorial state's likely unwillingness or inability to fulfill its obligations towards victims; obligations which include holding the perpetrators to account, but which go further, in a more restorative understanding of justice.

In the case of third states exercising their responsibilities in the global fight against impunity, the role and needs of victims have been more neglected. Participation in the criminal procedures depends on the state's domestic legal system, so that countries with a common law tradition, for instance, will leave very little space to victims apart from their role as potential witnesses (Kirchengast 2011). The costs and the complexity involved in criminal prosecutions based on universal jurisdiction force a very selective approach, which may appear at odds with the objective of using national criminal justice systems to "close the impunity gap" left by the failures of other national systems and the inability of the international criminal jurisdictions to cope with the immensity of the task. Repressive justice in third states is thus almost illusory for victims. Furthermore, reparation is the poor relation of the legal regime concerning universal jurisdiction, so that victims, short of obtaining criminal procedures against alleged perpetrators, cannot find refuge in programs of reparation aimed at, for instance, their physical or psychological rehabilitation, material support and/or collective measures of compensation.

This chapter looks at third states' obligations and responsibilities under international law regarding accountability for international crimes. Using Canada as an example, it also looks at the dilemma that third states face in implementing their obligations: they cannot prosecute all alleged war criminals found on their territory, and the other existing measures – such as expulsion to the country of origin – are unsatisfactory from international law and victims' perspectives. In this light, finally, this chapter proposes to reflect on what could be termed "alternative universal justice", or innovative forms of justice that would acknowledge the inherent practical impossibility of trying in a criminal court all potential suspects of international crimes present on a third state's territory while giving due recognition to the fundamental principles of justice, accountability and reparation.

Universal jurisdiction: (few) obligations under international law

At the heart of the system put in place by the ICC to ensure accountability for international crimes lies the principle of complementarity. States bear the primary responsibility to prosecute those responsible for genocide, crimes against humanity and war crimes. National prosecutions are called to play an increasingly important role in the global system put in place to fight against the impunity of those responsible of these crimes. The exercise of universal jurisdiction pursuant to legislations such as Canada's *Crimes against Humanity and War Crimes Act* can contribute to this endeavor.

In order to fulfill the promise of the new system of international criminal justice, it may indeed be vital that states are both able and willing to try those accused of international crimes, no matter where those crimes were committed and regardless of the nationality of the perpetrator or victims (*Darfur Report* 2005: 155). By acting locally to ensure justice for international crimes (mainly through extradition or prosecution), states can make a significant contribution to the "sustainable development" of the global accountability enterprise (Lafontaine and Elassal 2008). Clearly, states' policies regarding the prosecution of war criminals should be primarily guided by the extent of the legal obligations binding upon them. On that front, however, there is a gap between the promise of the new international criminal justice system, which places states as the primary duty-bearers for ensuring accountability for international crimes, and the actual obligations flowing from international law in that regard.

The *Rome Statute*, in its preamble and by implication of the complementarity principle (Arts. 1; 17), provides for states parties' duty to prosecute the international crimes contemplated therein. The Appeals Chamber of the ICC has recognized that states "have a duty to exercise their criminal jurisdiction over international crimes" (*The Prosecutor v. Germain Katanga and Mathieu Ngudjolo Chui* 2009: par. 85). However, there is no explicit obligation in the *Rome Statute* on the part of states parties to establish jurisdiction over the crimes and certainly no obligation to assert jurisdiction on the basis of universality (Akhavan 2010; Kleffner 2008). Regardless of the absence of a clear obligation in this regard in the *Statute*, many states have taken the opportunity presented by the need to modify their domestic law to implement their obligations under the *Rome Statute* to give their domestic courts jurisdiction to try these crimes on the basis of universality (Amnesty International 2010). This must be based either on these states' view that it is an obligation flowing from the *Statute*, as some states have argued,[3] or on the view, more widely shared, that other sources of international law allow, or sometimes mandate, the assertion of universal jurisdiction for ICC crimes.

Some treaties unquestionably provide for an obligation to prosecute or extradite (*aut dedere aut judicare*) some of the crimes under the jurisdiction of the ICC. The obligation *aut dedere aut judicare* is distinct from universal jurisdiction, but overlaps with it to some extent. No distinction will be made in this chapter between the two concepts, except to mention that as a practical matter, "when the *aut dedere aut judicare* rule applies, the state where the suspect is found must ensure that its courts can exercise all possible forms of geographic jurisdiction, including universal jurisdiction" (Amnesty International 2001: 11). With the notable exception of the *Convention on the Prevention and Punishment of the Crime of Genocide,* which however provides for a duty with respect to extradition (Art. 7), the obligation to extradite or prosecute is mandated for grave breaches of the Geneva Conventions, the First Protocol Additional (that is, certain war crimes committed in an international armed conflict), and for some crimes against humanity that are the subject of a specific convention, notably apartheid, enforced disappearances and torture. Hence, numerous ICC crimes – namely genocide, various crimes against humanity, and war crimes committed in a non-international armed conflict – are not covered by a treaty obligation to extradite or prosecute.

Customary international law may also impose such an obligation. It is outside the scope of this chapter to fully address the complex and controversial issue of whether there exists at customary law an obligation to extradite or prosecute all ICC crimes. Suffice it to say that the majority view seems to be that states are entitled but not obliged to assert universal jurisdiction for these crimes (Cryer *et al.* 2010: 51). Indeed, the obligation at international law to extradite or prosecute suspected international criminals may be limited to treaties which states have ratified and that provide for such an obligation, such as the Convention against Torture and the Geneva Conventions mentioned above. There may be an emerging rule at customary law obliging states to exercise universal jurisdiction over other ICC crimes, but a safer view at the moment is that the existing rule allows, rather than mandates, states to exercise universal jurisdiction over these crimes.

Therefore, there may be a gap at present in international law regarding the obligation to exercise universal jurisdiction over certain categories of ICC crimes. Faced with such a possible gap, which leads to possible inconsistency in the approach concerning varying types of conduct which are universally condemned, states can take one of two approaches: one is to exploit the gap, and thus justify inaction or selectivity, and the other is to fill the gap, and apply the same rule or obligation to all ICC crimes.

It is interesting to note that some national legislations or guidelines on the exercise of universal jurisdiction make specific mention of the state's obligation in the global fight against impunity. The South African legislation provides that the international obligations incumbent on the Republic are a priority consideration in the exercise of prosecutorial discretion (*Implementation of the Rome Statute of the International Criminal Court Act*, s. 5(1)(3)). Belgium is among the other states that specifically recognize in legislation the role of international obligations in the decision to prosecute (*Preliminary Title of the Code of Criminal Procedure*, ss. 10(1*bis*)). The Spanish law also specifically mentions international (treaty) obligations (*Ley organica del poder judicial*, s. 23(4)). The decision in the *SALC v. NDPP* case in May 2012 in South Africa, recognizing an obligation to investigate and prosecute international crimes "as far as possible", is a powerful judicial confirmation of the impact that genuine consideration of the state's responsibilities in the international fight against impunity can have in practice (par. 13.4).

In Canada, international obligations are supposedly taken into account in the exercise of prosecutorial discretion (Lafontaine 2012a). The first two prosecutions under the War Crimes Act, in *Munyaneza* and *Mungwarere* – for genocide, for crimes against humanity and in the former case for war crimes committed in a conflict not of an international character – are positive indications of the non-selective approach of the Canadian legal authorities as regards which international crimes will be prosecuted on the basis of universal jurisdiction. The political authorities, however, have arguably not hesitated to exploit the gap: "Canada is not the UN. It's not our responsibility to make sure each one of these [alleged war criminals present in Canada] faces justice in their own countries" (in Payton 2011). Clearly, the lightness of international obligations can provide a powerful justification for the lack of political will.

In July 2011, in a bold move to prove that Canada is not a safe haven for alleged perpetrators of international crimes, the Canadian authorities publicly released a list of 30 rejected refugee claimants, soliciting the public's assistance in hunting down the fugitives (Canada Border Agency Services 2011). Despite having reasonable grounds to believe the 30 suspects had committed or had been complicit in the commission of genocide, war crimes or crimes against humanity, the Canadian authorities did not intend to prosecute the accused once arrested. Indeed, all the 30 individuals were subjected to removal orders from Canada. Most immigration and refugee inadmissibility hearings being held *in camera*, the victims of these alleged offenders did not have a say in the expulsion process and could not voice their objections to the removal of their tormentors to countries where they would seldom be brought to justice for their actions.

Canada's approach highlights the difficulties of implementation of universal jurisdiction in practice and points to a difficult dilemma in the role that third states can play in ensuring justice for international crimes.

The "justice dilemma": prosecute or expel and the unsatisfactory reality of universal jurisdiction

> As Cesare Beccaria stated as long ago as 1764, "the conviction of finding nowhere a span of earth where real crimes were pardoned might be the most efficacious way of preventing their occurrence" and thus ensuring respect for the rule of law.
>
> (Cassese 1998: 17)

This is indeed the promise of universal jurisdiction, of the obligation to extradite or prosecute and of the creation of international criminal institutions. The end result for an alleged perpetrator of an international crime should be criminal investigation and prosecution, regardless of where their journey takes them.

Many states have adopted an aggressive "no safe haven" policy to ensure that their borders do not harbor international criminals. The policies encompass many remedies, both criminal and administrative, which, in Canada for example, could be grouped in three categories. The first category aims at preventing the admission to Canada of people who are or have been involved in war crimes, crimes against humanity or genocide. This includes the denial of visas overseas and denials at ports of entry. This effective measure has prevented roughly 2000 persons suspected of involvement in international crimes to gain access to Canada (Canadian Department of Justice 2008: 44). The other two categories apply once a suspect has entered or lives in Canada, which is particularly important for our purposes. A second category comprises the most repressive measures, which are prosecution in Canada under the War Crimes Act, extradition to a foreign government, and surrender to an international tribunal. A third category contains the other remedies, which are more focused on national interests than in ensuring that justice is done for the suspected crimes: revocation of citizenship under the Citizenship Act and deportation under the Immigration and Refugee Protection Act; exclusion from the protection of the 1951 United Nations Convention relating to the Status of Refugees; and inquiry for inadmissibility and removal from Canada under the Immigration and Refugee Protection Act.

According to the twelfth annual report of Canada's Crimes against Humanity and War Crimes Program, as of March 2011, 527 persons had been removed and two had been prosecuted since the program's inception in 1998. These numbers are telling, and in that regard the obvious should perhaps be recalled: deportation or removal of war criminals from Canada certainly cannot replace criminal prosecutions, nor can it be a substitute for extradition (LaForest 1991).[4] The over-reliance on administrative remedies, such as deportation and removal from the country, may serve the limited purpose of not allowing Canada to become a safe haven for war criminals, but it does very little to serve the broader objective of ensuring accountability for the core crimes. Deportation of alleged perpetrators of international crimes may be a first step in the right direction (Rikhof 2004), but for that to be true, it must remain just that, a first step. The ultimate aim is to ensure that justice, at home or abroad, is served.

While the overall budget of the Canadian war crimes program is $78 million for a period of five years (2005/06 to 2009/10), the cost of a single prosecution is evaluated at more than $4 million (Canadian Department of Justice 2008). According to that report, "[t]here is a strong cost effectiveness argument for using the criminal prosecution remedy sparingly" (2008: 48). This is clearly, in reality, the main guiding principle in the prosecutor's decision on whether to prosecute. The report, while confirming that

> [t]he 2007 decision of the War Crimes Steering Committee to place greater emphasis on immigration remedies (in terms of allocating resources) can be seen as appropriate from a cost effectiveness point of view given the apparent costs of prosecution cases and the budgetary limitations of the Program (2008: 48)

affirms at the same time that "[t]he limited resources available for criminal investigation, in relation to the inventory of serious cases, place an important limitation on the Program's contribution to the objective of denying safe haven through non-civil remedies" (2008: 61). The report thus concludes that "[t]here is considerable evidence that the Program will require increased financial resources if it is to be effective in addressing the no safe haven policy in the future" (2008: 60). We will come back to that. Clearly, financial considerations can severely restrict states' capacity to fulfill their international obligations.

Now, proponents of criminal prosecutions, particularly on the basis of universal jurisdiction, need to recognize that states have a legitimate interest in maintaining a manageable caseload; the caseload inevitably draws on public resources. States are also justified in taking into account the "potential political fallout of universal jurisdiction proceedings" (Broomhall 2003: 418). Though political and financial concerns should not be prioritized over the risk that alleged offenders go unpunished nor over the extent of Canada's international obligations in this regard, it has to be acknowledged that "[c]oncerns about the potentially real consequences of universal jurisdiction proceedings on interstate relations are not trivial" (Broomhall 2003: 418). In any case, the important obstacles that prosecutorial authorities may face in trying to gather evidence and witnesses testimonies abroad may very well, in practice, require a third state's cooperation, which may not always be forthcoming. Also, not all cases can meet the criteria of "reasonable prospect of conviction" necessary for the launch of a criminal procedure, notably whether there is sufficient (and sufficiently credible and accessible) evidence that could lead to a finding of guilt to the standard of "beyond a reasonable doubt". Even where information gathered by the authorities can lead to "reasonable grounds to believe" that a person has been involved in an international crime – the standard for refugee determination status, as an example – it is not necessarily the case that the authorities would be able to go to trial.

There is an apparently insoluble dilemma surrounding the available recourses to deal with war criminals present in third states like Canada. On the one hand, prosecution and extradition – the remedies most respectful of states' international responsibilities, if not obligations – are expensive, complicated and/or cumbersome. On the other hand, deportations and removals are quite unsatisfactory as they offer a very mild version of justice: there is no proper accountability of the alleged perpetrator, no satisfaction or reparation to the victims and very little truth telling associated with the processes. In some cases, the dilemma is even more complex: some individuals suspected of international crimes who are not welcome in a third state cannot be sent back, for fear of torture or other inhumane treatment or for fear that they would receive a trial that would be a "flagrant denial of justice" or other similar criteria (Lafontaine 2012b). In such cases, these individuals are caught in a legal void, with no official status in the third state, apart from being "unwelcomed", no prospect of finding refuge elsewhere, and often no chance at facing trial in the third state. Indeed, third states, for practical, evidentiary, financial, technical or policy reasons, often will not be willing or will be unable to bring these individuals before their courts (Rikhof 2012). This frequent and delicate situation, in which there is a collision of the fundamental rights of suspects – to life, to security of the person and to a fair trial – with those of victims – to justice, truth and reparation – is a major challenge for the implementation of international criminal justice at the national level and a thorny dilemma for states (Van Wijk 2013). Solutions have been crafted on a humanitarian basis, rightfully looking at the alleged perpetrator's untenable situation (Speckmann 2011). Some also insist on the need for prosecution (Vargas 2006). But what solutions can be envisaged that respect both the rights of suspects and those of victims?

A debate ensues between those who call for more justice – the "idealists" – and those who insist on third states' inherently limited role in the global endeavour of putting an end to impunity for international crimes – the "pragmatists" (see e.g. the public debate between Amnesty International and the Public Safety Minister with respect to the July 2011 hunt for fugitive alleged war criminals undertaken by the Canadian government: Kenney 2011; Neve and Vaugrante 2011). It is suggested that more thought should be invested in finding alternatives to these two apparently irreconcilable positions.

Alternative universal justice or some preliminary thoughts on ways out of the dilemma

The dilemma that third states confront in their dealings with war criminals who are present on their territory is comparable to the inherent limitations that international criminal justice has faced since its inception. In the recognition that criminal law cannot cope with the immensity of the task of ensuring justice for thousands of victims and just as many perpetrators, alternative measures were crafted to attain the goals of justice and reconciliation. These include truth and reconciliation commissions and other truth-telling mechanisms, traditional forms of justice such as the Gacaca in Rwanda, reparations programs for victims, and so on. "Transitional justice" encompasses various remedies, including criminal justice, that complement each other towards achievement of a common goal. These mechanisms were essentially conceived for the state where the crimes have occurred; very little thought, if any at all, was given to the possibility that similarly-inspired mechanisms be used by third states, which are also faced with daunting challenges once international criminals are found in their territories, often living among communities that include their very victims.

The principles that underlie transitional justice at the international level, among which figure prominently reconciliation and reparation to victims, can – and perhaps must – be transposed to third states such as Canada that are confronted with the difficult dilemma of dealing with alleged war criminals – and victims' communities – on their territories. Using Canada's legal and policy approach to war criminals present on its territory as an example, this part of the chapter offers preliminary thoughts on "alternative universal justice" measures that could perhaps, once fleshed out, contribute to minimizing the unsatisfactory consequences of the current state of affairs.

More resources for prosecution

The first reflection that needs to be made is the most obvious and the least "alternative". In the face of increased demands on states to contribute to the fight against impunity and considering that immigration flows necessarily require all states to seriously commit to "close the impunity gap", states' rhetoric regarding justice for international crimes needs to be met with hard cash. While resources will always be inevitable criteria guiding the exercise by states of their criminal jurisdiction over international criminals found on their territory, this consideration cannot be the main guiding principle of the policy in this regard. The Annual Reports of Canada's War Crimes Program give hints as to the limitations imposed by the budget allocated to the program, which remains at roughly $15 million per year since the coordinated program was established in 1998. The current budget has not taken account of "increases in salary or inflation that impact operational costs, or accommodation and corporate support costs. The result is a significant reduction in real dollar terms (adjusted for inflation) of the value of funds available for all program activities" (Canadian Department of Justice 2008: 52–3).

The budget that Canada allows for its War Crimes Program must be proportional to the extent of its international obligations (and responsibilities) and to the genuineness of its commitment to international criminal justice. This commitment must be directed at the proper functioning of the international institutions that have collectively been established for that purpose, such as the ICC, but states must commit equally to put to use their national institutions towards realization of the same fundamental objective of accountability. It seems beyond doubt that "the current level of program resources will be inadequate to achieving the Program's goals in the future" (Canadian Department of Justice 2008: 52). This situation has led numerous organizations and concerned individuals to steadily call for an increase in budget and has put into question Canada's role, once that of leadership, in the international criminal justice enterprise (CCIJ 2010; Shane 2011). The permanent funding given to the program in the 2011 federal budget was a first step in the right direction.

It must, however, be acknowledged that even if resources were significantly increased, numerous suspects of international crimes could not be prosecuted. Recourse to other remedies is essential in order to fulfill the War Crimes Program's objectives of ensuring both that Canada does not offer a safe haven to war criminals and that the principle of accountability is upheld.

Proactive stance on extradition and "concerned expulsions"

Considering the scarce resources for prosecution and the comparatively low costs of extradition or surrender procedures,[5] it seems that Canada should endeavor to promote more frequent recourse to the latter remedies. The procedures for transfers to international tribunals, including the ICC, and for extradition to third countries, are well provided for by legislation in the *Extradition Act*

(1999). Extradition is generally restricted to those states with which Canada has entered into an extradition treaty or which are designated as extradition partners by legislation (ss. 2–3). Extradition from Canada is usually done upon request from the third state or from the international tribunal.

Lack of request or lack of an extradition treaty with a given third state could be invoked as justification for the very rare recourse to extradition in war crimes cases.[6] However, the lack of an extradition treaty is not an obstacle, as s. 10 of the *Extradition Act* allows the Minister of Foreign Affairs, with the agreement of the Minister of Justice, to "enter into a specific agreement with a state or entity for the purpose of giving effect to a request for extradition in a particular case". Furthermore, although there are indeed few extraditions requests for war crimes worldwide, nothing prevents Canadian authorities from actively engaging with foreign governments with a view to encouraging extradition where circumstances so warrant (including fair trial and security concerns; Lafontaine 2012b). Just sharing the information about the presence of an alleged war criminal on Canadian soil can trigger an interest in seeking extradition. This proactive stance is clearly consistent with the *aut dedere aut judicare* principle discussed previously, which offers an alternative to the custodial state: prosecute or extradite. This shift would need more explicit cooperation between the actors of the War Crimes Program and the authorities responsible for extradition issues, including Foreign Affairs.

In fact, the proposal is often advanced that a sensible exercise of universal jurisdiction would take into account the possibilities that the suspect be tried in the territorial or national state. The "subsidiarity principle" refers to the idea that a state that wants to exercise universal jurisdiction should primarily defer to the territorial state or a state possessing another basis of jurisdiction if the latter is able or willing to prosecute (Lafontaine 2012b and authorities cited therein). The possibility of a trial abroad is also a factor that is taken into account in the prosecutor's decision to prosecute in Canada. The current passive attitude of custodial states as regards extradition is at odds with the idea that interstate cooperation is key to the fight against the impunity of perpetrators of international crimes, as demonstrated by the widespread use of *aut dedere aut judicare* clauses in treaties related to international crimes. However, importantly, if there cannot be genuine and fair prosecution elsewhere, Canada bears the legal and moral responsibility to conduct such proceedings before its courts (Rikhof 2009). Hence the importance, where real barriers to both prosecution and extradition exist, to deploy genuine efforts to promote accountability and to avoid making the "no safe haven" policy an unduly state-centric concept that becomes a safe conduit to impunity, as long as it is not "in our backyard".

Indeed, in a pragmatic understanding of third states' capacities as regards war crimes prosecution, where neither extradition nor prosecution is possible, states such as Canada should endeavor to adopt a collaborative approach with states where expulsion or deportation of an alleged war criminal is considered. "Concerned expulsions" – i.e. expulsions where the sending state tries to ensure that investigations and prosecutions will be undertaken by the receiving state – would alleviate the legitimate concern that the vast majority of alleged war criminals found on Canadian territory are expelled in conditions that are in contradiction with the obligations and responsibilities incumbent on all states in the fight against the impunity of alleged perpetrators of international crimes. Canada has some expertise in judicial cooperation, which could usefully be offered to the country to which the alleged offender is deported. Canadian authorities could thus contribute to the promotion of guarantees of non-repetition by training judges and prosecutors about the conduct of international crimes investigations and trials and by offering to share evidence gathered in Canada on a specific case, for instance. Generally speaking, some programs of international cooperation in Canada could be specifically targeted at "deportation countries", and could be implemented with the help of Canadian NGOs whose expertise touches upon judicial training and international criminal justice, such as Lawyers without Borders Canada or the Canadian Center for International Justice. Such measures could help to ensure that the destination countries of deported alleged war criminals are equipped for investigations and eventual criminal prosecutions.

The "Wanted by the CBSA" program launched in July 2011, referred to above, is in itself an innovative way of informing the public about measures taken towards alleged war criminals, but little or nothing appears to be done in relation to the country of destination so as to inform the authorities of the reasons for deportation and to offer assistance for investigations and prosecutions. This risky but promising program could be developed in a way that goes beyond the simplistic rhetoric of "these individuals have no right to be here and are being removed" (Payton 2011) to consider victims' interests in truth and accountability and Canada's responsibilities with respect to international criminal justice.

Alternative justice measures focusing on truth, reconciliation and reparation

As was discussed earlier, in some cases, neither prosecution nor expulsion is an option for a suspected war criminal. In general, there are also situations where expulsion is likely not the most favorable option in a holistic understanding of justice. For one thing, due to the long processing times of refugee or immigration claims in Canada, people suspected to be perpetrators of international crimes have very often forged strong family or professional ties with Canada by the time of the issuance of their removal order. Expulsions very often result in broken families and vulnerable economic situations if the offender happens to have children born on Canadian soil and is the main provider of the family. Expulsion to a state that the perpetrator left a long time ago is often not ideal for rehabilitation. For another thing, deportation may provide a sense of satisfaction for victims who are in Canada: because they know that the alleged perpetrator will not then enjoy the economic opportunities offered by Canada, and because expulsion of a person for their alleged past involvement in the commission of international crimes is a de facto official acknowledgement and denunciation of the actions of the individual. However, as noted above, expulsion is not accompanied with proper accountability of the alleged perpetrator, in Canada or abroad; there is no reparation to the victims and very little truth telling associated with the processes. It is perhaps time to craft innovative measures inspired by transitional justice, where the victims' interests in truth, reconciliation and reparation are paramount.

The idea of alternative justice is not foreign to Canadian criminal law. Section 717 of the *Criminal Code*, for instance, provides that alternative measures to prosecution can be envisaged provided these are not inconsistent with the protection of society and if certain conditions are met, including the existence of a program authorized by the Attorney General, the free participation and consent of the person alleged to have committed an offence and, most importantly, the acceptation of responsibility for the act or omission that forms the basis of the offence by that person.

Why couldn't a similar program specific to suspects of international crimes be designed? More often than not, individuals who have participated in core crimes no longer represent a danger to society, particularly to the society to which they integrated after the commission of the crimes (though, admittedly, the situation might be different in bordering states such as the Democratic Republic of the Congo for Rwandans, for instance, than in far-away lands such as Canada for the same nationals). Nothing prevents the crafting of a program in Canada or other states which could include public apologies to victims, public recognition of involvement in crimes, compensation to victims or to communities, community service with the victims' communities, etc. Measures could involve giving a number of hours per week to an NGO of the victims' community, or rendering a percentage of the suspect's salary to an NGO, in Canada or abroad, or to a Trust Fund for Victims – that of the ICC or that contemplated in the Canadian *War Crimes Act*, etc. Such programs could include measures in Canada and/or in the country where the crimes were committed, according to circumstances: notably the presence of communities of victims in Canada and the level of collaboration Canada enjoys with the territorial state. Such a program could be accompanied with removal from Canada or – why not – with the permission to stay in Canada if the suspect's compensation is considerable and remorse is genuine. The costs of such programs could be kept at a reasonable level, even if investigations would still be required to identify suspects. Such investigations and information gathering are already being done in relation to existing remedies as regards numerous potential suspects found on Canadian territory. Obviously, monitoring the program would imply that non-respect of the completion deadline, lack of genuine remorse or of full commitment, or any partial execution of an agreed measure could lead to the launch of a criminal prosecution, extradition or deportation, according to circumstances. Research into victims' needs in third states such as Canada (see Manirabona and Wemmers in this volume) and public consultation with victims could contribute to the design of a sensitive program that could be truly groundbreaking in the approach to universal justice.

Transparent decision-making process

The criteria upon which Canada decides whether to investigate or whether to prosecute are provided only in internal guidelines – the *Federal Prosecution Service Deskbook* – and in scarce information provided on the War Crimes Program's website (Lafontaine 2012a). No enforceable legal criteria exist to circumscribe the exercise of discretion. Other countries have asserted specific criteria in their legislations (e.g. Germany, *Code of Criminal Procedure*, s. 153f; South Africa, *Implementation of the Rome Statute of the International Criminal Court Act*, s. 5(1)(3); Belgium, *Preliminary Title of the Code of Criminal Procedure*, ss. 10 and 12; Spain, *Ley organica del poder judicial*, s. 23(4)). The importance of discretion in relation to the prosecution of international crimes is beyond doubt. The fact that certain states such as Germany and Belgium, where there is normally an obligation to prosecute, have adopted a special regime with respect to the prosecution of international crimes is quite telling in this regard.[7]

However, the need for broad prosecutorial discretion does not do away with the importance of transparency and accountability in the decision-making process. This is of particular concern for the victims, who are sometimes faced with the presence of an alleged perpetrator in their neighborhood and who may question the subsequent inaction from the prosecutorial authorities. Inaction that is not followed by explanation may significantly lessen victims' and the public's confidence in the administration of justice. It is thus crucial to ensure that the reasons of a decision not to prosecute are made available, as is frequently done by the German federal prosecutor (Gallagher 2009) or as is statutorily provided in the South African legislation (*Implementation of the Rome Statute of the International Criminal Court Act*, s. 5(5)).

The Canadian *Federal Prosecution Service Deskbook* recommends that where a decision is made not to institute proceedings, a record of the reasons for that decision be kept. It also indicates that in certain circumstances, such reasons may have to be explained to investigative agencies or to victims, and may sometimes be publicly communicated in order to maintain confidence in the administration of justice (s. 15.3.2). This recommendation is particularly important in the context of core crimes prosecutions, which will remain few in numbers in comparison to the number of potential suspects of war crimes present in Canada and to the much broader use of other remedies. We are not aware that such communications initiatives have ever been taken with respect to alleged war criminals in Canada.

Transparency to victims must be enhanced in the current Canadian War Crimes Program, as there is an opaque veil surrounding the process of deciding whether to prosecute. The War Crimes Program, initially quite proactive and visible, has obviously been hampered by budget restrictions, despite the energetic and competent presence of renowned lawyers and investigators among its staff: its website is now quite parsimonious of the information it shares and it is spread out between the Justice Department and other departments, such as the Royal Canadian Mounted Police and the Canadian Border Service Agency, so that a concerned citizen's search for information is made quite complicated. Furthermore, the annual reports are published late and are not easy to find (for example, as of July 2013 the only available report was the Twelfth Report, which summarizes the program activities from April 1, 2008 to March 31, 2011, also highlighting the delay in publishing some of the previous years' reports). In addition, as noted above, the administrative processes leading to deportation or expulsion are often confidential, except where they reach the judicial review stage, and it is almost impossible for victims to know what was taken into consideration in an assessment of exclusion or non-admissibility to refugee status. Information provided to victims may be key to their perceptions of justice and to their confidence in the judicial system in general, be it international or domestic (Wemmers and Raymond 2011). Such transparency is an almost costless measure that is particularly important in countries such as Canada, where victims have almost no possibility of seeking judicial review of a decision not to prosecute, which would obviously be the ultimate remedy to ensure transparency and accountability of the exercise of prosecutorial discretion (Lafontaine 2012a).

Crimes against Humanity Fund

Whether they rely exclusively on national jurisdictions or whether they provide for their own internal reparations schemes, international or internationalized criminal jurisdictions will count heavily on cooperation by states to ensure effective reparation to victims. In this spirit, states' obligations to cooperate with the ICC for the enforcement of orders for victim's reparations, whether monetary or non-monetary, should be duly reflected in national implementing legislations (see Art. 9.2 of the *Mutual Legal Assistance in Criminal Matters Act*, par. 132–134 and Clause 42).

An interesting consequence of the ICC *Statute* is the creation of reparation mechanisms in domestic legal systems, including in countries where victims normally have minimal involvement in criminal proceedings. For instance, Canada has created a "Crimes against Humanity Fund" as part of its national implementing legislation (*War Crimes Act*, s. 30). If such initiatives do not involuntarily act "at cross-purposes to the ICC Trust Fund for Victims" (Ferstman 2002: 686), they can be crucial tools for victims in national proceedings for ICC crimes and a positive indirect consequence of the complementarity principle. The Canadian Trust Fund is not yet operational and has therefore played no role in the two prosecutions undertaken thus far under the act. It currently plays no part in the general Canadian approach to justice for international crimes. Its potential, however – despite probable difficulties in funding and implementation – is tremendous (Manirabona 2011; Currie 2010). Considering the different categories of victims that international crimes create and their various needs, particularly where victims are in third states (Wemmers 2010a; Wemmers 2010b), the fund could channel innovative initiatives of reparation – think of scholarships or tax credits – including but not limited to psychological support of victims acting as witnesses in criminal trials in Canada. Reparation could be collective (see

Mégret in this volume) and could be done in synergy with the ICC Trust Fund if the situation calls for collaboration, or with the territorial state in certain circumstances.

Conclusion

It is now trite to say that the promise of the new system of international justice depends on states' capacity and will to put their legal systems to use for the global enterprise. It is also commonplace to argue that universal jurisdiction has a role to play in closing the impunity gap. Beyond the evidence and the rhetoric, many challenges remain: international obligations are inconsistent; practical and political obstacles lead to scarce prosecutions; extradition is underused; and victims' needs and rights are neglected. The recent use of universal jurisdiction not only in Western states such as Canada, Spain and Belgium but also by Senegal, South Africa and Argentina is a positive sign that the web is extending and closing on alleged war criminals. The next decades will require a move from an unduly state-centric "no safe haven" idea into a conscience of the necessity of being a proactive member of a global system directed at a single and common goal. This implies moving beyond the prosecute (little) or expel (a lot) dilemma and crafting alternative ways to ensure justice and reparation for victims of international crimes who are present in far-away lands.

Notes

1 The author wishes to acknowledge with gratitude the excellent research work of Evelyne Akoto in preparation for this chapter. She also thanks Titine Pétronie Kouendze Ingoba for a useful review of literature on certain areas of interest.

2 *Rome Statute*, Art. 75; *Internal Rules of the Extraordinary Chambers in the Courts of Cambodia*, r. 23(11).

3 See e.g. Dutch Explanatory Memorandum (*Memorie van Toelichting*) on the substantive implementing legislation (*Wet Internationale Misdrijven*) which states:

> Although not expressly provided for in the Statute, the majority of states – including the Kingdom – were always of the opinion that the principle of complementarity entails that states parties to the Statute are obliged to criminalize the crimes that are subject to the International Criminal Court's jurisdiction in their national laws and furthermore to establish extra-territorial, universal jurisdiction, which enables their national criminal courts to adjudicate these crimes even if they have been committed abroad by a foreign national
>
> (Kleffner 2008: 91)

4 The aims of extradition and deportation are clearly distinct. The object of extradition is to return a fugitive offender to the country which has requested him for trial or punishment for an offence committed within its jurisdiction. Deportation, on the other hand, is governed by the public policy of the state that wishes to dispose an undesirable alien.

5 The cost of prosecution is slightly over $4 million while extradition and surrender to an international tribunal range between $471,251 and $526,341 (Canadian Department of Justice 2008).

6 The 1983 *Rauca* case was the first war crimes extradition from Canada. He was extradited to Germany and died in prison while awaiting trial. Mr. Rauca was the last person to be extradited from Canada for war crimes until 2007, when Michael Seifert, a former German SS member, was extradited to Italy. The extradition of Jorge Vinicio Sosa Orantes to the United States for immigration fraud charges was a missed opportunity for Canada to extradite him to a country (Spain or Guatemala) where he would be tried for crimes against humanity (Moharib 2012).

7 In Germany, Ntanda Nsereko mentions that this discretion was designed "to save the German state from the financial burden and the heavy workload that the obligation to prosecute in all cases would engender" (2005: 127).

References

Akhavan, P. (2010) "Whiter National Courts? The Rome Statute's missing half", *Journal of International Criminal Justice*, 8: 1245–8.

Amnesty International (2001) *Universal Jurisdiction: The duty of states to enact and implement legislation*, London: Amnesty International Publications.

Amnesty International (2010) *Universal Jurisdiction: UN General Assembly should support this essential international justice tool*, available at: www.amnesty.org/en/library/info/IOR53/015/2010/en (accessed October 12, 2012).

Beccaria, C. (1880) *Dei Delitti e Delle Pene [On Crimes and Punishments]*, trans. by J. Farrer, London: Chatto and Windus.

Broomhall, B. (2003) *International Justice and the International Criminal Court*, Oxford: Oxford University Press.

Canada Border Services Agency (2011) *Government of Canada Enlists Help of Canadians to Enforce Canada's Immigrations Laws – Government will not tolerate war criminals in our communities*, available at: www.cbsa-asfc.gc.ca/media/release-communique/2011/2011-07-21-eng.html (accessed October 14, 2012).

Canada Border Services Agency, Citizenship and Immigration Canada, Department of Justice and Royal Canadian Mounted Police (2008) *Canada's War Program on Crimes against Humanity and War Crimes 2008–2011*, available at: www.cbsa-asfc.gc.ca/security-securite/wc-cg/bsf5039-eng.pdf (accessed October 5, 2012).

Canadian Center for International Justice and Partners (2010) *Letter to Federal Ministers of Finance and Justice*, available at: www.ccij.ca/webyep-system/program/download.php?FILENAME=74-4-at-File_Upload_25.pdf&ORG_FILENAME=Sign-on_letter_on_need_for_WCP_Funding_December_2010.pdf (accessed July 31, 2013).

Canadian Department of Justice (2008) *Crimes against Humanity and War Crimes Program – Summative evaluation final report*, available at: www.justice.gc.ca/eng/pi/eval/rep-rap/08/war-guerre/war.pdf (accessed July 31, 2013).

Cassese, A. (1998) "On the Current Trends Towards Criminal Prosecution and Punishment of Breaches of International Humanitarian Law", *European Journal of International* Law, 9: 2–17.

Cassese, A. (2006) "'Foreword' to Symposium on the 'Twists and Turns' of Universal Jurisdiction", *Journal of International Criminal Justice*, 4: 559–60.

CEG (2004) *Report of the Commonwealth Expert Group on Implementing Legislation for the Rome Statute of the International Criminal Court*, London: Westminster.

Citizenship Act 1985, Ch. 29, Ottawa: RSC.

Convention (I) for the Amelioration of the Condition of the Wounded and Sick in Armed Forces in the Field (1950), 75 UNTS 31.

Convention (II) for the Amelioration of the Condition of Wounded, Sick and Shipwrecked Members of Armed Forces at Sea (1950), 75 UNTS 85.

Convention (III) relative to the Treatment of Prisoners of War (1950), 75 UNTS 135.

Convention (IV) relative to the Protection of Civilian Persons in Time of War (1950), 75 UNTS 287.

Convention against Torture and Other Cruel, Inhuman or Degrading Treatment or Punishment (1987), 1465 UNTS 85.

Convention Relating to the Status of Refugees (1951), 189 UNTS 150.

Crimes against Humanity and War Crimes Act 2000, Ch. 24. Ottawa: SCC.

Cryer, R., Friman, H., Robinson, D. and Wilmshurst, E. (2010) *An Introduction to International Criminal Law and Procedure*, 2nd edn, Cambridge: Cambridge University Press.

Currie, R.J. (2010) *International and Transnational Criminal Law*, Toronto: Irwin Law.

ECCC (2011) *Internal Rules of the Extraordinary Chambers in the Courts of Cambodia*, available at: www.eccc.gov.kh/sites/default/files/legal-documents/ECCC%20Internal%20Rules%20(Rev.8)%20English.pdf (accessed June 15, 2013).

Extradition Act 1999, Ch. 18, Ottawa: SCC.

Federal Public Service of Belgium (1878) *Des Actions qui Naissent des Infractions c. I-II*, available at: www.ejustice.just.fgov.be/cgi_loi/loi_a1.pl?language=fr&la=F&cn=187804170&table_name=loi&&caller=list&F&fromtab=loi&tri=dd+AS+RANK&rech=1&numero=1&sql=(text+contains+("))#LNK0002 (accessed October 16, 2013).

Ferstman, C. (2002) "The Reparation Regime of the International Criminal Court: Practical considerations", *Leiden Journal of International Law*, 15: 667–86.

Gallagher, K. (2009) "Universal Jurisdiction in Practice – Efforts to hold Donald Rumsfeld and other high-level United States officials accountable for torture", *Journal of International Criminal Justice*, 7: 1087–116.

German Federal Ministry of Justice (1987) *Strafprozessordnung*, available at: www.gesetze-im-internet.de/englisch_stpo/englisch_stpo.html (accessed July 20, 2013).

Government of Canada (1985) *Criminal Code*, RSC: C-46.

Hay, J. (2004) "Implementing the ICC Statute in New Zealand", *Journal of International Criminal Justice*, 2: 191–210.

Immigration and Refugee Protection Act 2000, Ch. 27, Ottawa: SCC.

Implementation of the Rome Statute of the International Criminal Court Act 2002, No. 23642, Cape Town: SACC.

International Convention for the Protection of All Persons from Enforced Disappearance (2007), Doc.A/61/48.

International Convention on the Suppression and Punishment of the Crime of Apartheid (1976), 1015 UNTS 243.

International Criminal Court (n.d.) *Legal Basis*, available at: http://trustfundforvictims.org/legal-basis (accessed July 2013).

Italy v. Seifert (2007), BCCA 407.

Kenney, J. (2011) "Response to Open Letter from Amnesty International", available at: www.jasonkenney.ca/news/an-open-letter-to-amnesty-international/ (accessed August 2, 2013).

Kirchengast, T. (2011) "Les victimes comme parties prenantes d'un procès pénal de type accusatoire", *Criminologie*, 44(2): 99–123.

Kleffner, J.K. (2008) *Complementarity in the Rome Statute and National Criminal Jurisdictions*, Oxford: Oxford University Press.

Lafontaine, F. (2012a) *Prosecuting Genocide, Crimes against Humanity and War Crimes in Canadian Courts*, Toronto: Carswell.

Lafontaine, F. (2012b) "Universal Jurisdiction: The realistic utopia", *Journal of International Criminal Justice*, 10: 1277–302.

Lafontaine, F. and Elassal, E.F. (2009) "La prison à vie pour Désiré Munyaneza: Vers un 'développement durable' de la justice pénale internationale", *Le Devoir*, November 2, available at: www.ledevoir.com/2009/11/02/274892.html (accessed July 31, 2013).

LaForest, A.W. (1991) *Extradition To and From Canada*, 3rd edn, Aurora: Canada Law Books.

Ley organica del poder judicial (2009), BOE: 6/1985.

Manirabona, A.M. (2011) "Quelle réparation pour les victimes des crimes internationaux ayant immigré au Québec? Quelques commentaires à la lumière du jugement Munyaneza", *Journal International De Victimologie*, 9(3): 403–12.

Moharib, N. (2010) "Accused Guatemalan War Butcher Jorge Sosa Extradited to U.S.", *Calgary Sun*, September 22, available at: www.calgarysun.com/2012/09/22/accused-guatemalan-war-butcher-jorge-sosa-extradited-to-us (accessed October 16, 2012).

Mutual Legal Assistance in Criminal Matters Act 1985, Ch. 30, Ottawa: RSC.

Neve, A. and Vaugrante, B. (2011) "Amnesty International Canada Open Letter to Ministers Toews and Kenney about 'Wanted by the CBSA'", August 2, available at: www.amnesty.ca/news/news-item/amnesty-international-canada-open-letter-to-ministers-toews-and-kenney (accessed August 2, 2013).

Ntanda, N. and Daniel, D. (2005) "Prosecutorial Discretion before National Courts and International Tribunals", *Journal of International Criminal Justice*, 3: 124–44.

Payton, L. (2011) "War Crimes Prosecution not up to Canada, Toews Says", *CBC News*, available at: www.cbc.ca/news/canada/story/2011/08/03/war-crimes-suspect-toronto-arrest.html (accessed July 31, 2013).

Protocol Additional to the Geneva Conventions of 12 August 1949, and relating to the Protection of Victims of International Armed Conflicts (Protocol I) (1979), 1125 UNTS 3.

Public Prosecution Service of Canada (2013) *The Federal Prosecution Service Deskbook*, available at: www.ppsc-sppc.gc.ca/eng/fps-sfp/fpd/toc.html (accessed July 31, 2011).

R. c. Désiré Munyaneza (2009), QCCS 2201.

R. c. Désiré Munyaneza (2009), RJQ 1432.

R. c. Jacques Mungwarere (2013), ONCS 4594.

Re Federal Republic of Germany and Rauca (1983), DLR (3d) 638.

Rikhof, J. (2004) "Canada and War Criminals: The policy, the program and the results", paper presented to the 18th International Conference of the International Society for the Reform of Criminal Law, Montreal, August.

Rikhof, J. (2009) "Fewer Places to Hide? The Impact of Domestic War Crimes Prosecutions on International Impunity", *Criminal Law Forum*, 20: 1–51.

Rikhof, J. (2012) *The Criminal Refugee: The treatment of asylum seekers with a criminal background in international and domestic law*, Dordrecht: Republic of Letters Publishers.

Rome Statute of the International Criminal Court (1998), UNTS 2187.

Shane, K. (2011) "Former War Criminal Leadership Seen as Waning", available at: www.ccij.ca/media/ccij-in-the-news/index.php?DOC_INST=30 (accessed August 7, 2013).

South African Litigation Centre and Others v. The National Director of Public Prosecutions and Others (2012), NGHC: 77150/09.

Speckmann, D. (2011) "Briefing Paper: Balancing exclusion, prosecution and non-refoulement – the application of Article 1F of the Refugees Convention in The Netherlands", available at: http://ces.anu.edu.au/sites/ces.anu.edu.au/files/2011/2011%20BPS%20exclusion%20in%20the%20netherlands%20-%20speckmann.pdf (accessed July 31, 2013).

Statute of the Special Tribunal for Lebanon 2007, The Hague: S/RES/1757.

The Prosecutor v. Germain Katanga and Mathieu Ngudjolo Chui (2009), ICC-01/04–01/07–1497.

United Nations (1948) *Convention on the Prevention and Punishment of the Crime of Genocide*, available at: www.hrweb.org/legal/genocide.html (accessed August 7, 2013).

United Nations (2004) *Security Council Resolution 1564*, available at: http://daccess-ddsny.un.org/doc/UNDOC/GEN/N04/515/47/PDF/N0451547.pdf?OpenElement (accessed August 7, 2013).

United Nations (2005) *Report of the International Commission of Inquiry on Darfur to the United Nations Secretary-General*, available at: www.un.org/News/dh/sudan/com_inq_darfur.pdf (accessed July 31, 2013).

United Nations (2005) *Security Council Resolution 1593*, available at: http://daccess-dds-ny.un.org/doc/UNDOC/GEN/N05/292/73/PDF/N0529273.pdf?OpenElement (accessed August 7, 2013).

United Nations (2006) *Secretary General, High Commissioner for Human Rights Call for Urgent Action by Security Council to Halt Violence in Sudan*, available at: www.un.org/News/Press/docs/2005/sc8313.doc.htm (accessed July 31, 2013).

Van Wijk, J. (2013) "When International Criminal Justice Collides with Principles of International Protection: Assessing the consequences of ICC witnesses seeking asylum, defendants being acquitted, and convicted being released", *Leiden Journal of International Law*, 26(1): 173–91.

Vargas Santalla, E. (2006) "Ensuring Protection and Prosecution of Alleged Torturers: Looking for compatibility of non-refoulement protection and prosecution of international crimes", *European Journal of Migration and Law*, 8: 41–59.

Wemmers, J.M. (2010a) "Qui sont les victimes, et ont-elles toutes les mêmes droits?", in D. Lafortune, J. Poupart and S. Tanner (eds) *Questions de Criminologie*, Montreal: Les Presses de l'Université de Montréal.

Wemmers, J.M. (2010b) "The Needs of Victims of International Crimes", in R. Letschert, R. Haveman, A.M. de Brouwer and A. Pemberton (eds) *Developing Victimological Approaches to International Crimes*, Antwerp: Intersentia.

Wemmers, J.M. and Raymond, E. (2011) "La justice et les victimes: L'importance de l'information pour les victimes", *Criminologie*, 44(2): 157–69.

Part III

Victims and society

7 Framing reparation claims for crimes against humanity

A social psychological perspective

Katherine B. Starzyk, Danielle Gaucher, Gregory D.B. Boese and Katelin H. Neufeld

Crimes against humanity are acts of serious, widespread and systematic harm. Given their heinous nature, it seems people should unquestionably support reparations for such harms. Yet obtaining reparations for crimes against humanity can be difficult. Though most members of the public are usually willing to acknowledge at least some degree of wrongdoing, reparation campaigns are frequently met with indifference and sometimes actively opposed (Brooks 1999). In this chapter, we first describe how social psychologists aim to understand the causes of support for reparations; we then discuss the key theories (just world, system justification, and social identity) that organize much of social psychological research on reactions to intergroup harm and reparations. Finally, we provide suggestions for the design of reparation campaigns and highlight supporting research, much of it from our own work.

Social psychological approaches to understanding support for reparations

To understand how to frame reparation claims so that people are more likely to support them, it is useful to take an interdisciplinary perspective, as the methods and perspectives across disciplines are often complementary. Although social psychology is a relative newcomer to the area, we suggest that the discipline can make important contributions because social psychologists are experienced in evaluating the effects of situational factors as well as the underlying causes of behavior. Social psychologists can therefore help to understand when and why people are likely to support reparations. The research and analytic methods that social psychologists have used to study support for reparations are diverse, but most study reactions to reparations under controlled, experimental laboratory conditions. In one approach, the primary one we take, researchers have participants read a description of wrongdoing that includes or withholds details they think might influence whether participants support reparations. By holding details of the "crime" constant and only adding or removing a key factor, researchers can systematically observe whether the manipulated factor is responsible, at least in part, for people's subsequent reactions. For example, researchers may construct a passage that either does or does not label an intergroup harm as "genocide". Afterwards, participants complete measures assessing support for reparations as well as other social psychological constructs (e.g., collective guilt, empathy, intergroup attitudes). At the end of such studies, participants are always told what was misrepresented or omitted as well as the rationale for the manipulation(s).

Normally, participants are undergraduate students who are not members of the affected groups and who know little about the events they answer questions about. An advantage of this is that researchers can credibly manipulate aspects of the events. A possible disadvantage is that more informed participants might respond differently. Like our typical participants, though, the general public (at least in Canada) is often uninformed. In addition, such studies are sometimes complemented by studies in which participants are knowledgeable (and are even sometimes members of involved groups) and/or are asked to recall information rather than read passages. Such results are therefore likely to apply to the general public and members of majority groups, who are often the target of reparation campaigns.

Relevant social psychological theories

Several prominent social psychological theories are relevant to understanding reactions to reparations for crimes against humanity. In our work, which focuses on reactions to "historical" intergroup harms and current social injustices, we rely heavily on: belief in a just world (BJW) theory, system justification theory (SJT), and social identity theory (SIT). We describe these theories below, focusing on the aspects that help explain and predict reactions to reparations.

Belief in a just world theory

Belief in a just world theory (sometimes referred to as "just world theory") holds that people have a fundamental need to believe that the world is fair and just and that people get what they deserve (Lerner 1977, 1980). According to the theory, and the large amount of research that supports it, people hold a general "justice motive". This is an altruistic concern that justice is achieved, and people will go to great lengths to preserve this belief (Hafer and Bègue 2005). Any evidence of undeserved outcomes threatens this belief, and in turn motivates people to resolve the threat. Importantly, the response to such a threat can be prosocial. For example, people may resolve the threat of an innocent victim suffering by helping the victim. A prosocial response is more likely when people are able to help. In contrast, when people cannot help or it is likely that the victim will continue to suffer regardless of help, people may use alternate strategies to cope with the threat. For example, instead of helping, people may derogate the victim or come to view the victim negatively and therefore as deserving of their fate (Lerner and Simmons 1966) so that they can maintain the belief that good things happen to good people and bad things happen to bad people, or that people get what they deserve.

The majority of just world research focuses on people's reactions to dramatic cases of suffering, such as rape, and significant illness, such as HIV/AIDS and cancer. More recent research, however, demonstrates that people will also rationalize the more minor unfair outcomes that they personally experience in their everyday lives. For example, Gaucher *et al.* (2010) demonstrated that people will engage in compensatory rationalizations to help them preserve their belief in a just world. Specifically, they found that when people experience even minor uncontrollable *bad* events in their lives (such as a bad hair day), they will compensate for this misfortune by recalling uncontrollable *good* events. The reverse also holds true; after experiencing positive uncontrolled events (such as winning a small lottery), people recalled more negative past uncontrolled events. In this way, the perception is that good and bad rewards equal out and no one person ends up receiving more than their fair share; the belief that the world is just is maintained.

According to Lerner (1977), maintaining a belief in a just world is adaptive because it instills confidence that investing in long-term goals and delaying gratification is a safe and worthwhile endeavor (Hafer 2002; Hafer *et al.* 2005; Lerner 1977). Interestingly, people who score higher on belief in just world scales have better general wellbeing, suggesting there is a psychologically adaptive function to this belief (Furnham 2003). Though belief in a just world is typically conceptualized as a general justice motive held by everyone, some researchers have developed standardized measures to assess individual differences in this motivation (Rubin and Peplau 1973). Moreover, others have shown that this individual difference sometimes affects how people respond to injustice. For example, Gaucher *et al.* (2010) found that people with a higher motivation to view the world as just used more compensatory rationalizations.

System justification theory

Whereas just world theory focuses on how people rationalize underserved outcomes to make them appear fair, system justification theory focuses on people's tendency *to* justify and legitimize the socio-political systems within which they are forced to operate (Jost and Banaji 1994). According to system justification theory, not all injustice is rationalized equally. Injustice connected to one's socio-political system, such as one's government, is especially threatening because all people, to varying degrees, are motivated to justify and rationalize away the moral and other failures of their socio-political systems. People are most likely to justify a socio-political system when they cannot easily escape it, when the system is threatened, and when the system strongly influences personal outcomes. Citizens are therefore particularly likely to support their governments when they cannot physically leave (e.g., by emigrating to other provinces or countries), when internal or external groups are criticizing or attacking the government (e.g., during times of war), and when they are highly dependent on the government (e.g., during a recession).

One reason people will justify their socio-political systems is that it is psychologically uncomfortable to believe that something illegitimate/unfair has control over them. Thus, the motive to defend one's socio-political systems is partly a result of people's fundamental need to perceive order in the world; system justification helps people to meet the need to attain certainty and create a stable worldview. Of course, people can fulfill the need to believe that the world operates systematically and non-randomly by perceiving control from multiple, interchangeable sources. One possible source is a sense of *personal control* over events in the world. People, however, sometimes face a loss of personal control. In such cases, they can compensate for the loss of personal control by increasing their reliance upon *external* sources of control, such as the government. In support, Kay *et al.* (2009) found that people whose sense of personal control had been threatened were more likely to engage in system justification (i.e., to defend the legitimacy of the current government). Existential needs, such as the need to perceive a safe environment, and relational needs to bond with others who also tend to justify the system are also theorized to underlie system justification tendencies (Jost *et al.* 2009).

A central tenant of SJT is that people hold a general preference for the status quo. Kay and colleagues experimentally demonstrated that people tend to construe "whatever currently is" as "the way it should be," across a number of domains (i.e., political structure, public policy, and gender inequality), as well as that system threats operate much like self-threats, invoking defensive processes (2009). For example, in an experiment concerning gender diversity in Canadian parliament, researchers manipulated participants' need to justify the socio-political system and the apparent status quo by implying that there were relatively few or many women working in politics. Participants who were motivated to justify their socio-political systems deemed gender arrangements as most ideal if they believed the arrangements reflected the status quo. Thus, participants who thought there were few (rather than more) women in politics were less supportive of female politicians (Kay *et al.* 2009). In addition to providing direct evidence for a motivated status quo bias, this research highlighted the power of the status quo for determining people's social ideals.

Building on system justification theory, some of our recent research suggests that people may forgo justice concerns within systems that they are motivated to justify, but not in irrelevant systems. In a study focusing on the lack of clean running water in 28 percent of Canada's First Nations' homes, we (Neufeld *et al.* 2013) manipulated the feasibility of providing clean running water to this group and the relevance of the system to participants – we randomly assigned Canadian undergraduate students to learn that the issue was local and therefore occurred in a relevant system (i.e., Canada) or in a foreign system (i.e., Australia). Aside from these manipulations, participants' experiences were identical across conditions. Consistent with system justification theory, participants who thought the issue was an Australian one supported that country's government taking action regardless of feasibility. In contrast, solution feasibility *did* matter in the context of a local system: when participants believed the issue was Canadian, those who received feasibility information demonstrated greater support for government action, empathy, and moral outrage, and judged what they learned about the issue to be more accurate.

Social identity theory

Social identity theory (SIT) holds that people derive an identity based on their group memberships (Tajfel and Turner 1986). Moreover, people seek to maintain a positive view of their social identities – that is, they seek to maintain positive distinctiveness. For marginalized groups, this can be difficult. If the group boundaries are thought to be easily permeable, individuals may simply leave the group and join a more favorably received group. When one cannot easily leave a marginalized group, positive distinctiveness can be achieved through various self-enhancement strategies. In-group favoritism, the tendency for people to give more valued resources to their own rather than to an out-group, is perhaps the most widely researched positive distinctiveness strategy. Although the motivation to justify important socio-political systems may override the tendency toward in-group favoritism, people show a pervasive in-group bias. That is, they tend to give preferential treatment to members of their own group. In-group bias occurs for non-arbitrary groups (such as race, culture, gender, etc.) as well as arbitrary ones (such as groups created in the laboratory based on a coin toss). Indeed, much of the supporting evidence for in-group bias effects comes from laboratory experiments invoking the *minimal group paradigm*. Within this paradigm, participants are brought into the lab and then randomly assigned to a group based on some "minimal" classification scheme, such as a coin toss or preference for a particular item. Participants in their assigned "group" are then asked to distribute resources between their group and an out-group. In-group bias emerges time and again. People consistently distribute more of the valued resources to their in-group than their out-group.

The motivation to protect important identities also affects responses to the commission of major harm. For example, when confronted with an in-group's transgressions, people rarely report "collective guilt" (Iyer *et al.* 2004; Wohl *et al.* 2006) – an emotion that "stems from the distress that group members experience when they accept that their in-group is responsible for immoral actions that harmed another group" (Branscombe and Doosje 2004: 3). Interestingly, and in support, Peetz and colleagues (2010) report that the average German reports as much collective guilt as do Canadians for the Holocaust.

Importantly, however, whether they belong to a perpetrator or victim group, not all group members speak with a single voice. For example, sampled in 2002 when the issue of reparations for slavery re-emerged, 37 percent of African Americans did not believe that the US government should offer cash payments to descendents of slaves (Viles 2002). Similarly, not all perpetrator group members fail to perceive continued suffering or oppose reparations. For example, the CURE group (Caucasians United for Reparations and Emancipation) once actively advocated for reparations for US slavery (CURE 2008). Thus, some people may be persuaded to support reparations even when they symbolically belong to the perpetrator group.

Lessons for framing reparation campaigns from social psychology

Collectively, research findings on just world, system justification, and social identity make several suggestions about human nature. Specifically, they suggest that people are "built" to think about justice (BJW) and to justify their social systems (SJT); that such justice and system motivations are adaptive in that they satisfy a broad constellation of underlying psychological needs (BWJ; SJT; SIT); and that people are inherently "groupish" in that they easily form and often maintain group boundaries through in-group biases. The phenomena illustrated by all three theories conspire against people's general acceptance, adoption and support of reparations – but they also shed light on when people will support reparations. We provide some suggestions below for designing reparation campaigns that follow from these theories and describe evidence to support our suggestions. In no way do we mean to present these as prescriptive, because some may not fit with victim group values or be a good match to a particular reparation campaign.

Show how reparations are feasible and highlight their possible benefits

Reparations are often both financially and psychologically costly. One may, however, make even very expensive reparation packages seem more attractive. Although people do not necessarily make decisions rationally (Tversky and Kahneman 1974), we propose that people are more likely to support reparations if they seem feasible and likely to be beneficial.

Reparations seem "feasible" when people think they are realistic or that they could be provided. In some cases, it may be easy to provide reparations. In other cases, it may be difficult or seem painful to provide reparations, but nonetheless *seem* feasible. It is possible that people will perceive reparations as more feasible in times of abundance or when they think providing reparations will not compromise valued social resources. Separate from the idea of feasibility, "potential benefit" refers to whether people believe there will be positive outcomes to providing reparations. Feasibility therefore refers to the ability to provide reparations, whereas potential benefit refers to the possible "rewards" associated with providing reparations. Of course, these are related concepts. People may be unwilling to perceive ineffectual reparations as feasible, but, conversely, be more willing to perceive beneficial reparations as more feasible. By demonstrating possible benefit, groups campaigning for reparations may justify the financial and psychological expenditure.

One possible benefit of providing reparations is ending continued victim suffering. Although scholars argue that reparations in many cases do not truly "repair" the wrongdoing (e.g., Brooks 1999; Minow 1998), the general public may perceive that they do. People may sometimes also perceive victims who continue to suffer as more deserving of reparations. Consistent with this, legal scholar Matsuda (1987) suggests that groups must emphasize that they are still suffering psychologically, physically or materially as a consequence of the original harm in order to be successful in obtaining reparations. In some cases, victim suffering may be unclear, for a variety of reasons. For example, victims may hide how they continue to suffer. Yet when continued suffering is not obvious, people may be reluctant to distribute valued resources and acknowledge culpability, even implicitly.

Supporting the above, Starzyk and Ross (2008) examined the effects of feasibility and continued suffering on support for reparations for a government-sponsored harm against a Black community in Canada. Undergraduate student participants read a description of the forced relocation of Africville, which occurred in Halifax, Nova Scotia, in the 1960s (Clairmont and Magill 1999). They learned that the City of Halifax bulldozed Africville without the residents' permission or consultation; that the residents were unhappy in their new homes, though they had amenities such as running water, electricity and sewage service; and that residents believed the city confiscated the land for economic rather than humanitarian reasons. At the time of the study, former Africville residents and descendents were publicly seeking reparations for the relocation, but participants in the study typically knew nothing about the events or the reparation campaign. This ignorance allowed the researchers to manipulate the presentation of both the feasibility of providing reparations and the group's continued suffering: the descriptions stated either that the confiscated land was undeveloped and still available or that it was no longer available (feasibility manipulation) and depicted the residents either as continuing to suffer psychologically and materially from the relocation or as doing reasonably well. When reparations were presented as feasible, participants expressed greater compassion for victims who continued to suffer. In addition, these participants perceived the situation as more unjust, reported more sympathy, and judged reparations more favorably. Consistent with just world and system justification theories, when reparations seemed impractical (i.e., the land was no longer available), continued victim suffering did not affect participants' assessments of the magnitude of the injustice and their expressions of sympathy. Unexpectedly, participants also objected (relatively speaking) to compensating non-suffering victims when reparations were feasible, possibly because they perceived them as undeserving of compassion or not as victims – because they were not suffering.

In summary, Starzyk and Ross (2008) found that demonstrating victim suffering mattered. Importantly, though, victim suffering should not be perceived as too great to "fix", as intractable suffering should threaten the belief in a just world and socio-political systems. In such cases, people may blame the victims for their difficulties or respond in some other negative way rather than responding sympathetically. Providing an example of how highlighting victim suffering can sometimes backfire, Imhoff and Banse (2009) found that people responded in a *more* prejudiced manner when presented with evidence of Jews' ongoing suffering due to their past history of victimization.

To understand the effects of potential benefits associated with reparations, Starzyk and Boese (2012) manipulated the perception of potential benefit by asking participants to consider either the potential costs or the potential benefits of providing reparations. Participants who considered the potential benefits, rather than costs, of providing reparations supported an official government apology more.

In sum, allowing people to see the continued suffering of "victim" groups while highlighting the feasibility and benefits of reparations may be one avenue to increase people's support for reparations.

Avoid disparaging the groups and systems whose support for reparations you are seeking, or provide ways for them to feel better in the face of social psychological threats

Groups seeking reparations and governments wanting to provide reparations must remember that people are strongly motivated to view their in-groups positively and that reminders of in-group wrongdoing will likely threaten this positivity. Canadian Prime Minister Stephen Harper's 2006 apology (CBC News 2006) for the Chinese Head Tax provides an excellent example of how one may genuinely acknowledge a grave harm in a relatively non-threatening way (Dyzenhaus and Moran 2006). In his apology, he first emphasized the gravity of the harm and accepted moral responsibility for "shameful policies". He then clearly praised both the harmed minority group and the majority in his apology and therefore supported the positivity of both social groups. Harper described how the Chinese-Canadian community "continues to make such an invaluable contribution" to Canada while at the same time emphasizing that every country makes mistakes and that Canadians are "good", "just" and "decent". Additionally, he affirmed the current system by stating that the harm "lies far in our past" and was "a product of a profoundly different time" in which such discrimination was legal. Thus, those campaigning for reparations may sometimes at least consider constructing messages in ways that validly acknowledge what happened without unnecessarily disparaging the group that caused the harm, or while providing ways for them to feel better in the face of such criticism. For example, Gunn and Wilson (2011) found that group affirmation (writing about a value that is important to the group) helped men to take on greater collective guilt and support reparations for discriminatory practices against women.

Although affirming the goodness of the perpetrator group is often an effective means of garnering their support for reparations, victim groups may find this approach unsatisfactory. Indeed, in some cases, it may be more important to voice messages that may threaten the perpetrator group even though doing so may jeopardize the success of a reparations campaign. For example, Chief Justice Murray Sinclair (Chairperson of the Truth and Reconciliation Commission of Canada; Puxley 2012) as well as some scholars (e.g., Churchill 2001; Stannard 1993) and members of the public (e.g., Annett 2001) suggest, sometimes strongly, that the term "genocide" should be used to describe what happened in Canada's Indian Residential Schools. Beginning in the mid-1800s, for over a century, the Government of Canada operated church-run Residential

Schools for the purpose of "civilizing" the Aboriginal Peoples of Canada. These schools were used to extinguish Aboriginal Peoples' culture, language and way of life. Many students who attended these schools experienced neglect, abuse and illness they likely would not have experienced otherwise, all factors that arguably contributed to high rates of student deaths.

How might non-Aboriginal Canadians respond to the label genocide being applied to Indian Residential Schools? On the one hand, given almost universal opposition to genocide, non-Aboriginal Canadians might feel morally compelled to take the issue seriously and respond accordingly when faced with a portrayal of Indian Residential Schools as genocidal. On the other hand, non-Aboriginal Canadians might simply feel threatened or unfairly criticized by the label and might therefore respond defensively to protect the reputations of the groups and social systems involved. To evaluate these options, Boese and Starzyk (2012) examined how non-Aboriginal Canadians react if the label genocide is used to describe what happened in Indian Residential Schools. Non-Aboriginal Canadian students read one of two brief passages about Indian Residential Schools and provided their opinions about the harm. Those who read a "genocide" version of the passage reported *less* compassion for the victims, perceived the schools as *less* harmful, and felt *less* optimism for the future of Canada's Aboriginal peoples, compared to those who read a "standard" version of the passage. Powerful words such as genocide may be inflammatory for those who are symbolically or actually culpable.

In sum, presenting people with the facts of what happened while taking care not to invoke defensive processes is another avenue for increasing support for reparations.

C Give outsiders an inside view through education and perspective taking

Members of victim, perpetrator, and third-party groups often have very different narratives of harmful events. For example, victim (versus perpetrator or third-party) group members tend to be more knowledgeable about the harm-doing and feel the events are more relevant – in some cases, harms that occurred long ago may seem like they happened only yesterday. Sahdra and Ross (2007) suggest that harmful events are less accessible to "high identifiers" because they are inconsistent with their basic ideas ("schemas") about their group. These authors manipulated in-group identity and found that people recalled fewer in-group harms when primed to highly identify with their group. In a similar study focusing on memory, Peetz and colleagues (2010) found that perpetrator group members psychologically distanced harmful events when threatened and thereby experienced less collective guilt as well as supporting reparations less. Specifically, Peetz and colleagues (2010) showed that Germans distanced the events of the Holocaust more if they felt unjustly blamed by other nations. When reparations are provided, narratives of past events held by perpetrator, victim, and third-party groups may converge if these various parties negotiate a revised history in the process of reparations, as they often do (Brooks 1999). Groups may, however, use strategies to develop a common narrative before reparations are provided, and doing so should lead to increased support for reparations. One possible strategy to develop a common narrative is education.

Education may be useful because people have more difficulty rationalizing or denying the reality of the situation in the face of well-constructed and convincing arguments (such as those sometimes provided in education campaigns). By making it difficult for people to reasonably justify their conclusions (Blader and Tyler 2002), such arguments can limit the effects of motivated reasoning (Kunda 1990: 480–98) and increase the likelihood that people will ultimately judge a harm to be unjust (Biernat and Fuegen 2001; Jones *et al.* 1995; Miron and Branscombe 2008; Miron *et al.* 2010). Consistent with this, Boese and Starzyk (2012), in the study described above, also found that providing detailed information about Indian Residential Schools offset the tendency of non-Aboriginal Canadians to respond defensively to the label genocide. Unfortunately, the process of educating a population can be lengthy and expensive and thus may not always be a readily available option. Moreover, governments and other perpetrator groups are unlikely to want to voluntarily educate the general public about past wrongdoing. If they educate their citizens at all, most governments and perpetrator groups are likely to wait until they have acknowledged the wrongdoing through an apology or some other form of reparation. Even then, they may not proceed with education or commemoration immediately. Nonetheless, it may be useful for victim groups to mount smaller education campaigns when they can. For example, prior to obtaining reparations, the Chinese Canadian community developed a documentary entitled *In the Shadow of Gold Mountain* (Cho 2004) and tied showings of the documentary to the campaign for reparations.

A related alternative to education is perspective taking, the process of "stepping into the shoes of the other". There is good evidence to suggest that perspective taking can motivate people to engage in prosocial behavior (e.g., Batson and Shaw 1991; Davis 1994; Dovidio *et al.* 2006; Eisenberg and Miller 1987) because doing so causes people to experience empathy, which is an emotion that allows people to understand the behavior and thoughts of others. Perspective taking necessarily requires some education, but not a great deal, and so it may be more efficient and less expensive than an education campaign. In one study, Gryba and Starzyk (2011) examined the effects of perspective taking by asking participants either to remain objective or to imagine how an Indian Residential School survivor felt as they read one survivor's personal story. Participants who took the survivor's perspective responded more empathetically and positively toward Aboriginal Canadians.

Conclusion

Social psychological factors influence people's reactions to reparations. In this chapter, we have focused on the motivations to view the world as fair and just and socio-political systems as legitimate as well as the importance of perceiving one's social groups positively, providing examples of supporting research from our labs, though several other social psychologists (some of which we have highlighted briefly here) are conducting important complementary research. Based on our and others' research, we argue that campaigns that effectively balance the victim group's interests and social psychological motivations such as those we describe are likely to have the best chance of evoking broad social support for reparations.

References

Annett, K. (2007) *Unrepentant: Kevin Annett and Canada's genocide*, available at: http://topdocumentaryfilms.com/unrepentant-kevin-annett-canadas-genocide/ (accessed July 4, 2013).

Batson, C.D. and Shaw, L.L. (1991) "Evidence for Altruism: Toward a pluralism of prosocial motives", *Psychological Inquiry*, 2: 107–22.

Biernat, M. and Fuegen, K. (2001) "Shifting Standards and the Evaluation of Competence: Complexity in gender-based judgment and decision-making", *Journal of Social Issues*, 57: 707–24.

Blader, S.L. and Tyler, T.R. (2002) "Justice and Empathy: What motivates people to help others?", in S.L. Blader and T.R. Tyler (eds) *The Justice Motive in Everyday Life*, New York: Cambridge University Press, 226–50.

Boese, G.D.B. and Starzyk, K.B. (n.d.) *The Social Psychology of Genocide Denial: Do the facts matter?* unpublished manuscript, Winnipeg: University of Manitoba.

Branscombe, N.R. and Doosje, B.E.J. (2004) *Collective Guilt: International perspectives*, New York: Cambridge University Press.

Brooks, R.L. (1999) *When Sorry Isn't Enough: The controversy over apologies and reparations for human injustice*, New York: New York University Press.

Caucasians United for Reparation and Emancipation (2008) "CURE: Reparations education and advocacy", available at: www.reparationsthecure.org/ (accessed December 17, 2012).

CBC News (2006) "PM Unveils Redress for Head Tax on Chinese", June 22, available at: www.cbc.ca/news/canada/story/2006/06/22/chinese-apology.html (accessed June 22, 2006).

Cho, K. (2004) *In the Shadow of Gold Mountain*, available at: www.nfb.ca/film/in_the_shadow_of_gold_mountain/ (accessed June 24, 2013).

Churchill, W. (2001) *A Little Matter of Genocide: Holocaust and denial in the Americas 1492 to the present*, San Francisco: City Lights Publishers.

Clairmont, D.H. and Magill, D.W. (1999) *Africville: The life and death of a Canadian black community*, Toronto: Canadian Scholars' Press.

Davis, M.H. (1994) *Empathy: A social psychological approach*, Boulder, CO: Westview Press.

Dovidio, J.F., Piliavin, J.A., Schroeder, D.A. and Penner, L. (2006) *The Social Psychology of Prosocial Behavior*, Mahwah, NJ: Lawrence Erlbaum Associates Publishers.

Dyzenhaus, D. and Moran, M. (2006) *Calling Power to Account: Law, reparations and the Chinese Canadian head tax case*, Toronto: University of Toronto Press.

Eisenberg, N. and Miller, P.A. (1987) "The Relation of Empathy to Prosocial and Related Behaviors", *Psychological Bulletin*, 101: 91–119.

Furnham, A. (1993) "Just World Beliefs in Twelve Societies", *Journal of Social Psychology*, 133: 317–29.

Furnham, A. (2003) "Belief in a Just World: Research progress over the past decade", *Personality and Individual Differences*, 34 : 795–817.

Gaucher, D., Hafer, C.L., Kay, A.C. and Davidenko, N. (2010) "Compensatory Rationalizations and the Resolution of Everyday Undeserved Outcomes", *Personality and Social Psychology Bulletin*, 36: 109–18.

Gryba, C. and Starzyk, K.B. *The Effects of Perspective Taking and Victim Alcoholism on Reactions to Aboriginal Canadians*, unpublished data, Winnipeg: University of Manitoba.

Gunn, G.R. and Wilson, A.E. (2011) "Acknowledging the Skeletons in our Closet: The effect of group affirmation on collective guilt, collective shame, and reparatory attitudes", *Personality and Social Psychology Bulletin*, 37: 1474–87.

Hafer, C.L. (2002) "Why we Reject Innocent Victims", in C.L. Hafer (ed) *The Justice Motive in Everyday Life*, New York: Cambridge University Press, 109–26.

Hafer, C.L. and Bègue, L. (2005) "Experimental Research on Just-Word Theory: Problems, developments, and future challenges", *Psychological Bulletin*, 131: 128–67.

Hafer, C.L., Bègue, L., Choma, B.L. and Dempsey, J.L. (2005) "Belief in a Just World and Commitment to Long-Term Deserved Outcomes", *Social Justice Research*, 18: 429–44.

Iyer, A., Leach, C.W. and Pedersen, A. (2004) "Racial Wrongs and Restitutions: The role of guilt and other group-based emotions", in N.R. Branscombe and B. Doosje (eds) *Collective Guilt: International perspectives*, Cambridge: Cambridge University Press, 262–83.

Imhoff, R. and Banse, R. (2009) "Ongoing Victim Suffering Increases Prejudice: The case of secondary anti-semitism", *Psychological Science*, 20: 1443–7.

Jones, W.H., Kugler, K. and Adams, P. (1995) "You Always Hurt the One You Love: Guilt and transgressions against relationship partners", in J. Tangney and K.W. Fischer (eds) *Self-Conscious Emotions: The psychology of shame, guilt, embarrassment, and pride*, New York: Guilford Press, 301–21.

Jost, J.T. and Banaji, M.R. (1994) *The Role of Stereotyping in System Justification and the Production of False Consciousness*, New York: Psychology Press.

Jost, J.T., Federico, C.M. and Napier, J.L. (2009) "Political Ideology: Its structure, functions, and elective affinities", *Annual Review of Psychology*, 60: 307–37.

Kay, A.C., Gaucher, D., Peach, J.M., Laurin, K., Friesen, J., Zanna, M.P. and Spencer, S.J. (2009) "Inequality, Discrimination, and the Power of the Status Quo: Direct evidence for a motivation to view what is as what should be", *Journal of Personality and Social Psychology*, 97: 421–34.

Kunda, Z. (1990) "The Case for Motivated Reasoning", *Psychological Bulletin* 108: 480–98.

Lerner, M.J. (1977) "The Justice Motive: Some hypotheses as to its origins and forms", *Journal of Personality*, 45: 1–52.

Lerner, M.J. (1980) *The Belief in a Just World: A fundamental delusion*, New York: Plenum Press.

Lerner, M.J. and Simmons, C.H. (1966) "Observer's Reaction to the 'Innocent Victim': Compassion or rejection?", *Journal of Personality and Social Psychology*, 4: 203–10.

Matsuda, M.J. (1987) "Looking to the Bottom: Critical legal studies and reparations", *Harvard Civil Liberties–Civil Right Law Review*, 22: 362–97.

Minow, M. (1998) *Between Vengeance and Forgiveness: Facing history after genocide and mass atrocities*, Boston: Beacon Press.

Minow, M. (2002) *Breaking the Cycles of Hatred: Memory, law, and repair*, Princeton: Princeton University Press.

Miron, A.M. and Branscombe, N.R. (2008) "Social Categorization, Standards of Justice, and Collective Guilt", in A. Nadler, T. Malloy and J. Fisher (eds) *Social Psychology of Intergroup Reconciliation*, Oxford: Oxford University Press, 77–97.

Miron, A.M., Branscombe, N.R. and Biernat, M. (2010) "Motivated Shifting of Justice Standards", *Personality and Social Psychology Bulletin*, 36: 768–79.

Neufeld, K.H., Starzyk, K.B., Boese, G.D.B. and Gaucher, D. (2013) "The Effects of Efficacy Framing and System Threat on Support for Addressing Social Injustice", poster presented to the 14th Annual Meeting of the Society for Personality and Social Psychology, New Orleans, January.

Peetz, J., Gunn, G.R. and Wilson, A.E. (2010) "Crimes of the Past: Defensive Temporal Distancing in the Face of Past In-group Wrongdoing", *Personality and Social Psychology Bulletin*, 36: 598–611.

Puxley, C. (2012) "Residential Schools Called a Form of Genocide", *The Globe and Mail*, available at: www.theglobeandmail.com/news/national/residential-schools-called-a-form-of-genocide/article547129/ (accessed June 23, 2013).

Rubin, Z. and Peplau, A. (1973) "Belief in a Just World and Reactions to Another's Lot: A study of participants in the National Draft Lottery", *Journal of Social Issues*, 29: 73–93.

Sahdra, B. and Ross M. (2007) "Group Identification and Historical Memory", *Personality and Social Psychology Bulletin*, 33: 384–95.

Stannard, D.E. (1993) *American Holocaust: Columbus and the conquest of the New World*, New York: Oxford University Press.

Starzyk, K.B. and Boese, G.D.B. (2012) *The Effect of Potential Benefit on Support for Reparations for Intergroup Harm*, unpublished document, Winnipeg: University of Manitoba.

Starzyk, K.B. and Ross, M. (2008) "A Tarnished Silver Lining: Victim suffering and support for reparations", *Personality and Social Psychology Bulletin*, 34: 366–80.

Tajfel, H. and Turner, J.C. (1986) "The Social Identity Theory of Intergroup Conflict", in S. Worchel and W.G. Austin (eds) *Psychology of Intergroup Relations*, Chicago: Nelson Hall, 7–24.

Tversky, A. and Kahneman, D. (1974) "Judgment Under Uncertainty: Heuristics and biases", *Science*, 185: 1123–31.

Viles, P. (2002) "Suit Seeks Billions in Reparations", *CNN*, March 27, available at: http://archives.cnn.com/2002/LAW/03/26/slavery.reparations (accessed June 24, 2013).

Wohl, M.J.A., Branscombe, N.R. and Klar, Y. (2006) "Collective Guilt: Emotional reactions when one's group has done wrong or been wronged", *European Review of Social Psychology*, 17: 1–37.

8 The healing state?

Residential schools and reparations in Canada

Andrew Woolford[1]

What does the state do when it engages in reparative processes? Moreover, how do we assess the role of the state in reparations? In many respects, the state's capacity as distributor of public goods and opportunities, and as sanctifier of official truths, marks its contribution to reparative politics. However, the state does more than compensate and acknowledge the past when it takes part in reparations. The state also works on itself, the nation and victims through policies of redress.

When we speak of the state, however, it is important to note that the state is not a monolith; it is a space where multiple actors compete over various forms of power. Such a notion is captured in the works of Pierre Bourdieu and Loïc Wacquant, who understand the state as a "splintered space of forces vying over the definition and distribution of public goods" (Wacquant 2009: 289; see also Bourdieu 1994, 1999). In short, the state is understood from this perspective as a diverse field of activity – Bourdieu (1994) refers to this as the bureaucratic field – in which institutions and actors affiliated with the state collectively negotiate its many dimensions.

In this chapter, an understanding of the state as a set of competitive interactions within the bureaucratic field is used to analyze state involvement in collective healing projects, such as that currently underway in Canada under the auspices of the 2006 Indian Residential School Settlement Agreement (IRSSA). The IRSSA is built around two distinct parts: compensation and a truth and reconciliation commission, accompanied by a formal apology. My primary focus will be on the compensation and the official apology,[2] and I will demonstrate that these reparative measures have not met with widespread approval from Indigenous residential school survivors. Based upon survivor criticisms of these measures, I will contend that the state's involvement in redress reflects colonial and neoliberal tendencies within Canada's bureaucratic field.

Residential schools as a state project

In *Thinking Like a State*, James Scott examines the ways in which the state seeks to make its subject and environment more legible and hence manageable (Scott 1998). He views the project of rationalizing and standardizing the social and natural worlds as characteristic of the high-modernist, authoritarian state. Such states, he suggests, are particularly prone to utopian forms of social engineering.

Residential schooling as seen in Canada exhibits several aspects of thinking like a state. At root, residential schools were about land acquisition, nation-building, and reducing the costs of governing Indigenous peoples. In the 1870s, when industry-oriented assimilative schooling began to emerge on the continent to replace or adapt the mission-based schools of old, a caste of reformers, economists, government agents, military officers and others began to raise questions about how to resolve the so-called Indian problem. In their view, extermination in the form of the Indian Wars that had taken place in the US was too expensive a solution to this problem (Miller 1996). In addition, perceptions of Indian dependence on government handouts, as well as their resistance to leaving their allegedly backward ways of life behind, were thought to require a radical intervention. However, there was not unity around potential solutions to this "Indian problem". While some suggested that Indigenous peoples should simply be left to fade into oblivion or annihilation upon reserves, others hoped to remake the Indian as a Christian European. Still others felt it was only possible to give Indians a leg up on the social evolutionary ladder and that the humanitarian goals of Christian uplift were racially improbable. During this crucial period, those calling for a policy of destructive non-intervention were marginalized, whereas Christian humanists and social Darwinists were able to come together under the notions of civilization and assimilation (see Fear-Segal 2007; Hoxie 1983).

Thus, in a grand attempt at re-writing Indigenous–non-Indigenous relations, assimilative schooling rose to the fore as the answer to the Indian problem. The Indian problem, in simple terms, was that Indigenous populations held relationships with their traditional territories that did not align with European property regimes. Their sedentarization was perceived to be essential to their survival, since semi-nomadic patterns of existence would not fit under the emerging economy. But Indigenous adults had proven resistant to previous government attempts to incorporate and enfranchise them within a European way of life. Therefore, the government turned its attention to children, and boarding schools were the flagship institutions for effecting their assimilation. But, on a broader level, it is no coincidence that the Indian Act (1876) was established just prior to the onset of the residential schooling system. Twinned together, these polices sought to fashion a legible Indian in the place of diverse Indigenous societies. The Indian Act defined who was and who was not an Indian and governed the lives of Indians in their near entirety, including their education.

Whereas in the US Indigenous boarding schools would primarily consist of large-scale institutions operated by the state under the auspices of the Indian service (see Adams 1995; Szasz 1999), in Canada, Christian denominations were tasked with the job of running schools. This decision was based upon the 1879 Davin Report in which the author, Nicholas Flood Davin, summarizes his whirlwind study of US policies of Indigenous education. Despite his admiration for the US system, and his preference for boarding over day schools, Davin did not feel that the US model could be applied wholesale in Canada, and instead advised the Canadian government to make use of the existing network of Christian missions in order to deliver schooling (Davin 1879; Miller 1996; Milloy 1999). This decision would have serious repercussions, as the Canadian state often distanced itself from the day-to-day operations of the schools, instead opting to try to govern assimilative education through the denominations, which were required to manage their funds under exceedingly tight budgets (Miller 1996). For their part, the churches also contributed to the stagnancy and despair of Canadian residential schooling, as they were quick to lobby against any proposed reforms to this system that were perceived to infringe upon their control of Indigenous schooling (Milloy 1999; Reyhner and Eder 2004).

The per capita funding formula used for Indian residential schools left these institutions chronically underfunded. Schools were established in areas where church missions already existed; the schools were often in expanded or repurposed mission buildings. Many of the buildings were decrepit, poorly ventilated and inadequately heated for winter months. Students spent half their day in work and half in scholastic or religious education. The work, originally conceived as a means to transfer employable skills to Indigenous children, became a necessity for sustaining the poorly funded schools. Overworked, underfed, poorly clothed and inadequately housed in crowded dormitories, the students were susceptible to communicable diseases and other ills that put their lives at risk. In addition, they experienced an all-out assault on their cultures. From the moment they entered a residential school, they were subject to assimilative interventions. Traditional clothes were removed, hair was cut, names were changed, and languages and cultural practices were forbidden. Now in a world of intense loneliness, they were separated from parents and relatives for ten months of the year, if not more. Physical, emotional, sexual and spiritual abuse was common, from both staff and fellow students, and Indigenous cultures were derided (Fontaine 2010; Grant 1996; Haig-Brown 1988; Johnston 1988; Knockwood 2001; Miller 1996; Milloy 1999). Although some Indigenous students cite positive experiences of teachers and education, the overarching purpose of the school was, as Deputy Superintendent Duncan Campbell Scott made plain in 1920:

> To get rid of the Indian problem … Our object is to continue until there is not a single Indian in Canada that has not been absorbed into the body politic, and there is no Indian question, and no Indian Department.
>
> (quoted in Titley 1986: 50)

Only around 30 percent of Indigenous children attended residential schools between 1879 and the 1960s (Miller 1996), but the schools have affected far greater numbers. Moreover, the residential school system was complemented by other institutional mechanisms that attacked Indigenous cultures. Day schools communicated similar messages of cultural inferiority. Indigenous forms of governance were replaced with a European model (Ladner 2012). Indigenous rituals, such as the potlatch and sun dance, were outlawed (Bracken 1997; Cole and Chaiken 1990). And Indigenous territory was marked with boundaries and exploited for its resources (Woolford 2011). Together, these networked harms have resulted in continuing suffering for many Indigenous peoples, including present-day child removals, addiction, suicide, un- and underemployment, and ongoing cycles of violence and abuse (Blackstock 2008; Wesley-Esquimaux and Smolewski 2004).

When examining the bigger picture of the colonial assault on Indigenous peoples in Canada, the challenge of redress seems insurmountable. Thus, the IRSSA and the government apology, like many such reparative projects, seek to take the messiness and multidimensionality of historical suffering and shape it into a manageable, workable form. The desire to create a useable past is not surprising, but it does result in the constant danger of producing overly reductive narratives of past injustices and their contemporary ramifications. However, since the focus of this chapter is on the state, the key question here is whether such redress mechanisms represent a meaningful transformation of state practices. Here the thoughts of philosopher Jürgen Habermas are quite pertinent. When engaged in a debate with revisionist German historians, Habermas wrote:

> As before, there is the simple fact that subsequent generations also grew up within a form of life in which that was possible. Our own life is linked to the life context in which Auschwitz was possible not only by contingent circumstances but intrinsically. Our form of life is connected with that of our parents and grandparents through a web of familial, local, political, and intellectual traditions that is difficult to disentangle – that is, through a historical milieu that made us what and who we are today. None of us can escape this milieu, because our identities, both as individuals and as Germans, are indissolubly interwoven with it.
>
> (Habermas 1991: 232)

This moral reflection can be imported to Canada; Canadians can ask not only of themselves, and their identity as Canadians, but also of their political institutions: Have we significantly altered the colonial form of political life that made residential schools possible?

I will argue that the bureaucratic field in Canada has undergone superficial alterations, but that it nonetheless maintains its basic shape in relation to Indigenous peoples. Having effectively eliminated Indigenous forms of governance, the state has over the past four decades begun to offer limited forms of self-governance to Indigenous groups, mostly in the form of municipal-like powers. In addition, the state has made glacial movements toward the settlement of outstanding land claims and treaty violations and has removed some of its more notorious laws: for example, those that prohibited Indigenous cultural practices such as the potlatch; that forbid the hiring of lawyers by Indigenous groups seeking to pursue land claims; and that removed Indian status from Indigenous women who married non-Indigenous men. Finally, the state has begun to redress its history of forced assimilation. However, the Canadian state has engaged in such practices in ways that often simply affirm the status quo, providing

Indigenous groups and individuals minor redress while simultaneously continuing to seek to adapt them to mainstream Canadian life.

The Indian Residential School Settlement Agreement

In 1990, Indigenous leaders began to discuss residential school abuses in a more public manner than ever before. This occurred alongside the work of the Royal Commission of Aboriginal Peoples, which in preparing for its 1996 report consulted with Indigenous individuals on a broad array of issues, including residential schools. Also in 1996, Alberni residential school survivors began the first class-action lawsuit for residential schools against the United Church of Canada and the federal government. Soon, more survivors added their names to class-action lawsuits. According to the federal government's Resolution Framework to Resolve Indian Residential School Claims, as of 2004, more than 12,000 survivors of physical and sexual abuse at Indian Residential Schools had filed for compensation from the federal government (Indian and Northern Affairs Canada 2002). The threat of an avalanche of settlements forced the government to undertake an alternate strategy to resolve the injustices of residential schooling.

One of the government's first moves was to consider an apology. Other groups involved in residential schooling had already expressed their remorse. The United Church issued an apology in 1986, followed by the Oblates of Saint Mary in 1991, the Anglican Church in 1993, and the Presbyterian Church in 1994. The federal government would present its statement of reconciliation in 1998, when Minister of Indian and Northern Affairs Jane Stewart spoke to a group of residential school survivors at the release of *Gathering Strength: Canada's Aboriginal Action Plan*, which directed $350 million toward the creation of the Aboriginal Healing Foundation to facilitate community-based healing projects (Corntassel and Holder 2008). However, critics felt the statement was insincere, in large part because it focused almost exclusively on those who had suffered physical or sexual abuse within the schools, eliding broader issues of cultural loss and community disruption.

The government's statement of reconciliation and its funding of the Aboriginal Healing Foundation did not quell the lawsuits. For this reason, in 2002, the federal government sought to expedite the settlement process through its introduction of the Indian Residential Schools Resolution Framework (Indian and Northern Affairs Canada 2002). The key to this framework was to settle legitimate claims outside of the courts in an alternative dispute resolution (ADR) process, which the government claimed would handle up to 18,000 claims over a seven-year period in an equitable and just manner (Indian and Northern Affairs Canada 2002).

The ADR process was roundly criticized even when it had barely begun. The Assembly of First Nations (AFN) estimated that ADR settlements would be too stingy to satisfy residential school survivors (Assembly of First Nations 2004). In addition, the AFN noted that the ADR program focused solely on physical and sexual abuse, ignoring the residential school assault on Indigenous cultures, languages and families (Assembly of First Nations 2004). Concerns were also raised that the ADR process would simply enrich lawyers and mediators, leaving very little in settlement for residential school survivors. For this reason, a push was made toward a lump-sum compensatory scheme similar to that offered to Japanese internment camp victims after World War II (Barkan 2000; Torpey 2006).

Such a deal was reached on May 8, 2006 and is referred to as the Indian Residential School Settlement Agreement (IRSSA), which has several components. First, this settlement provides at least $1.9 billion dollars for common experience payments (CEP), which are payments allotted to any individual who attended a residential school, regardless of their experience. This includes a base of $10,000 for the first year and $3000 for every year thereafter. Second, the settlement features an Independent Assessment Process (IAP) for those who suffered sexual or serious physical abuses, or serious psychological trauma as a result of abuse. Amounts from this process can range between $5000 and $275,000, or more if a loss of income can be demonstrated. These amounts are determined through a points system, which involves an itemization of the types of harm suffered while in a residential school. Finally, collective reparations were also made, adding another $125 million to the Aboriginal Healing Foundation and setting aside $60 million for a Truth and Reconciliation Commission and a further $20 million for community commemorative projects (Indian Residential Schools Settlement Agreement 2006). In addition, the federal government also agreed to provide a public apology, which was delivered on June 11, 2008, this time in front of the House of Commons. Here, Prime Minister Stephen Harper stated, "The government now recognizes that the consequences of the Indian residential schools policy were profoundly negative and that this policy has had a lasting and damaging impact on aboriginal culture, heritage and language" (Harper 2008).

In some respects, Harper went further than previous governments in acknowledging the harms of residential schools. Whereas the 1998 statement of reconciliation limited itself to expressing remorse for physical and sexual abuse within the schools, the 2008 apology recognized the wider harms of residential schools to Indigenous communities. Nonetheless, survivors giving testimony to the Truth and Reconciliation Commission of Canada (TRC) have in large part expressed a healthy degree of skepticism with respect to this apology. For some, the apology was simply too little and too late:

> And I just want to say to the Prime Mister that apologized, shame on you yourself; shame on the government. And I, I didn't, I just will not accept that apology; it's just too late. And I'm not going to, I'm ... It's just too late for apologies, even for my family and everybody; and, like my dad, my stepmother. And then I thought, I can't really think like that either too, because they had gone to residential school themselves. So until then I don't know what's going to make things right, except to tell our story.
>
> (Anonymous 2011a)

> The ironic thing is that Harper, what's he, who is he, Prime Minister Harper, whom I couldn't stand to begin with, this sanctimonious nincompoop, anyway, did his big apology for the residential school. What, three, four months after Danny died. I was enraged by that too, as if some words are going to make up for all the lives that are, have been ruined. Yet really, it's not just my life, my other son's life has been ruined, my granddaughter's life has been ruined. And the cycle just keeps on generating. The trauma just goes on and on and on.
>
> (Anonymous 2011b)

Others bristled at the inconsistencies of the apology, contending that it acknowledged past harms without doing enough to change the contemporary treatment of Indigenous peoples in Canadian society.

> Well, I think, I think the Canadian public really needs to be educated. I think they have to get a feel for this. They have to appreciate what occurred, understand the reasoning behind it, and to make sure it never happens again. And I think Canada could be one of the leading countries in the world in doing that. But we, we, we have to follow through with, with what we say we're gonna do. For example, the Prime Minister made the apology, and now the efforts, not only the Truth and Reconciliation Commission has to take place, like the Healing Foundation lost its funding, and that's really gonna affect our community. So, it seems Canada says one thing, but then they don't follow through, and that's really disturbing and it's confusing for people 'cause we're saying we want to deal with it in a constructive way, but then Canada's bureaucracy, or whatever you want to call it, is acting a different way.
>
> (Anonymous 2010a)

> What did Harper do since the apology? Well, now, he's starting to implement a system where they do mandatory punishment, where he's gonna punish people. And who are the people that he's punishing? It's our people! But what about the healing process? Yes, they did Aboriginal Healing Foundation and they did a lot of support, but that kind of thing has to keep on. What Marie Wilson and the rest of the Commissioners are doing – that's a step in the right direction. That's the healing process. It's gonna take a long time.
>
> (Anonymous 2011c)

The latter speaker ends, as did several others, viewing reconciliation and social healing as more likely to come about through telling their stories than through apologies and compensation. As participants in the TRC process, it is likely that they feel some hope that this forum will be able to educate Canadian society and begin a process of change and relationship-building for Indigenous and non-Indigenous peoples in Canada. However, they find it hard to reconcile the apology delivered by Harper with his other actions, such as the Safe Streets and Communities Act,[3] which threatens to increase Aboriginal overrepresentation in Canadian prisons through mandatory minimum sentences; his 2009 statement during a press conference at the G20 meetings in Pittsburgh that Canada has "no history of colonialism" (quoted in Henderson and Wakeham 2009: 1); and recent efforts to cut back funding for Indigenous representative organizations and increase accountability for Indigenous governments.

Notwithstanding survivors' expressions of hope for the TRC, it has not been an entirely unproblematic venture. The TRC made a later start than expected, in part as a result of conflict between the initial commissioners. Judge Harry LaForme resigned as Chief Commissioner in October 2008. It was reported that he had a dispute with the AFN and the other two commissioners. It was also mentioned that he saw the survivor testimony component of the TRC events as potentially divisive and thought that more emphasis needed to be placed on reconciliation rather than truth-seeking so as to build national unity. The two remaining commissioners later resigned in June 2009 (Canada Newswire 2008). Justice Murray Sinclair took over as Chief Commissioner on 3 June 2009 and the TRC has moved ahead under his leadership.

This early dispute raised concerns that the TRC could become a project in nation-building and governance through forced closure. Although the initial power struggle was won by those seeking to direct the TRC toward prioritizing the stories and experiences of cultural harm and abuse within the residential schools, questions remain. Will the Indian Residential School TRC offer an adequate reckoning with the Canadian past? Will Canadians embrace its telling of their history even if it tarnishes a positively held Canadian national identity? Will the telling of the past be limited and circumscribed by political and legalistic concerns? These questions are central to evaluating the reconciliation sought through the TRC, and it is still too early to pass judgment on its success in meeting its goals. However, it is fair to say that public and media attention to the TRC has been less than desired, and many Canadians remain largely unaware of what is underway at various TRC-sponsored events and community meetings across the country. It is also the case that restrictions against mentioning perpetrator names, the exclusion of day schools and non-recognized residential schools from the process, and the lack of attention to broader colonial processes of land dispossession and the loss of self-determination threaten to shape the sort of truth the TRC produces and to impose closure (Chrisjohn and Wasacase 2009; Henderson and Wakeham 2009; James 2012; Patzer 2012).

With respect to the common experience and independent assessment compensation programs, some early evidence of the use of these instruments can be noted. The compensation offered is settlement in the true sense of the word (Brooks 2003), since it is conducted in a language intended to prevent further liability on the part of the government and churches, and to represent a full and final resolution to the *Baxter v. Canada* class-action lawsuit. The CEP merely marks the time one spent in a residential school without addressing directly the cultural harm of this schooling experience. The most prevalent complaint about the CEP recorded in TRC statements is that because of poor record-keeping at the schools, survivors are often not given full compensation for the years they attended.

> Before, before it, okay, there was a thing where they said you, you send for your records, so I did, I sent for my records right away, and they sent me 28 pages with my name on it. And from what I understood, each page represents a quarter, so I, I still have those, those 28 pages. And the sad part was, I was paid one year. They didn't pay me for the other five. They said they couldn't verify, and I said, like, I thought to myself, holy cripes, just like I'm victimized again. And I thought, well, no amount of money is gonna, is gonna heal me. You know they could pay me all the money they want, but it's up to me, though I did appeal it … no money, amount of money is gonna, is gonna release what's inside that I have, you know, I'm going to do that in my own time, in my own way.
>
> (Anonymous 2012a)

> I went through the CEP, common experience process and I applied for twelve years of residential school and I got eight years back. And I was rejected four years, 'cause the government said I went to day school those four years from grade nine to twelve. So I was rejected, another form of rejection I thought and I was very angry about this and today I'm still angry over that, I still want to pursue it.
>
> (Anonymous 2010b)

After feeling that their stories have gone too long unheard and unacknowledged, it is not so much the lack of compensation that hurts survivors, but rather the feeling that their suffering is going unrecognized. Moreover, they sense that they are doubted and discredited, and these feelings bring back memories of how they were treated at the residential schools – as unreliable, untrustworthy, tainted individuals.

Unlike the CEP, the Individual Assessment Process (IAP) deals with specific instances of harm, although it does so in an actuarial manner that asks claimants to identify instances of physical, sexual or psychological abuse that they have suffered individually rather than collectively. In this manner, harm is itemized and made calculable – it is delineated, counted, measured, estimated, and compensated. Through such practices, the past is managed more than it is made usable, as deeply social and ontological damage perpetrated through forced assimilation is transformed into a discrete set of reparable acts. The IAP form is a 28-page document that demands a great deal of personal and descriptive information from the applicant. In addition, various forms of verification or proof are required, such as a doctor's note to confirm that one is too ill to attend a hearing. The complexity of the application means applicants will in most cases require the assistance of lawyers in filling out its details, adding one further level of translation (and cost), as their personal experiences of harm are converted by professionals into the terms demanded by the form and by the process. Survivors often note the byzantine nature of the process, and the expenses paid to lawyers in order to navigate it.

> The waiting period takes too long, nobody explains anything to us. For instance, my IAP is going on three years now, in all those years I've had three different caseworkers looking at my file and my lawyer was never notified that one of the caseworkers, when she left her position it was sitting on someone's desk for about six months. Until I told my lawyer to look into it, then I find out another caseworker took over, just as he was phoning. We get all this run around, he doesn't get no information, I didn't even get no information about this residential school until I read it through the newspaper.
>
> (Anonymous 2010c)

> But by the time I got my pay out of it all, and the lawyer fees taken off, the lawyer collected, for my case alone, just me, her portion of it was like ten thousand five hundred; for her. So I only came, came out of it with like, twenty-five thousand.
>
> (Anonymous 2011d)

Moreover, the process is very invasive, and this experience is magnified for survivors who have spent a portion of their lives in the surveillance space of the residential schools. And, in the end, its calculus of suffering is difficult for survivors to negotiate, as they are left unsure how to parcel their pain into the categories of harm offered by the IAP forms.

> When I applied for the IAP, we were told to gather documents, everything, treatment, medical, high school, elementary, treatment centers, our relationships if we were ever sexually abused and our education, if we took other courses. ... Sometimes I think they're getting too personal when they do that especially with your marriage life. They don't need to know how many times I married or lived common law with people, that's none of their damn business. All I was there for was to talk about the abuse and physical abuse and the stuff I saw going in the residential schools.
>
> (Anonymous 2010d)

> The IAP is asking me ... to measure the amount of hurt and pain I have experienced in the residential school. What I find most difficult is trying to separate my whole life experience from what happened to me in the school and the events before and after the residential school. I feel there is a connection from when I lived on the reserve, when I left the reserve, and came home after being in the hospital for 10 years.
>
> (Anonymous 2012b)

The hearing for the IAP is also designed to contain suffering within terms convenient to governance. Survivors must rehearse and learn to present their pain in a manner that fits state categories of suffering. But, ultimately, their pain is under evaluation, and institutional actors not so far removed from those who were its originators adjudicate the veracity of their suffering. This has the potential effect of furthering traumatization.

> I had my residential school survivor hearing recently and gave my testimony. It was hard, difficult and stressful. The hearings are designed to determine just how much abuse one has suffered and how much the government should pay that individual … The only saving grace of this process is that there would be money set aside to pay for therapy. Though I must admit I was disheartened to learn that it would be perhaps another entire year before I get that paid for by the government. In the meantime, I have to continue to suffer through my pain while the government looks over my case to determine if I'm telling the truth … They treated me as though I were only concerned about a large financial gain. A large financial gain would never, no matter how large it is, give me a normal life. My life and history would still be messed up … Throwing money is just another way for them [the government] to wipe their hands of this country's botched history.
>
> (Courchene 2010: A13)

Finally, the retelling of one's traumatic experiences in such an environment does not have the cathartic effect of the speaking cure some hope will derive from such truth-telling occasions.

> And now after so many years, the last few years it starts coming out, the pain and there's nothing I can do except try and forget it, it will never happen again. But people always ask you to repeat it, repeat it in these IAP meetings that I had, three of them already. I'm going for my fourth one and it's still. They think it's easier talking about it but it isn't.
>
> (Anonymous 2010e)

> That's why I was always afraid of her. But I think there was a lot of shame in telling that story, too. Because I remember when she hit me, too, I wet my pants. And that, so I was very much ashamed … So, when I, I wrote out the IAP, I wouldn't even mention that part of it, you know. There's a lot of shame in it. So, … you know, that, you wet yourself and everything, eh.
>
> (Anonymous 2012c)

Reading and listening to statements made by survivors for the TRC does not give one the impression that the IRSSA compensation (CEP and IAP) and the apology are advancing individual healing. If this is the case, what is the state accomplishing through its engagement with such processes? Why would the state be willing to invest a great deal of time and resources in such a project if not with the hope of improving the lives of survivors and their communities?

Healing like a state

There are several existing critiques of the ways that the state engages with reparations processes. For some, such reparative agreements are viewed as means for the state to gain or restore legitimacy (Moon 2009), rehabilitate its institutions and operations (Humphrey 2003), engage in nation-building (Corntassel and Holder 2008; Wilson 2001), or govern the victim group to ensure both finality and certainty within the social order (Woolford 2005, 2010). Indeed, in a feat of statecraft, reparations are often used in an attempt to accomplish all of these things. By statecraft I mean the capacity of the state to direct material (e.g., money, economic opportunities) and symbolic (e.g., truth and commemoration) resources toward the strengthening of state power. Thus, the distribution of material and symbolic resources through reparations is not merely a means of serving the justice needs of victims. Rather, through involvement in reparations, state actors re-negotiate the state's public image and status, thereby remaking the state in the aftermath of unsavory events. The hope is that by assuaging past state injustices, a reinvigorated state can renew its claim to hold a fair and legitimate monopoly of power in society. In addition, through reparations state actors re-negotiate the status of victims by creating mechanisms through which victim demands upon the state become legible, calculable, and final. For victims, the ability to cause the state uncertainty – e.g., through lawsuits, collective action, and public messaging – is their greatest source of power; the state seeks to reduce this power through reparative settlements and thereby to create more manageable victims.

In presenting this summary of reparative statecraft, however, it is important not to simply reduce the state to a conspiratorial, singular entity that is necessarily unified in its action. As defined earlier, the state is a splintered space of interactions between the multiple institutions and actors that comprise the bureaucratic field. So what does it mean to say that the state seeks legitimacy, nation-building, institutional rehabilitation, or certainty through reparations? These objectives do not arise randomly, and yet they cannot be located within the intentionality of a single all-powerful actor or group of actors.

Within the bureaucratic field one finds actors and institutions with varying degrees of power and sway in determining state involvement in reparative processes. One also finds pervasive discourses, or approaches to problematizing and addressing state concerns. For example, in my previous research on the British Columbia Treaty Process (Woolford 2005), I examined how federal and provincial government positions within treaty negotiations developed through interactions between different levels of government (federal, provincial, municipal and Indigenous), government ministries (e.g., Indian Affairs, Justice and Finance), frontline staff such as treaty negotiators and counsel, resource interests, public organizations such as churches and citizen groups, and other public actors. Through these interactions, the state forms its negotiation mandate. However, certain actors within these negotiations hold greater power in defining this mandate. In particular, the ministries of Finance and Justice were most forceful in setting the limits of reparative policy, imposing certain visions of settlement upon the treaty process, such as: no apologies or regret for wrongful land appropriation could be expressed prior to full and final settlement of the treaty; monetary distribution could not be termed compensation prior to settlement, since this would signal wrongdoing and liability on the part of the federal government; and, although First Nations would not be asked to cede, surrender and release their traditional territories to the government, as had been typical of earlier treaties, language was still required to ensure that there was certainty in the form of no future Indigenous claims on territory and resources that were not fully explicated in the treaty document (Woolford 2005). Some negotiators felt these and other aspects of the government mandate to be too restrictive, and sought to massage them at the treaty tables to better fit the interests of First Nations seeking treaty settlement. However, these individuals lacked the autonomy to do much more than superficially adjust the mandate, and any significant change to the mandate would require a lengthy process of consultation and multi-level approval.

One sees similar sets of interactions when looking at the formation and implementation of the IRSSA. Here, as well, ministries such as Justice and Finance have sought to establish justice parameters that prioritize state objectives such as restoring legitimacy, better fitting Indigenous groups into a hegemonic vision of the Canadian nation state, and achieving certainty and finality through the waiving of any further rights to redress. Indeed, even before the IRSSA came into existence, efforts were underway to limit and restrict its reparative ambit. In the late 1990s, the Working Group on Truth and Reconciliation and Exploratory Dialogues began to consult with survivors, Indigenous and non-Indigenous governments, the churches, Indigenous healers and leaders, and legal counsel. In these early stages, one already sees a process of narrowing the pool of victims eligible for reparations, as Métis and Inuit representatives were largely absent from the table as negotiations to form the IRSSA were underway. Moreover, the suffering caused by day schools to Indigenous children and communities received little attention during these preliminary discussions. Finally, even though the framework for the IRSSA would be drawn from Assembly of First Nations proposals for reparative settlements, IRSSA negotiations came under increasing government control, as even the mediator for the negotiations, Frank Iacobucci, appeared to represent the interests of the federal government in the negotiations rather than acting as a neutral facilitator (Petoukhov 2011). Thus reasons of state began to trump the needs of survivors and other victims of Canadian colonialism from the very formation of the IRSSA onward, and the justice on offer was bracketed by the concerns of multiple government parties concerned as much with the desires of the state as the needs of victims. In this respect, one can understand how the CEP and IAP compensation payments have become so heavily formalized and bureaucratic, as they are deployed as tools to bring to an end the class-action lawsuits that represented too much uncertainty to governments, as well as to clearly demarcate a set of eligible victims and to transform their suffering into a payable quantity, rather than a more amorphous moral debt.

Under Stephen Harper's Conservative government, greater uniformity has been imposed on the bureaucratic field than was noticeable under previous governments. The neoliberal marching orders extend beyond the line ministries down to peripheral bureaucratic field institutions, such as non-profit social service agencies that find themselves threatened with funding loss if their public advocacy is discerned to imply a critique of government policy. Under such conditions, survivors appear quite aware that the government that is supposed to be offering them justice for past wrongs is hard at work at other objectives, and that the broader policy framework is one that contradicts and even sullies the apology and compensation they have received. Thus, recent developments such as the mandatory minimum sentences included in the Safe Streets and Communities Act (2012), the goal to foster First Nations voluntary acceptance of fee simple landownership, reductions in funding to Indigenous representative organizations, accountability mechanisms intended to discipline Indigenous governments, and other such interventions, strike them as inconsistent with the actions of a state that purportedly wants to deal with its past. In this manner, while survivors are offered opportunities to receive compensation, to hear a government apology, and to have their experiences of residential schools made part of the official record, they also see their communities and organizations weakened, child welfare policies that remove Indigenous children from their homes in numbers greater than at the height of the residential school system, and horrendous rates of Indigenous overrepresentation in Canadian prisons.

Indeed, in light of these shifts in the bureaucratic field it is no wonder that survivors find the state's reparative efforts to be too little, too late, re-traumatizing, overly bureaucratic, unfair, insincere and self-contradictory. The state has not done the work on itself that it expects survivors to do upon themselves. Instead, it offers victims minimal compensation and public acknowledgment with one hand while with the other it squeezes them. The colonial mesh thus continues to tighten across the Indigenous world, since the goals of nation-building, cost reduction, and land acquisition are still apparent within or underneath Canadian redress policies. As such, residential school reparations do not offer a significant or sufficient departure from the thinking like a state that made residential schools possible.

Notes

1 I would like to acknowledge the support of the Truth and Reconciliation Commission of Canada for making possible the research that is the background to this chapter. Thank you also to Christopher Powell, Jeremy Patzer, Natalia Ilyniuk, Jo-Anne Wemmers and all of the participants in the Healing and Reparations for Victims of Crimes against Humanity Workshop for their comments and thoughts on this chapter and on the presentation on which it is based.

2 At the time of writing, the Truth and Reconciliation Commission was still in progress.

3 Bill C-10, passed in 2012.

References

Adams, D.W. (1995) *Education for Extinction: American Indians and the boarding school experience, 1875–1928*, Lawrence: University Press of Kansas.

Anonymous (2012a) Statement to the Truth and Reconciliation Commission of Canada [oral testimony], June 14, Truth and Reconciliation Commission of Canada National Event in Saskatoon, SK, file: 2011–1776, Saskatoon, SK, TRC Digital Archive.

Anonymous (2012b) Statement to the Truth and Reconciliation Commission of Canada [oral testimony], April 13, Truth and Reconciliation Commission of Canada National Event in Victoria, BC, file: 2011–3967, TRC Digital Archive.

Anonymous (2012c) Statement to the Truth and Reconciliation Commission of Canada [oral testimony], April 13, Truth and Reconciliation Commission of Canada National Event in Victoria, BC, file: 2011–3967, TRC Digital Archive.

Anonymous (2011a) Statement to the Truth and Reconciliation Commission of Canada [oral testimony], November 23, Truth and Reconciliation Commission of Canada Regional Event at Fort Simpson, NT, file: 2011–2687, TRC Digital Archive.

Anonymous (2011b) Statement to the Truth and Reconciliation Commission of Canada [oral testimony], October 13, Truth and Reconciliation Commission of Canada Regional Event in Enderby, BC; file: 2011–3291, TRC Digital Archive.

Anonymous (2011c) Statement to the Truth and Reconciliation Commission of Canada [oral testimony], February 5, Truth and Reconciliation Commission of Canada, One Spirit Convention, Ottawa, ON, file: 01-ON-28 05FE11–009, TRC Digital Archive.

Anonymous (2011d) Statement to the Truth and Reconciliation Commission of Canada [oral testimony], September 28, Truth and Reconciliation Commission of Canada, Regional Event at Inuvik, NT, file: 2011–0325, TRC Digital Archive.

Anonymous (2010a) Statement to the Truth and Reconciliation Commission of Canada [oral testimony], July 15, Truth and Reconciliation Commission of Canada Regional Event in Fort Good Hope, NWT, file: 01-NWT-JY10–022, TRC Digital Archive.

Anonymous (2010b) Statement to the Truth and Reconciliation Commission of Canada [oral testimony], June 18, Truth and Reconciliation Commission of Canada National Event in Winnipeg, MB, file: 02-MB-18JU10–063, TRC Digital Archive.

Anonymous (2010c) Statement to the Truth and Reconciliation Commission of Canada [oral testimony], September 28, Truth and Reconciliation Commission of Canada Regional Event in Inuvik, NT, file: 2011–0325, TRC Digital Archive.

Anonymous (2010d) Statement to the Truth and Reconciliation Commission of Canada [oral testimony], June 16, Truth and Reconciliation Commission of Canada National Event in Winnipeg, MB, file: 02-MB-16JU10–129, TRC Digital Archive.

Anonymous (2010e) Statement to the Truth and Reconciliation Commission of Canada [oral testimony], June 17, Truth and Reconciliation Commission of Canada National Event in Winnipeg, MB, file: 02-MB-17JU10–035, TRC Digital Archive.

Assembly of First Nations (2004) "Residential School Briefing Note for National Chief Matthew Coon Come", Ottawa: The Assembly of First Nations.

Barkan, E. (2000) *The Guilt of Nations: Restitution and negotiating historical injustices*, New York: W.W. Norton & Company.

Baxter v. Canada (2006) CanLII 41673.

Blackstock, C. (2008) "Reconciliation Means Not Saying Sorry Twice: Lessons from child welfare in Canada", in M.B. Castellano, L. Archibald and M. Degagne (eds) *From Truth to Reconciliation: Transforming the legacy of residential schools*, Ottawa: Aboriginal Healing Foundation, 163–78.

Blackwater v. Plint (1998), 52 B.C.L.R. (3d) 18.

Bourdieu, P. (1999) "The Abdication of the State", in P. Bourdieu (ed.) *The Weight of the World: Social suffering in contemporary society*, Cambridge: Polity Press, 181–8.

Bourdieu, P. (1994) "Rethinking the State: Genesis and structure of the bureaucratic field", *Sociological Theory*, 12(1): 1–18.

Bracken, C. (1997) *The Potlatch Papers: A colonial case history*, Chicago: University of Chicago Press.

Brooks, R.L. (2003) "Reflections on Reparations", in J. Torpey (ed.) *Politics and the Past: On repairing historical injustices*, Lanham: Rowman and Littlefeld, 103–14.

Chrisjohn, R. and Wasacase, T. (2009) "Half-Truths and Whole Lies: Rhetoric in the 'apology' and the Truth and Reconciliation Commission", in G. Younging, J. Dewar and M. DeGagné (eds) *Response, Responsibility, and Renewal: Canada's truth and reconciliation journey*, Ottawa: Aboriginal Healing Foundation, 217–29.

Cole, D. and Chaikin, I. (1990) *An Iron Hand Upon the People: The law against the potlatch on the northwest coast*, Vancouver: Douglas and McIntyre.

Corntassel, J. and Holder, C. (2008) "Who's Sorry Now? Government apologies, Truth Commissions, and self-determination in Australia, Canada, Guatemala, and Peru", *Human Rights Review*, 9: 465–89.

Courchene, R. (2010) "Letter to the Editor", *Winnipeg Free Press*, March 26.

Davin, N.F. (1879) *Report on Industrial Schools for Indians and Half Breeds*, Ottawa, Minister of the Interior.

Fear-Segal, J. (2007) *White Man's Club: Schools, race, and the struggle of Indian acculturation*, Lincoln, NE: University of Nebraska Press.

Fontaine, T. (2010) *Broken Circle: The dark legacy of Indian residential schools, a memoir*, Victoria: Heritage House.

Grant, A. (1996) *No End of Grief: Residential schools in Canada*, Winnipeg: Pemmican Publications Inc.

Habermas, J. (1991) *The New Conservatism: Cultural criticism and the historians' debate*, Cambridge, MA: MIT Press.

Haig-Brown, C. (1988) *Resistance and Renewal: Surviving the Indian residential school*, Vancouver: Tillicum Library.

Harper, S. (2008) *Prime Minister Harper Offers Full Apology on Behalf of Canadians for the Indian Residential Schools System*, available at: www.aadnc-aandc.gc.ca/eng/1100100015644/1100100015649 (accessed October 1, 2012).

Henderson, J. and Wakeham, P. (2009) "Colonial Reckoning, National Reconciliation? Aboriginal peoples and the culture of redress in Canada", *ESC: English Studies in Canada*, 35(1): 1–26.

Hoxie, F. (1983) *The Final Promise: The campaign to assimilate the Indian, 1880–1920*, Lincoln: University of Nebraska Press.

Humphrey, M. (2003) "From Victim to Victimhood: Truth Commissions and trials as rituals of political transition and individual healing", *Australian Journal of Anthropology*, 14(2): 171–187.

Indian and Northern Affairs Canada (2002) *Resolution Framework to Resolve Indian Residential School Claims*, available at: www.ainc-inac.gc.ca/ai/rqpi/info/nwz/2002/20021212_is-eng.asp (accessed April 12, 2010).

Indian Residential Schools Settlement Agreement (2006), "Detailed Notice for the Indian Residential School Settlement", Ottawa: Government of Canada, available at: http://www.residentialschoolsettlement.ca/detailed_notice.pdf. (accessed April 12, 2010).

James, M. (2012) "A Carnival of Truth? Knowledge, ignorance and the Canadian Truth and Reconciliation Commission", *The International Journal of Transitional Justice*, 6: 182–204.

Johnston, B. (1988) *Indian School Days*, Norman: University of Oklahoma Press.

Knockwood, I. (2001) *Out of the Depths: The experiences of MiKmaw children at the Indian residential school at Shubenacadie, Nova Scotia*, Halifax: Fernwood Publishing.

Ladner, K. (2012) "Political Genocide: Killing nations through legislation and slow moving poison", paper presented at The Colonial Genocide and Indigenous North America Workshop, Winnipeg, September.

Miller, J.R. (1996) *Shingwauk's Vision: A history of Native residential schools*, Toronto: University of Toronto Press.

Milloy, J.S. (1999) *A National Crime: The Canadian government and the residential school system, 1879 to 1986*, Winnipeg: University of Manitoba Press.

Moon, C. (2009) "Healing Past Violence: Traumatic assumptions and therapeutic interventions in war and reconciliation", *Journal of Human Rights*, 8(1): 71–91.

Patzer, J. (2012) "Residential School Harm and Colonial Dispossession: What's the connection?", paper presented at The Colonial Genocide and Indigenous North America Workshop, Winnipeg, September.

Petoukhov, K. (2011) "An Evaluation of Canada's Truth and Reconciliation Commission through the Lens of Restorative Justice and the Theory of Recognition", unpublished thesis, University of Manitoba.

Rehak, P. (2008) "Justice Harry S. LaForme Resigns as Chair of the Indian Residential Schools Truth and Reconciliation Commission", *Canadian Newswire*, October 20, available at: www.newswire.ca/en/story/372423/justice-harry-s-laforme-resigns-as-chair-of-the-indian-residential-schools-truth-and-reconciliation-commission (accessed October 12, 2012).

Reyhner, J. and Eder, J. (2004) *American Indian Education: A history*, Norman, OK: University of Oklahoma Press.

Scott, J.C. (1998*) Thinking Like a State: How certain schemes to improve the human condition have failed*, New Haven and London: Yale University Press.

Szasz, M.C. (1999) *Education and the American Indian: The road to self-determination since 1928*, Albuquerque: University of New Mexico Press.

Titley, E. Brian (1986). *A Narrow Vision: Duncan Campbell Scott and the administration of Indian affairs in Canada*. Vancouver: University of British Columbia Press.

Torpey, J. (2006) *Making Whole What has been Smashed: On reparations politics*, Cambridge, MA: Harvard University Press.

Wacquant, L. (2009) *Punishing the Poor: The neoliberal government of social insecurity*, Durham: Duke University Press.

Wesley-Esquimaux, C.C. and Smolewski, M. (2004) *Historic Trauma and Aboriginal Healing*, Ottawa: Aboriginal Healing Foundation.

Wilson, R. (2001) *The Politics of Truth and Reconciliation in South Africa: Legitimating the Post-Apartheid State*, Cambridge: Cambridge University Press.

Woolford, A. (2011) "Transition and Transposition: Genocide, land, and the British Columbia Treaty Process", *New Proposals: Journal of Marxism and Interdisciplinary Inquiry*, 4: 2.

Woolford, A. (2010) "Governing Through Repair: Transitional justice and Indigenous peoples in Canada", paper presented at "Facing the Past: Finding remedies for grave historical injustice" workshop, Utrecht, May.

Woolford, A. (2005) *Between Justice and Certainty: Treaty-making in British Columbia*, Vancouver: University of British Columbia Press.

9 Transitional justice in Bosnia-Herzegovina

Understanding accountability, reparations and justice for victims

Nicholas A. Jones, Stephan Parmentier and Elmar G.M. Weitekamp

Following a period of mass atrocity and violations of human rights, the damage resulting from the crimes committed impacts the entirety of the society and particularly the victim/survivors in a far-reaching and exceptionally complex manner. During this time of societal evolution, the emerging state is faced with many questions in regard to the processes and mechanisms employed in addressing these dark times. Despite repeated examples of confronting these atrocities over the past few decades, "the world community is still left with questions about the validity and utility of the mechanisms that we have initiated" (Weinstein *et al.* 2010: 28). Furthermore, as noted by Valiñas, Parmentier and Weitekamp (2009: 1), the process of transitional justice rarely accounts for the "views and expectations of the local population", instead being directed by elites that have historically shaped legislation as well as justice policies and practices. The possibility exists that these elites are too distanced from the very root of the experiences of those they seek to help, which may in part provide an explanation for Shaw and Waldorf's (2010: 2) contention that transitional justice has come under increased scrutiny by the victims it is supposed to serve.

This chapter addresses two key questions from the perspectives of persons who were victimized during the Bosnia-Herzegovina conflict. First, are the interventions employed where transitional justice is undertaken meeting the needs of victims of the mass crimes committed during the conflict? Second, what factors impact victims' perceptions? We present the results of our analyses after providing a short review of the transitional justice literature and conclude with a discussion on how we can use the experiences of victims to inform legal reform, practice and research.

Transitional justice: definitions and theoretical background

Siegel (1998: 431) defines transitional justice as "the study of choices made and the quality of justice rendered when states are replacing authoritarian regimes by democratic institutions". Philpott (2007: 94) complements this definition by referring to transitional justice as "the sum of activities through which states and citizens redress past political injustices", thereby adding the actions that accompanies the decisions that are made. Transitional justice occurs in different cultural, social and political environments, and while stakeholders seek very similar outcomes the different mechanisms for achieving them leads to diverse results (Clark 2009). Nevertheless, commonalities exist. According to Jones *et al.* (2012: 554), "core components across a variety of models include accountability, truth, trust, reconciliation, healing, forgiveness, peace and justice". Furthermore, in order to reflect the entirety of the victim/survivor context in which they are located, achieving these elements needs to be undertaken within a reparative framework that encapsulates the "(1) individual, (2) societal, (3) national, and (4) international perspectives" (Danieli 2008: 343). In order for transitional justice to move a post-conflict society toward stability and a lasting peace (suggestive of reconciliation) the response should be multifaceted in order to address the needs of the victims, to hold offenders accountable and to acknowledge that other members of the society were also harmed (Clark 2009; Danieli 2008; Weitekamp *et al.* 2006). Proponents of transitional justice models increasingly suggest the necessity of a holistic approach that enables the state, the community and individuals to confront the past in a manner conducive to a better future. It is our contention that a restorative justice approach can play a pivotal role as a component of the broader response.

Much of the previous scholarship on transitional justice has focused on the analysis and evaluation of the diverse range of mechanisms employed in the pursuit of transitional justice (Jones *et al.* 2012: 554). Yacoubian (2003: 135) discussed five responses taken by the international community: "1) doing nothing; 2) granting amnesty; 3) creating a truth commission; 4) domestic prosecutions; and 5) creating ad hoc tribunals". Typically, the responses carried out tend to reflect a "western, liberal tradition of accountability for crimes" (Lambourne 2009: 30) with a reliance on criminal prosecutions.

Reparative justice, the provision of reparations to victims of crime, has been seen as the "most common form of justice in the past" (Weitekamp 1993: 70). While interest in this approach waned in both acceptance and practice in the twentieth century it did not disappear, remerging in the 1970s and 1980s as an alternative to retributive justice (Weitekamp 1993). Notions of reparation to victims of gross violations of human rights have garnered greater international acceptance in recent times with "the acceptance of internationally accepted human rights norms as a basis for reparations" (Cunneen 2008: 359). The United Nations directed efforts toward "re"-focusing on victims, the harms experienced by these people and the need for reparations have included:

- The creation of the Van Boven/Bassiouni principles[1];
- *The Basic Principles and Guidelines on the Right to Remedy and Reparation for Victims of Violations of International Human Rights and Violations of Humanitarian Law* (E/CV.4/2005/L.48, adopted April 13, 2005);
- *The Basic Principles of Justice for Victims of Crime and Abuse of Power* (A/Res 40/34), and;

- *The Set of Principles for the Protection and Promotion of Human Rights Through Action to Combat Impunity* (E/CN.4/2005/102/ADD.1) (see Cunneen 2008; Danieli 2008).

According to Walgrave (2008: 621), restorative justice is "an option on doing justice after the occurrence of an offense that is primarily oriented towards repairing the individual, relational and social harm that is caused by an offence". As an option, restorative justice is often viewed as various processes, based on a fundamental set of principles that may vary depending on the socio-political, historical and cultural landscape in which they are used. Weitekamp *et al.* (2006: 11) have identified a number of such principles including personalism,[2] reparation, reintegration and participation. When reflecting on the definition and set of principles provided by Walgrave we find that there is a great deal of overlap between reparative and restorative justice. "It is interesting to note that in the historical background and development of restorative justice that the terms restitution, reparation, compensation, atonement, redress, community service mediation and indemnification have been used interchangeably in the literature" (Weitekamp *et al.* 2006: 8). Each perspective, while remaining cognizant of the contributions retributive justice provides in the context of mass violations of human rights, calls for a paradigmatic shift that returns the primary focus of addressing these crimes to the redress and repair of the victims' needs as opposed to the acts committed by the perpetrators. This approach has gained more interest in response to the acknowledged shortcomings of the retributive approach in addressing victim's needs (Weitekamp *et al.* 2006; Danieli 2009).

The restorative and retributive perspectives both seek similar outcomes surrounding the establishment of the truth regarding the events that transpired, acknowledging the harm done to victims, holding offenders accountable, re-establishing victims' power and esteem, reintegrating the victim and offender into society in a respectful manner, as well as restitution and compensation to victims and reconciliation (Cunneen 2008: 365). Additionally, active victim participation in the decision-making regarding the manners and forms that reparations will take is central to both approaches.

> Reparative justice insists that every step throughout the justice experience as a whole – from the first moment of encounter of the *Court* with a potential witness through the follow-up of witnesses after their return home to the aftermath of the completion of the case – presents an opportunity for redress and healing.
>
> (Danieli 2009: 356)

With respect to process, restorative justice's voluntary approach, which engages both victims and offenders in a dialogue, is argued to provide a more promising method of working toward the goals of transitional justice than retributive, accusatory approaches. By providing a safe, voluntary space for dialogue, it creates "an opportunity … to restore the harm done and to reconcile the relation"

(Weitekamp *et al.* 2006). These dialogical processes may facilitate the undoing of what Danieli (1988: 220) refers to as the *conspiracy of silence* wherein the healing for survivors of mass trauma is impeded as a result of survivors' experiences receiving a "pervasive societal reaction comprised of indifference, avoidance, repression, and denial". At an individual and local level, the repair to these relationships may further engage members of the larger society in productive conversations acknowledging the trauma that the victims have experienced and their roles in the conflict as perpetrators or observers. It may further raise this consciousness within the international realm, thereby intersecting the individual, societal, national and cross-national perspectives noted by Danieli that are required to address mass victimization.

The TARR model

The model of transitional justice examined in the current investigation is the TARR model originally proposed by Parmentier (2003), which was based on the identification of four key issues surrounding post-conflict justice:

- seeking truth (T) about the what occurred during the conflict;
- ensuring accountability (A) of perpetrators for their criminal acts;
- providing reparation (R) to victims; and
- the promotion of reconciliation (R).

As a result of continued analysis and revision, this model has been expanded to include three additional components (consideration of the physical, material and emotional traumas experienced; building trust as a component of reconciliation; and dialogue in various forms) as well as refinement of accountability into two separate but related categories, which are imposed obligations and active participation (Weitekamp and Parmentier 2012). Previous analyses carried out by Jones and colleagues (2012) suggest that trust and reconciliation were essentially measuring a single outcome. Therefore the final model, TARR–III, involves the interplay of seven components:

1 trauma
2 dialogue
3 truth
4 reparation
5 imposed obligations
6 active participation
7 reconciliation.

The objectives of the TARR–III model are twofold. First is the attempt to "understand the recent developments that are gradually leading away from situations of impunity towards situations of post-conflict justice in the face of a democratic transition". The second objective is to integrate a restorative justice perspective into responses to mass violence (Weitekamp *et al.* 2006: 218). The first objective reflects acknowledgment that exemption from punishment must be addressed through interventions that ensure the accountability of the perpetrators (Danieli 2009; Jones 2010; Valiñas *et al.* 2009; Weinstein *et al.* 2010). The second objective is consistent with incorporating restorative justice principles within the context of transitional justice. For example, Van Ness (1996: 29–30) argued that, in the context of international human rights – the focus of these mass crimes – there are five areas in which restorative justice theory shares commonalities with international criminal justice:

1 States must balance the interests of victims, offenders and the public.
2 Victims and offenders must have access to formal and informal dispute resolution mechanisms.
3 Crime prevention requires comprehensive action by government and community.
4 Government's role in responding to particular crimes should be to provide impartial, formal judicial mechanisms for victims and offenders.
5 The community must help victims and offenders reintegrate.

The TARR–III model's concepts of dialogue (or dialogical processes) as well as conceptualizations of accountability that differ from the retributive sanctions of punishment are particularly salient in this context. However, given the gravity of the crimes addressed in periods following mass victimization this does not suggest that punishment must be ignored or done away with. As noted by Villa-Vicencio (2008: 387), "Restorative justice seeks to recover dimensions of justice often lost within institutional retributive justice processes. It does not necessarily reject all punitive measures associated with the retribution justice." The value of the TARR model as described by Weitekamp *et al.* (2006: 22–3) goes beyond the creation of another typology for transitional justice, because it pieces together and demonstrates the interconnectedness of its constitutional components: concepts already identified by a number of studies in the area of post-conflict justice.

Previous research examining the various configurations of the TARR model has highlighted a number of important findings. Early scholarship demonstrated the centrality of "seeking the truth" as a cornerstone of the respondents' requirements for achieving justice (Valiñas *et al.* 2009). The authors contended that previous manipulations of facts were a crucial element in creating the conditions conducive for violence and that truth seeking was vital in order to provide a foundation for progressing toward a shared future. It was further demonstrated that official sites for truth-telling processes (such as courts and Truth and Reconciliation Commissions) were more strongly endorsed by participants than were venues that are more informal, as the formal site provided "an official endorsement of the stories of suffering and violations" (Valiñas *et al.* 2009: 63). Increased recognition of the long-term harms of psychological trauma for victims of these crimes was also apparent, given that psychologists were third-ranked as a venue for "telling their stories". Finally, informal processes were "regarded as positive by a considerable amount of respondents ... and while it seems clear that not all respondents would feel ready to engage in such initiatives, a considerable number would be prepared for it" (Valiñas *et al.* 2009: 63).

In the TARR models, accountability was determined as having two separate but related components: active responsibility and imposed obligations. Active responsibility involves offenders taking a personal and active approach to undoing the damage they caused through confession and/or apology; imposed obligations are more formal reparative measures, such as paying money to victims or returning property, that are ordered by organizations such as courts or commissions (Valiñas *et al.* 2009; Jones *et al.* 2012). Increases in the self-reported suffering of victims were correlated with both types of accountability; however, only active participation was positively correlated with trust and/or reconciliation (Jones *et al.* 2012). This was posited to be related to higher levels active participation compared to imposed obligations, "showing the role of confessions and apologies for perceptions of what constituted truth" (Jones *et al.* 2012: 558). Interestingly, it was observed that dialogue had a much stronger relationship with active responsibility than with imposed obligations, suggesting that dialogical approaches were more effective in achieving the former than the latter.

As noted above, scholars have found that perceptions of what might constitute meaningful reparations to victims were related to trauma, dialogue and both active responsibility and imposed obligations. Reparations that are positively perceived by victims/survivors are closely linked to both truth and accountability, reflecting the outcomes of truth seeking and actions carried out to increase accountability (Valiñas *et al.* 2009). This demonstrates the centrality of accountability as important in addressing victims' suffering (Jones *et al.* 2012: 558). Surprisingly, however, perceived support for reparations (as for truth and imposed obligations) was negatively associated with trust and/or reconciliation. In addition to suggesting that the measures of reconciliation require further refinement, it has been argued that, "if reconciliation is associated with impunity, then it is quite reasonable to see how the measures of truth, reparation and imposed obligations could be negatively associated with reconciliation" (Jones *et al.* 2012: 560). What did appear to ameliorate participants' concerns with an offender's exemption from punishment, and hence a more positive correlation with reconciliation, was active participation on the part of the offender, which was more likely to occur in dialogical processes.[3]

Evaluating the TARR model

This research examined data collected through a self-administered, population-based survey in Bosnia-Herzegovina in June 2006. The participants surveyed for the original research were selected through a quota sampling procedure and undertaken through convenience and snowball sampling techniques (Valiñas *et al.* 2009: 10). This process reduced, to the greatest degree possible, selection bias while also targeting pre-determined criteria of interest including geographical distribution, religious affiliation (ethnicity),[4] age and gender. Data were collected from 855 participants (N=855), and of this total 51 percent were male and 49 percent were female. The average age of the respondents was 40 years with a range from 18 to 84 years. According to the investigators, their sample "met their objective as 79 percent of the respondents were indeed between 25 and 64 years old" (Valiñas *et al.* 2009: 14). Of the respondents, 663 (77.5 percent) had experienced physical suffering, 722 (84.4 percent) suffered material losses, and 726 (84.9 percent) had experienced emotional suffering. These figures indicate that most respondents experienced some degree of victimization and in many cases multiple forms of suffering.

Building on previous research, we examined the factors impacting the participants' perspectives of various components of the TARR model (accountability, reparation and justice processes). Regression models were used to test the relationships between each of the demographic variables, the degree of suffering and the variables associated with the TARR model. Indicators representing the respondent's level of education, religious affiliation (ethnicity),[5] gender, age, and self-reported suffering (physical, material and emotional) were included in models that investigated their relationships with accountability, reparation and justice processes. The measurement of the variables followed the analytical process previously undertaken by Jones *et al.* (2012). Trauma was measured by responses to questions regarding the degree to which participants experienced 1) physical, 2) material and 3) emotional suffering. Imposed obligations were measured using three obligations imposed on perpetrators: 1) payment of money to victims; 2) the return of stolen property or goods; and 3) carrying out community service. Active responsibility was measured by perpetrators providing 1) confessions and 2) apologies. Reparation was measured in two ways: 1) individual reparations, which included survey questions where participants responded to "I" or "me" questions such as "if I could tell others about my experience during the war"; and 2) collective reparations, which included questions that spoke to the collectivity such as memorialization and "if truth about all the facts and events of the war would be known". Finally, justice processes were divided into three categories examining the continuum from the very informal to the formal: 1) informal dialogical,[6] 2) truth commission, and 3) courts (inside Bosnia-Herzegovina).

Results

Beginning with accountability, the first model examined the impact of the demographic characteristics and indicators of the degree of suffering on imposed obligations. The model was statistically significant and accounted for 2.9 percent of the variance in participants' perceptions of imposing obligations on the perpetrators (adjusted $R^2=0.029$, $\alpha=0.005$). Only one of the independent variables, the "degree of suffering", had a statistically significant association with imposed obligations ($\beta=0.145$, $\alpha=0.003$). The second model used the same set of independent variables to explain perceptions about active responsibility. Again, the model was statistically significant and accounted for 5.2 percent of the variance in participants' perceptions of active responsibility on the part of the perpetrators (adjusted $R^2=0.052$, $\alpha=0.000$). Inconsistent with the first model, however, only religious affiliation (ethnicity) had a statistically significant relationship with active responsibility (Catholic dichotomous variable, $\beta=0.119$, $\alpha=0.031$ and Muslim dichotomous variable, $\beta=0.269$, $\alpha=0.000$).

Turning now to reparations, we analyzed two models: one examining individual reparations as the dependent variable, the other collective reparations. In the case of individual reparations, the model was statistically significant and explained 3.8 percent of the variance in respondents' perceptions (adjusted $R^2=0.038$, $\alpha=0.003$). The only independent variable that had a statistically significant relationship with reparations was the self-reported "degree of suffering" ($\beta=0.151$, $\alpha=0.004$). For collective reparations the analysis also revealed that the model was statistically significant (adjusted $R^2=0.026$, $\alpha=0.007$). However, none of the independent variables included in the model had a statistically significant association with reparations.

With respect to the type of justice (or "venue" where it may be sought, suggesting a continuum from dialogically-based to formal retribution-based approaches) three regression models were estimated that examined the relationships of the independent variables and informal dialogical processes, the truth commission, and courts inside Bosnia-Herzegovina. Only the model testing informal dialogical processes was statistically significant (adjusted $R^2=0.085$, $\alpha=0.000$), accounting for 8.5 percent of the variance in respondents' perceptions of these processes.[7] The independent variables driving this model were "degree of suffering" ($\beta=0.141$, $\alpha=0.002$) and the religious affiliation dichotomous variable for being Muslim, as opposed to Catholic or Orthodox ($\beta=0.226$, $\alpha=0.000$).

Given the relationship between the variable indicating "degree of suffering" and the variables measuring religious affiliation (ethnicity), a series of supplementary analyses were conducted. A chi-square test explored the relationship between the different components of suffering (physical, material and emotional) to see if differential experiences occurred for each religious (ethnic) group. The results of the analysis suggested that there was a statistically significant difference between the three groups with respect to physical and material suffering but not emotional suffering. Respondents who self-identified as Muslim (Bosnians) reported a higher degree of physical suffering than did the Catholics (Croats) or the Orthodox (Serbians) ($\chi^2=47.02$, df=6, $\alpha=0.000$).[8] With respect to material suffering the results were similar across all three groups, with the respondents who self-identified as Muslim (Bosnians) reporting a higher degree of material suffering than did the Catholics (Croats) or the Orthodox (Serbians) ($\chi^2=24.895$, df=6, $\alpha=0.000$).[9]

Discussion

The results of the analyses reported above suggest that many standard demographic variables (age, gender and level of education) do not have a statistically significant relationship with the respondents' perceptions regarding the imposition of obligations on perpetrators, active responsibility on the part of the perpetrators, individual reparations, or the use of informal dialogically-based processes. The variables that had the strongest influence on the respondents' perceptions were the "degree of suffering" that they experienced and their religious (ethnic) affiliation.

Accountability was conceptualized as having two separate but related components, imposed obligations and active responsibility. The only independent variable that had a statistically significant impact on the imposition of obligations on the perpetrators was the degree of suffering. This suggests that as a person's severity of suffering increases there is an accompanying desire to impose formal sanctions on those who harmed them. It might also suggest an increased longing for vengeance, wherein victims wanted the perpetrators to be held fully accountable for their crimes.

The second component of accountability, which is active responsibility, posits that confession and/or apology demonstrates that the perpetrator is – at least to some degree – contrite following their actions. In this instance, the only variable that had a statistically significant relationship with the perceptions of active responsibility was religious affiliation (ethnicity). Muslims (Bosnians) as opposed to Catholics (Croatians) and Orthodox (Serbians) demonstrated a stronger acceptance of confessions and apologies. Given that this group reported higher levels of physical and material suffering, this is a somewhat counterintuitive result. These findings suggest that victims with a higher degree of suffering are more supportive of the notion that offenders take a more active role in making amends. There may be social psychological and/or religious explanations for this finding, which would further support the usefulness of an integrated, multidisciplinary disciplinary approach to understanding transitional justice as suggested by Danieli (2009). For example, perhaps some of the answers lay within a religious exploration of forgiveness and reconciliation. Philpott's (2007) discussion of the influence of religious accounts provides one possible explanation. He argued that reconciliation is "far more than a relinquishment of claims owed by perpetrators, but also as an action that involves the victim's own will to restore and that often helps him to recover his own sense of agency" (Philpott 2007: 98). While reconciliation is common among many religions, in the case of Islam, "forgiveness is meant to be conditional upon the prior repentance of perpetrators, whereas Christian theologians are more willing to commend unilateral forgiveness on the part of victims, though they are divided on the issue" (Philpott 2007: 98). Despite experiencing a higher degree of suffering, the Bosnian Muslims are more likely to support confessions and apologies. Perhaps this is because for them it is a precondition of moving toward forgiveness and reconciliation and is therefore sought after, whereas for the other groups, it is not considered necessary and therefore they are not as bound by those sentiments.

Perceptions about individual reparations were influenced by the suffering experienced by respondents. This suggests that the greater the degree of trauma experienced by an individual, the greater the need for hearing the truth and discovering answers to the "why" and "what" questions. Being able to make sense of their victimization requires ending impunity, acknowledgement of one's suffering, and claiming redress (Danieli 2009). We contend that achieving this resolution is a key feature of a restorative approach as it responds to the shortcomings of retributive justice, particularly in terms of "healing and restorative truth, meaning the truth that places facts and their meaning within the context of human relationships" (Weitekamp *et al.* 2006: 3).

The interplay between trauma, truth, accountability, reparation and dialogue, as discussed by Jones *et al.* (2012), enable us to make linkages between "degree of suffering" and "religious affiliation" and their impact on the respondents' positive or negative perceptions toward dialogical approaches. Bosnian Muslims perceived that their suffering was higher than other groups, but also reported greater support for the use of informal processes. That outcome is consistent with previous research suggesting that dialogical models may facilitate getting answers to one's questions and receiving an apology, and may possibly increase the chances for reconciliation (Jones *et al.* 2012). Additionally, this finding may also suggest that when there is a perception of a higher degree of suffering within a group, informal processes may become more important than formal individualized approaches based on traditional retributive justice. However, it must be noted that despite our support for incorporating restorative approaches into transitional justice, we recognize that the socio-political, historical and cultural contexts in which these conflicts arise must also be taken into account. Furthermore, restorative approaches cannot be considered a panacea that will address all the ills created by these crimes. As a result, these approaches are to be viewed as *complementary* to other forms of healing and redress, such as psychological counseling for victims, retributive actions to end impunity, and reparative measures at a state and international level.

Notes

1. According to Cunneen (2008), the van Boven / Bassiouni principles reflect the work of the United Nations firstly in 1989 when they commissioned Theo van Boven as the Special Rapporteur on the Prevention of Discrimination and Protection of Minorities; and the again in 1998 when Bassiouni "was appointed to further revise the principles developed by van Boven on the right to reparations for victims of gross violations of human rights" (358). These gave rise to the discussions in the UN that finally led to the adoption of the *Basic Principles and Guidelines on the Right to a Remedy and Reparation for Victims of Gross Violations of International Human Rights Law and Serious Violations of International Humanitarian Law* (General Assembly, 24 October 2005, A/C.3/60/L.24) which are one in the same.
2 According to Roche (in Weitekamp *et al.* 2006: 11) personalism incorporates the view that "crime is a violation of people and their relationships rather than a violation of law".
3 It is interesting to note that in the Rwandan and Cambodian contexts it was observed that victims of crimes against humanity considered three components of the TARR model (accountability, truth and reparation) as preconditions for achieving reconciliation (Raymond 2010). Raymond noted that accountability, although defined as punishment and typically through incapacitation, was seen more as a deterrent, a preventative measure against future crimes, and recognition of the victim's experience, and not necessarily as retaliation. Truth was important with regard to finding out what happened and as a means of recognition of their victimization.
4 In the original analysis conducted by Valiñas *et al.* (2009), religious affiliation was used as a proxy measure for ethnicity as it provided the "primary distinction between different national groups (or ethnic groups)" (11). While it was noted in the original

research that this measure had limitations, it continues to be used in this research as it "it is more commonly used in order to inquire about a person's ethnicity since the concept of 'ethnicity' is not yet well interiorised by all individuals" (11).

5 The survey included Catholic, Jewish, Muslim, Orthodox and Other as potential responses. Based on the descriptive statistics only the Catholic, Muslim and Orthodox categories had enough cases to be usable for the analyses. In order to proceed with the analysis, these three classifications were coded into dichotomous (yes/no) variables.

6 Included: 1) in public events such as workshops or roundtables, 2) in small groups in the community (with members of other ethnic groups present), and 3) in small groups in the community (members of other ethnic groups NOT present).

7 The issue with both models is likely best explained by the high degree of skewness observed in the values of both dependent variables (TRC and courts). We considered dichotomizing the variables and performing a logistic regression but this would not have addressed the skewness issue. It might be possible to log the values and proceed with the analysis, but the interpretation of those results could be meaningless. This remains an issue to be explored further.

8 At the lowest level of reported suffering, "very little", there was a 15 percent lower response among the Bosnian Muslims (35.2 percent) than for the Croatian Catholics (51.1 percent) and the Serbian Orthodox (49.3 percent). At the highest level, "very much", the results were 31.7 percent, 17.6 percent and 26.5 percent respectively.

9 At the lowest level of reported suffering, "very little", there was around a 50 percent difference in the percentage providing a lower response among the Bosnian Muslims (6.9 percent) than for the Croatians Catholics (12.4 percent) and the Serbian Orthodox (17.9 percent). At the highest level, "very much", the results were 50.0 percent, 62.2 percent and 56.7 percent respectively, demonstrating less of a difference at the highest level but nevertheless a difference.

References

Clark, P. (2009) "Establishing a Conceptual Framework: Six key transitional justice themes", in P. Clark and Z.D. Kaufman (eds) *After Genocide: Transitional Justice, post-conflict reconstruction and reconciliation in Rwanda and beyond*, New York: Columbia University Press, 191–207.

Cunneen, C. (2008) "Exploring the Relationship Between Reparations, the Gross Violation of Human Rights, and Restorative justice", in D. Sullivan and L. Tift (eds) *Handbook of Restorative Justice: A global perspective*, New York: Routledge, 355–68.

Danieli, Y. (1988) "Confronting the Unimaginable: Psychotherapists' reactions to victims of the Nazi Holocaust", in J.P. Wilson, Z. Harel and B. Kahana (eds) *Human Adaptation to Extreme Stress: From the Holocaust to Vietnam*, New York: Plenum Press, 219–38.

Danieli, Y. (2008) "Essential Elements of Healing after Massive Trauma: Complex needs voiced by victims", in D. Sullivan and L. Tift (eds) *Handbook of Restorative Justice: A global perspective*, New York: Routledge, 343–54.

Danieli, Y. (2009) "Massive Trauma and the Healing Role of Reparative Justice", *Journal of Traumatic Stress*, 22(5): 351–7.

Jones, N.A. (2010) *The Courts of Genocide: Politics and the rule of law in Rwanda and Arusha*, New York: Routledge.

Jones, N.A., Parmentier, S. and Weitekamp, E.G.M. (2012) "Dealing with International Crimes in Post-War Bosnia: A look through the lens of the affected population", *European Journal of Criminology*, 9(5): 553–64.

Lambourne, W. (2009) "Transitional Justice and Peacebuilding after Mass Violence", *The International Journal of Transitional Justice*, 3(1): 28–48.

Parmentier, S. (2003) "Global Justice in the Aftermath of Mass Violence", *International Annals of Criminology*, 41(1–2): 203–24.

Philpott, D. (2007) "What Religion Brings to the Politics of Transitional Justice", *Journal of International Affairs*, 61(1): 93–110.

Raymond, É. (2010) "Justice pour les crimes contre l'humanité et génocides: Point de vue et attentes des victimes", unpublished thesis, University of Montreal.

Shaw, R. and Waldorf, L. (2010) "Introduction: Localizing transitional justice", in R. Shaw, L. Waldorf and P. Hazan (eds) *Localizing Transitional Justice: Interventions and priorities after mass violence*, Stanford: Stanford University Press, 3–27.

Siegel, R.L. (1998) "Transitional Justice: A decade of debate and experience", *Human Rights Quarterly*, 20(2): 431–54.

United Nations. (1993) Study concerning the right to restitution, compensation and rehabilitation for victims of gross violations of human rights and fundamental freedoms. Commission on Human Rights: Sub-Commission of Prevention of Discrimination and Protection of Minorities. Mr. Theo van Boven, Special Rapporteur – Forty-fifth session (E/CN.4/sub.2/1993/2July1993).

United Nations. (2000) Civil and Political Rights, Including the Questions of: Independence of the Judiciary, Administration of Justice, Impunity: The right to restitution, compensation and rehabilitation for victims of gross violations of human rights and fundamental freedoms. Commission on Human Rights. Mr. Cherif Bassiouni, Special Rapporteur – Fifty-sixth session (E/CN.4/2000/62 18 January 2000).

Valiñas, M., Parmentier, S. and Weitekamp, E.G.M. (2009) *Restoring Justice in Bosnia and Herzegovina: Report of a population-based survey* no. 31, Leuven: Leuven Centre for Global Governance Studies.

Van Ness, D.W. (1996) "Restorative Justice and International Human Rights", in B. Galaway and J. Hudson (eds) *Restorative Justice: International perspectives*, Monsey: Criminal Justice Press, 17–36.

Villa-Vicencio, C. (2008) "Transitional Justice, Restoration, and Prosecution", in D. Sullivan and L.Tift (eds) *Handbook of Restorative Justice*, New York: Routledge, 387–400.

Walgrave, L. (2008) "Restorative Justice: An alternative for responding to crime?" in S.G. Shoham, O. Beck and M. Kett (eds) *International Handbook of Penology and Criminal Justice*, Boca Raton: CRC Press, 25–50.

Weinstein, H., Fletcher, M., Laurel, E., Vinck, P. and Pham, P.N. (2010) "Stay the Hand of Justice: Whose priorities take priority?", in R. Shaw and L. Waldorf (eds) *Localizing Transitional Justice: Interventions and priorities after mass violence*, Stanford: Stanford University Press, 27–48.

Weitekamp, E.G.M. (1993) "Reparative Justice: Towards a victim oriented system", *European Journal of Criminal Policy and Research*, 1(1): 70–93.

Weitekamp, E.G.M. and Parmentier, S. (2012) "On the Road to Reconciliation: An attempt to develop a theoretical model which applies restorative justice mechanisms in post-conflict societies", in E. Plywaczewski (ed.) *Current Problems of the Penal Law and Criminology*, Warsaw: Wolters Kluwer Publishing, 795–804.

Weitekamp, E.G.M., Vanspauwen, K., Parmentier, S., Valiñas, M. and Gerits, R. (2006) "How to Deal with Mass Victimization and Gross Human Rights Violations: A restorative justice approach", in U. Ewald and K. Turković (eds) *Large-Scale Victimization as a Potential Source of Terrorist Activities*, Amsterdam: IOS Press, 217–41.

Yacoubian, G.S. (2003) "Evaluating the Efficacy of the International Criminal Tribunals for Rwanda and the Former Yugoslavia: Implications for criminology and international criminal law", *World Affairs*, 165(3): 133–41.

10 The art of acknowledgment

Re-imagining relationships in Northern Ireland

Jill Strauss

This is a unique time in Northern Ireland as it transitions from overt violence to relative peace.[1] After 800 years of tensions between Protestants and Catholics[2] in Northern Ireland, culminating in the extreme violence of a period known as the Troubles (1968–1998[3]), there is now relative peace in the region since the 1994 ceasefires and the 1998 Good Friday Agreement. As a result of these recent historical developments there are currently people alive with first-hand experience of the Troubles and, at the same time, there is a younger generation growing up in a more segregated society than that of their parents and grandparents. This setting provides a unique opportunity to explore how we repair relationships within communities that have been torn apart after years of violence and humiliation.

This chapter focuses on reparation, as for example apology or other symbolic forms of restitution (Zehr 2002), at the level of the community, and in particular the relationships between the members of different social identity groups. According to Bell, within the transitional justice field there is an increasing "recognition that if a shift is to be successful, transitional societies must enact it in various extra-legal and non-executive domains" (2011: 325). In this chapter, we will present the findings from an ethnographic case study that assessed whether art combined with conflict resolution approaches can create alternative paths for individuals in situations of inherited conflict to accept the validity of each other's perspectives, and the significance of this for the parties involved.

After discussing the notion of empathy, we will describe how validation, recognition and acknowledgment can transform relationships. Following this, we will consider how art can support the conflict transformation process through an examination of a storytelling and visual art project that took place in Portadown, Northern Ireland in 2008 with an intergenerational group of Catholics and Protestants as part of the author's doctoral research. The chapter closes with an analysis, using a restorative lens, of three of the five artworks that came out of the project; these artworks were made by the young participant artists as creative attempts to "put right the wrongs" (Zehr 2002: 19) they heard in the older people's stories about life during and before "the Troubles".

Empathy

Is art a means through which we can generate empathy for the other? It is in times of transition that we can engage with multiple perspectives, imagine alternatives, and encounter "the other" in non-adversarial ways enabling us to reimagine our relationships. In her article, "Contemporary Art and Transitional Justice in Northern Ireland: The Consolation of Form", Vikki Bell argues that in a transitional context, "artworks become sites in which the assumptions of transition are opened up for critical reflection, probing the notion of what constitutes Peace and its conditions of possibility" (2011: 325). Furthermore, according to Cohen, a work of art:

> Allows us to experience, perceive, or understand something previously unknown about ourselves. Conversely, it is by attending to what is evoked within us that we are able to understand the poetic image. Understanding [an artwork] can alter a [viewer] who enters into a state of receptivity to the poetic image, to its resonances and reverberations within the [viewer], and to the [continued] inversions between them.
>
> (Cohen 2003: 268)

What Cohen refers to as "resonances and reverberations" can also be called empathy. Cohen goes on to use this analogy to explain that interdependence as well as empathy is necessary for parties in conflict to transform negative relationships into positive ones. In other words, it is not enough to understand and accept "the other's" experience; we must also value them and appreciate our mutual dependence. We cannot survive in isolation, just as we cannot be in conflict alone.

Pranis *et al.* maintain that "[h]ow we're treated, how we participate, who's involved, … how we're heard: these factors give us a sense of whether or not we've experienced justice" (2003: 17–18). Some writers such as Bennett (1998) view empathy as primarily understanding the other person's emotions. According to Bennett, when we are empathetic, we are experiencing "the imaginative intellectual and emotional participation in another person's experience". In order to be able to take on the perspective of another "[w]e need to get inside the head and heart of the other" (Bennett 1998: 207).

However, Rothman (1997) does not believe that empathy for another's emotional state is required for reframing the "us vs. them" scenario. He considers that "analytic empathy" is not only sufficient but necessary if the underlying causes of blaming and scapegoating are to be addressed as well. "Analytic empathy" involves understanding the other's motivations and behaviors rather than their emotional state. This allows parties in conflict to appreciate each other's aggressive actions as being not unlike their own. Once we no longer perceive the other party as very different from ourselves, they are in theory no longer an adversary. Also, we are less inclined to blame someone when we understand why they have acted the way they have (Rothman 1997).

The theory, however, does not take into consideration that there is often a "mismatch between people's need to tell their stories and express their suffering and their former enemy's capacity to listen" (Cohen 2003: 270). Therefore, initiatives bringing together individuals and groups after violent conflict should include "conflict resolution training to improve skills in communication, negotiation, and problem solving" (Babbitt 2003: 102). If the conditions are created for empathetic listening, then it follows that for the speaker, the validation of knowing that they have been heard and their story accepted should help (Deutsch 2006b) even if the acknowledgement does not come from the perpetrator (Jelin 2003).

"Validation", "recognition" and "acknowledgment" are all words used to describe the experience of being listened to respectfully and compassionately. This can transform an individual's feelings of hurt, pain, isolation and disenfranchisement to feelings of relatedness and a desire for others to have a similar opportunity (Bush *et al.* 1994; Hamber 2006; Lindner 2009; Kayser 2000). This is particularly necessary in Northern Ireland because during this time of transition from violent conflict to relative peace, many believe that the other religious identity group has misrepresented their respective history or side of the story and that the world does not understand or know the truth about how they have each been wronged. Perhaps this is because, as Morrow argues, "[i]n the absence of victory, where one party may be more able to shape and control the flow of information, truth recovery will be a process of accusation as much as of vindication for both communities" (2008: 6). While Bell argues that a lack of a "collective meaning" of the past is a hindrance to peace-building because "[p]eace can never be simply done with the past" (2011: 342), this flexibility could also be potentially useful for a society attempting to re-imagine and redefine itself.

The project

In 2008, an ethnographic case study conducted by the author involving an intergenerational group of Protestants and Catholics from Northern Ireland undertook a six-month storytelling and art-making project to achieve mutual validation and respect in the present as an antidote to a history of mutual humiliation and violent conflict. The project design included listening and paraphrasing activities and storytelling circles. This created the conditions for the older people to reflect on their past lives and for the younger people to explore ways of interpreting those memories and feelings creatively in a visual form, and in the process for Protestant and Catholic, old and young, to develop empathy for "the other" and recognition of their respective truths.

This case study took place at the Millennium Court Arts Centre in Portadown. Even though the population is 45 percent Catholic, Portadown is considered a Protestant town because it is best known for the recurring violence surrounding the annual Protestant Orange Order parades during the summer marching season. As previously noted, there is no agreed-upon historical narrative so these performances serve to remind Catholic and Protestant alike of the Protestant claim to the land. In fact, marching itself is symbolic in Northern Ireland, making concrete not only memory but also power and access (Jarman and Bryan 1997). As Northern Ireland native Bill Rolston explains, "[f]or us the Twelfth [of July] is an annual reminder, like so many smaller daily reminders, that we were losers in the struggle over the establishment of the state" (1991: 18).

At the same time, not only the Catholics may feel threatened. For some Protestants, there is deep insecurity due to a lack of a sense of belonging in Ireland (Graham 1994; Reid 2004; Graham 2007; Dunlop 1995). Another native of the North, Frank Ormsby, has reflected that "[t]o be native to a province colonised by one's ancestors, at home and yet 'alien' ... is to be perpetually unsure of one's place" (1979: 4). Northern Ireland has suffered a long history of insecurity and mutual humiliation (Stokes 2006). Kay Pranis, a leader in restorative justice maintains that "[t]he fear of not belonging and the pain of feeling that one doesn't belong are at the root of much violence and harm in the world" (2012: 34). For this reason, contested territory is one of the ways conflict is exhibited in the North.

Contestation is also exhibited in Northern Ireland through symbols and images. The artist Rita Duffy points out the "sophisticated visual sense" in Northern Ireland. The people learn from childhood to identify and use a "rich language of signals and symbolism" to articulate cultural difference and sectarianism through flags, murals, graffiti, banners and curb painting instead of canvas that defines and demarcates both territory and identity (quoted in Pryor 2008: 43). Moreover, one image can "have layers of meaning" even for one person and "different people can see very different meanings in the same symbol" (Bryan and Gillespie 2005: 13). Likewise, "[w]hat is forgotten in one situation may be recalled in another". This suggests that identity itself is never fixed nor uniform, but rather it has the fluidity necessary for individuals to navigate their locations across a range of discourses and subject positions (Norquay 1999: 20).

The first part of the cross-community project involved conflict resolution and storytelling workshops, which took place from May 21 to July 2, 2008. The workshops were followed by a month of art-making and then a two-month exhibit entitled "Impressions" in August and September. This project was voluntary; it turned out that the participants had no reservations about working collaboratively with members of the other religious identity group and were interested in partnering with individuals from a different generation. Nevertheless, there were cases of validation that will be described below. For the workshops, the group of twelve, comprising five young people and seven older people, met once a week over a six-week period. The younger participants were 20 to 23 years old (plus one, who worked for the host gallery, was 30 years of age and from the Republic of Ireland) and the older participants ranged in age from 60 to 70 years. This meant that the younger group members were about the same ages as the older people had been during the Troubles 40 years earlier.

This intergenerational project also involved remembering, storytelling, and recording as artistic acts similar to the making of visual and performance pieces. Of interest was how the older people would recount their narratives and what they would choose to tell as a creative act. Likewise, which stories would inspire the young artists when determining what to interpret visually? This collaborative approach created the opportunity for the young participant artists to walk in the shoes of the storytellers in order to interpret visually the older people's stories empathetically, thereby collaboratively creating something new in the process (Deutsch 2006a; Zehr 2005; Pranis 2003). The resulting artwork reflected how Northern Irish artists each looked at another's (the storyteller's) past through the lens of her present, in the process envisioning a different future for Northern Ireland. In this way, they went from the individual to their hopes for their society (Cohen 2003).

The art

Are some expressions of validation more effective than others? Can visuals communicate emotion and information more effectively than words (Rose 2007)? Described here are three of the five artworks created for this intergenerational and cross-community project. Gail and Emily,[4] two textile artists, created the first two artworks disussed. These young women are Protestant and as they are both from the Portadown area, they not oblivious to the contested issues around symbols in the North of Ireland. The third artwork presented is by Nola, a young Catholic artist.

Gail

Gail chose to take on and re-imagine one of her religious identity group's most contested emblems – the marching banner. Gail wanted to re-imagine and reframe the banner (Figure 10.1), which she called the *Banner of Hope*. Her chosen design is in keeping with the traditional Orange Order Banner of a center motif with words and other images surrounding it; however, the content is untraditional. The usual center design often commemorates a past victorious battle over the Catholics. Instead, in the center Gail sewed the region of Northern Ireland in green surrounded by many flags to represent the diversity of immigrants that now live there. For over a century Ireland thought of itself as a place of emigration, but it is now a place of immigration as people seeking safety from violence now make their homes there. The central image is surrounded by several embroidered vignettes of the stories that grabbed Gail's imagination.

One of the stories she chose to depict (Figure 10.2) was recounted by a Catholic woman who told of how 50 years ago, her sister worked in one of the linen factories in Portadown. The linen industry in the North was "a main source of survival especially for the Catholic community given the discriminatory employment practices in the ship-building industries [the other main employment]" (Bell 2011: 333). Protestants owned the factory her sister worked in, and in the summer time, they would hang bunting on the walls and across the ceiling of the factory. Hanging red, white and blue colored bunting, the colors of the flag of the British Union flag or the Union Jack, is very popular in the summer as part

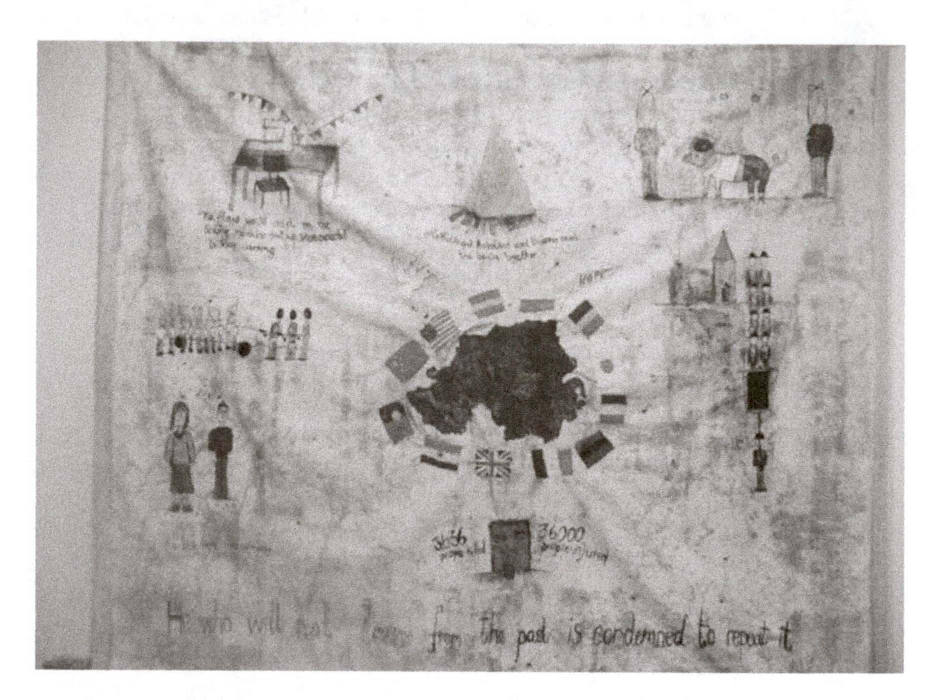

Figure 10.1 Banner of hope.

Figure 10.2 Close-up of sewing vignette.

of the Protestant Orange Order marching season celebrations. Over time, the bunting would fall and get stuck in the sewing machines. Nevertheless, the workers were not allowed to cut and untangle the bunting from their machines and were even expected to continue sewing. One day, in frustration, the storyteller's sister cut the bunting that had entwined itself in her sewing machine. As a result, she was treated very badly by her fellow workers. She was ostracized, and forced to go home by her employer. Upon hearing what had happened to his daughter, her father insisted that she go back to work the following day because the family needed her salary. When his daughter refused, he went and begged for his daughter's job back. She returned to her job but things were never the same. Five decades later, this story of injustice was empathetically portrayed by a Protestant: sewn onto fabric, as the storyteller's sister had sewn fabric, on a banner that is a symbol like the red, white and blue bunting of the Orange Order and their sectarian dominance.

In addition, Gail does not try to explain her religious identity group's actions or in other ways excuse them. Instead she has made public the wrong, thereby removing the shame and silence, and in this way has attempted to make things right. According to the storyteller, there was a real feeling of validation when she saw Gail's banner. She hugged Gail when she first saw it, and then she called her sister to tell her. After all these years there was some sort of acknowledgment, some validation of the humiliation and ostracization she had felt and perhaps some sense that she had been in the right. Perhaps this is why at the exhibition opening the storyteller said "[t]hey were really listening to us". This vignette was the best example of how visual depictions of one's experiences of injustice and humiliation can be made right when the story is made public, portrayed empathetically and given validation at an institutional level for others to see.

Emily

Like Gail, Emily, who is also Protestant, looked to the rituals of her religious identity group. In *Us and Them* (Figure 10.3), she takes on the duality of Northern Ireland directly by re-imagining her community's flag as a symbol of unity and disunity. In this case, she incorporated the flag of the United Kingdom with the flag of the Republic of Ireland, often referred to as the Tricolour, to be what could be called a cross-community (Protestant and Catholic) or bi-national flag. However, "[t]he Irish Tricolour and the Union Flag are not simply pieces of cloth but represent a whole range of beliefs and identities" (Bryan and Gillespie 2005: 13). In response to the stories she heard, she explored one way to create a symbol of unity in a bi-national flag. The matter of one flag and what it will include and exclude is a timely issue for a society in transition.

This artwork comes directly out of a group dialogue during which the Catholics in the group shared their painful memories of sectarian bonfires at which the flag of the Irish Republic was burned. They also talked about how much they hated territory demarcation and Orange Order marches that led to an increase in

Figure 10.3 Us and Them.

bias attacks against Catholics during the summer marching season. As Emily described later, it was very hurtful to hear these criticisms from people she now considered her friends, because these are traditions that are important to her, that she enjoys and takes pride in. However, she seemed to assume that of course she would stay in the room and listen. This is to her credit, because she could have walked out at any time.

Emily practiced her listening skills during the conflict resolution workshops, stayed, and heard what the others had to say, and out of that process the artwork described above was inspired. The Public Conversations Project, an organization that trains people in how to have potentially divisive dialogue in a constructive and productive way, describe this willingness to stay in the room and listen even when it is hard to hear what is being said as "listening with resilience" (Herzig and Chasin 2006: 9; 11). In a post-project interview, Emily said that she "learned that listening involves more than just hearing the words someone said and it took effort for me to understand the ideas and feelings that each person was trying to communicate".

Rather than visually depicting any of the older participants' stories, Emily attempted here to address a wrong she had become recently aware of and to make things right by giving equal recognition to the two main religious identity communities. The power of the work lies in the marrying of the flag of the Republic of Ireland, which is associated with political nationalism (Wilson

2000) and separation from Britain, with the Union flag signifying the colonizer and "almost a millennium" of oppression for some Catholics (Santino 2001: 11). The artist is forcing the viewer to engage with a potentially difficult political reality by imagining these two mutually exclusive symbols in a unified composition. Whether her flag is considered blasphemous or prophetic only time will tell. Gallery visitors expressed strong opinions both for and against the flag design, in some cases even responding to previous visitors' opinions in the gallery comment book. Worth noting here is that in the 2008 Northern Ireland Life and Times Survey, 28 percent of 18–24 year olds (the peers of the artists involved in this project) felt that a new neutral flag for Northern Ireland was needed but only 6 percent thought it should be the Union flag and the Irish Tri-Color side by side (ARK 2009). However, it is not evident that these respondents considered the creative design possibilities of some kind of incorporation.

Nola

Another young artist, Nola, who is Catholic, embraced the idea of memory and the inheritance of memory while generating emotions for the viewer in the present. She chose to work with Nellie, a Protestant and former housing worker (social worker) on the Garvaghy Road in Portadown. The Garvaghy Road and Drumcree Church are best known for the annual standoff over Protestant Orange Order marches through this Catholic area every July. Nellie was aware that as a Protestant working for the state, whose job it was to go into people's homes uninvited to assess and report on them, she was "the other" in many ways – and yet she was always offered a cup of tea in a china cup. This was significant and quite moving to Nellie, who was sensitive to the fact that as a Protestant representing a government agency she was not necessarily welcome in these homes, especially at a time when security forces in the name of the state were regularly searching Catholic homes for weapons (White and Falkenburg White 1995). These uninvited intrusions into their homes could have only felt humiliating to Catholics (just as they would to anyone). Yet, or perhaps because of this, she was always treated as an invited guest. Perhaps they recognized in Nellie a friend rather than a foe, but by treating her as a guest rather than an intruder the Catholic women changed the power dynamic of their relationship with Nellie, if not the state, by refusing to give up their dignity. This was the story that most touched and inspired Nola to create her installation entitled *Empathetic Perception* (Figure 10.4).

Nola broke china cups and saucers and then she repaired them with glue, wire, string, and bandages to symbolize how people have been broken or damaged; the scars do not always heal but there is also resilience. In addition, when a china cup has a chip or a crack it is usually repaired and kept in the family. Nola talked about the high value placed on porcelain and how we pass it down from generation to generation, like other traditions – something those of us of European descent can relate to. Nola also highlighted that just as we inherit

Figure 10.4 Empathetic Perception.

objects from our elders, so too our beliefs and attitudes, good and bad, as for example sectarianism (religious intolerance) and other forms of hate.

Nola was inspired by Nellie's compassion, as well as her own community's dignity, fragility and resilience, all embodied in the offer of a cup of tea to an uninvited visitor. This installation piece may not necessarily heal a wound or right a wrong; it does validate a more nuanced appreciation of small acts of maintaining one's dignity and survival in the face of terrible injustice and both direct and indirect violence. In addition, seeing the cups and saucers on pedestals highlighted their perceived value, though they were in various states of disrepair, which generated a lot of thoughtful and sometimes anxious conversation among gallery visitors.

Lessons learned

Among the lessons learned from the project, several participants emphasized the importance of listening in order to better understand the other. "There's skill to actually listen and to be able to interpret what these people have to say. It was very humbling for me". In the same post-project interview, Nola mentioned that the project experience had affected her so much that she was teaching her sisters the listening skills she had learned in our workshops. Similarly, Gail's portrayal of the abuse of power made tangible, in red, white and blue marching season bunting caught in a sewing machine, proved powerful acknowledgement for the elder storyteller and her sister. During one workshop, Gail had raised the difficult question about why more people did not try to stop the violence during the Troubles. An important insight into that generation for her was that whereas she had "always thought that the problems were with the older people … these people who were put through the mill, they just want to move past the hatred". Likewise, when Nola reflected on what she had learned during our project, she commented that while her "life has been defined by the Troubles", she "didn't even know what it was like before or during the main part of the Troubles". Similarly, another of the young participant artists remarked on the significance of hearing "the reality of it from both sides" and how "you never find out about these things just reading about it in the paper".

The exhibition as a whole created a great sense of pride for all the participants and a sense of wonder that they had all created this together. There was a sense of collective accomplishment and validation. At the exhibition opening, the young people brought their parents and grandparents and the older people brought their children and grandchildren, furthering the intergenerational impact and validation of our collaborative endeavor. During the opening, one of the older participants marveled at our ability to respond sensitively and thoughtfully from our individual perspective in different ways that provides nuanced understandings of often complex situations: "[w]e all heard the same stories but the art is so different". In fact, all the storytellers praised the art: "[the artists] had respect for our stories and they had respect for us, to give us the space and the time … they were really listening to us to create such fantastic work".

Along with the history that was learned, relationships across generations and across religious divides developed. For example, one participant in her late sixties told me how much it meant to her that on one occasion, 20-year-old Gail had not only greeted her at the train station but also sat and talked with her during the hour-long journey from Belfast to Portadown as she would with any friend. Emily, one of the younger participants, came to value these relationships as well. Initially Emily thought of her participation in the Communities of Interest project as a way to exhibit her art at the Millennium Court Arts Centre. However, she said that this changed for her as she became friends with the other participants during the dialogue activities. She came to look forward to the workshops and seeing her new friends each week, or seeing them in the streets of Portadown and "saying hi".

Conclusion

This ethnographic case study set out to assess whether art combined with conflict transformation approaches can create alternative paths for individuals in situations of inherited conflict to accept the validity of each other's perspectives and the significance of this for the parties involved. To the extent that they were challenged to conceptualize something they had not seen for themselves, the artist participants saw themselves as walking in another's shoes when they visually portrayed the older people's stories. However, the artists had something of themselves in each piece as well, for something in a story had to resonate in each of them to be able to envision the artwork they created. At the same time, though, they accepted the older people's narratives as their truths. Hamber maintains that genuine healing is communicated through the context, processes and relationships in and around how the object or apology is envisioned and created (2004). Therefore, it seems to be the relationships created during the workshops, as much as the artworks, that engender empathy and conciliation.

The job of the artist is to use his or her imagination to envision alternatives, to imagine something new, and that is what these young artists have done. They have looked at the past through the lens of their present and created their vision of their future. In creating something new, each of these artworks examine one life from two different points of view (Kaminsky 1992). At the same time, as a group project the artworks are varied in terms of themes, mediums and content, so perhaps multiple voices is more accurate. As Northern Ireland continues to look at its past through the lens of its present to create a new future it needs to find ways to acknowledge and validate the multiple voices present in its society as a whole.

Notes

1 Many people commonly use the word "conflict" as a synonym for violence. Likewise, the term "post-conflict" is used to describe the circumstances of societies once overt violence and war have ended. However, if conflict is a natural normal experience of living in a diverse world, then humans will always have disagreements, misunderstandings or competing wants and needs. Furthermore, like most everywhere in the world there is still both direct and indirect violence. Therefore, instead of "post-conflict" the phrase "time of transition", i.e. from overt violence to relative peace, is used to describe and identify the current situation in Northern Ireland.

2 The two largest religious identity groups in Northern Ireland are Protestant and Roman Catholic. These are the two main groups that have been at odds to varying degrees over many generations (Dunlop 1995; Hall 2008, 1989; Darby 1986). There are overlaps between Protestant, Unionist and British on the one hand, and Catholic, Nationalist and Irish on the other. However, these vary based on individual and group politics and/or religious identity. Because of these complexities, it was decided to use the same group identification that people in Northern Ireland use based on religious affiliation, with the understanding that there are exceptions to every generalization.

3 The origin date and duration of the Troubles are also contested history in the North of Ireland. For some the Troubles began "almost a millennium ago", for others with Partition and then the establishment of the Republic of Ireland in the mid-twentieth century, or in 1969 (Santino 2001) or with the Civil Rights Movement in 1968. 1968 is considered the beginning of the Civil Rights Movement in Northern Ireland and the nonviolent civil rights marches were, at least in part, the impetus for the escalation of this most recent period of overt violence in the North. Therefore, for the purposes of this case study, the Troubles are considered to have begun in 1968.

4 All project participants' names have been changed. All quotations used in this account of the project are taken from post-project interviews with project participants in August and September 2008.

References

ARK (2009) *Northern Ireland Life and Times Survey 2008*, Belfast: UK Data Service.

Babbitt, E.F. (2003) "Evaluating Coexistence: Insights and challenges", in A. Chayes and M. Minow (eds) *Imagine Coexistence: Restoring humanity after violent ethnic conflict*, San Francisco: Jossey-Bass.

Bell, Vikki (2011) "Contemporary Art and Transitional Justice in Northern Ireland: The consolation of form", *Journal of Visual Culture*, 10(3): 324–53.

Bennett, M.J. (1998) *Basic Concepts of Intercultural Communication: Selected readings*, Yarmouth: Intercultural Press, Inc.

Bryan, D. and Gillespie, G. (2005) *Transforming Conflict: Flags and emblems*, Belfast: Institute for Irish Studies.

Bush, R., Baruch, A. and Folger, J.P. (1994) *The Promise of Mediation: Responding to conflict through empowerment and recognition*, San Francisco: Jossey-Bass.

Cohen, C. (2003) "Engaging with the Arts to Promote Coexistence", in A. Chayes and M. Minow (eds) *Imagine Coexistence: Restoring humanity after violent ethnic conflict*, San Francisco: Jossey-Bass.

Darby, J. (1986) *Intimidation and the Control of Conflict in Northern Ireland*, Syracuse, NY: Syracuse University Press.

Deutsch, M. (2006a) "Cooperation and Competition", in M. Deutsch, P.T. Coleman and E.C. Marcus (eds) *The Handbook of Conflict Resolution: Theory and practice*, San Francisco: Jossey-Bass.

Deutsch, M. (2006b) "Justice and Conflict", in M. Deutsch, P.T. Coleman and E.C. Marcus (eds) *The Handbook of Conflict Resolution: Theory and practice*, San Francisco: Jossey-Bass.

Dunlop, J. (1995) *A Precarious Belonging: Presbyterians and the conflict in Ireland*, Belfast: Blackstaff Press.

Graham, B. (1994) "No Place of the Mind: Contested Protestant representation of Ulster", *Ecumene*, 1(3): 257–81.

Graham, B. (2007) "Heritage and the Construction of Place and Identity", paper presented at "The Representation of Place by Collectors and Through Collections" conference, Belfast.

Hall, M. (1989) *Ulster: The hidden history*, Belfast: Pretani Press.

Hall, M. (2008) *Divided by History? A grassroots exploration*, Newtonabbey: Farset/Inishowen and Border Counter Initiative.

Hamber, B. (2004) "Public Memorials and Reconciliation Processes in Northern Ireland", paper presented at the "Trauma and Transitional Justice in Divided Societies" conference, Warrington, March.

Hamber, B. (2006) "Narrowing the Micro and the Macro: A psychological perspective on reparations in societies in transition", in P. de Greiff (ed.) *Handbook of Reparations*, New York: Oxford University Press.

Herzig, M. and Chasin, L. (2006) *Fostering Dialogue Across Divides: A nuts and bolts guide from the public conversations project*, Watertown, MA: Public Conversations Project.

Jarman, N. and Bryan, D. (1997) *From Riots to Rights: Nationalist parades in the North of Ireland*, Coleraine: Centre for the Study of Conflict, University of Ulster, available at: http://cain.ulst.ac.uk/csc/reports/riotstorights.pdf (accessed April 8, 2010).

Jelin, E. (2003) *State Repression and the Labors of Memory*, in C. Calhoun (ed.) *Contradictions*, Minneapolis: University of Minnesota Press.

Kaminsky, M. (1992) "Myerhoff's 'Third Voice': Ideology and genre in ethnographic narrative", *Social Text*, 33: 124–44.

Kayser, U. (2000) *Creating a Space for Encounter and Remembrance: The healing of memories process*, Johannesburg: Truth and Reconciliation Commission.

Lindner, E.G. (2009) "Emotion and Conflict", in C.E. Stout (ed.) *Contemporary Psychology*, Westport, CT: Praeger Publishers.

Morrow, D. (2008) "Shared or Sacred? Attitudes to community relations among young people 2003–2007", in D. Schubotz and P. Devine (eds) *Young People in Post-Conflict Northern Ireland*, Lyme Regis, Dorset: Russell House Publishing.

Norquay, N. (1999) "Identity and Forgetting", *The Oral History Review*, 26(1): 1–21.

Ormsby, F. (1979) *Poets for the North of Ireland*, Belfast: Blackstaff Press.

Pranis, K. (2012) "The Restorative Impulse", *Tikkun*, 27(1): 33–4.

Pranis, K., Stuart, B. and Wedge, M. (2003) *Peacemaking Circles: From crime to community*, St Paul, MN: Living Justice Press.

Pryor, K. (2008) *The Northern Ireland Collection*, Wolverhampton: Wolverhampton Arts + Museums.

Reid, B. (2004) "Labouring Towards the Space to Belong: Place and identity in Northern Ireland", *Irish Geography*, 37(1): 107–8.

Rolston, B. (1991) *Politics and Painting: Murals and conflict in Northern Ireland*, London: Associated University Press.

Rose, G. (2007) *Visual Methodologies: An introduction to the interpretation of visual materials*, 2nd edn, London: Sage.

Rothman, J. (1997) *Resolving Identity-Based Conflict in Nations, Organizations and Communities*, San Francisco: Jossey-Bass.

Santino, J. (2001) *Signs of War and Peace*, New York: Palgrave.

Stokes, P.A. (2006) "The Troubles in Northern Ireland, 1968–2005: A case of humiliation", *Social Alternatives*, 25(1): 17–21.

White, R.W. and Falkenberg White, T. (1995) "Repression and the Liberal State: The case of Northern Ireland, 1969–1972", *Journal of Conflict Resolution*, 39(2): 330–52.

Wilson, R. (2000) *Flagging Concern: The controversy over flags and emblems*, available at: http://cain.ulst.ac.uk/dd/papers/flags.htm (accessed July 14, 2013).

Zehr, H. (2002) *The Little Book of Restorative Justice*, Intercourse, PA: Good Books.

Zehr, H. (2005) *Changing Lenses: A new focus for crime and justice*, 3rd edn, Scottdale, PA: Herald Press.

Part IV

Collective reparations and the law

11 The case for collective reparations before the International Criminal Court

Frédéric Mégret

Many have predicted that collective reparations would significantly shape the reparations regime of the International Criminal Court (ICC) (Ferstman 2002) and that the argument for the ICC to award such reparations is intuitively strong. Yet the degree to which collective reparations should be prioritized is not a matter of universal agreement among victims, let alone among international lawyers and policy makers. This chapter seeks to assess some of the challenges of making the case for collective reparations and, in the process, to provide a more principled defense of the need to prioritize collective reparations than has arguably been offered so far. In developing its argument, this chapter notes that great latitude was initially given to the court in terms of defining its principles of reparation[1] and that, although this latitude will gradually narrow, much still remains to be decided and much will depend on actual practices of reparation. The Trust Fund for Victims (TFV) will also have a key role and will, in all likelihood, be less hamstrung by restrictions, given its more flexible and administrative mode of operation even when acting as an implementer of court awards.

Before going into the details of the argument, it is necessary to identify what is understood by "collective reparations" in the context of international criminal justice (it may have a number of other meanings in other contexts). Interestingly, the term is not defined in the *Rome Statute* and may therefore have been subject to different interpretations. There are essentially three ways in which collective reparations can be understood, only one of which this chapter is concerned with. The first is reparations that are really individual reparations but whose precise disbursement is awarded to an intermediary "group"[2] or through an intergovernmental, international or national organization approved by the TFV (*Rules of Procedures and Evidence* 1995, r. 98.4). These reparations are not truly collective and the "collective" element only intervenes as a sort of intermediary operational variable.

The second way in which one can talk of collective reparations is as reparations awarded to "organizations or institutions that have sustained direct harm to any of their property which is dedicated to religion, education, art or science or charitable purposes, and to their historic monuments, hospitals and other places and objects for humanitarian purposes" (*Rules of Procedures and Evidence* 1995, r. 85(b)). Here, the emphasis is on formal collectivities, essentially the moral persona. Again, this is not what this chapter is focused on.

The third meaning of collective reparations is reparations that are awarded to a group or category of persons as such (e.g. a particular ethnic, racial, political or religious group, or civilians) (*Rules of Procedures and Evidence* 1995), quite independently of the group or category's legal existence. While these various forms of collective reparations are not necessarily incompatible, the only meaning this chapter is concerned with is the final sense: i.e. reparations for the benefit of a given group in the broad sense, regardless of the way the reparations are administered or whether they in first analysis merely benefit a representative institution rather than the group as such. For example, collective reparations might involve monetary compensation for harm suffered by the community as a whole, or rehabilitation programs that target the group, particularly groups with a symbolic dimension (Mégret 2009).

The chapter begins by suggesting that there has been a discreet emphasis on individual reparations in the ICC regime, and finds that focus to be problematic. It goes on to examine several arguments in favor of collective reparations, ultimately offering a strong principled defense of collective reparations.

The problem with individual reparations

An individualist bias?

It is clear that both individual and collective reparations are recognized under the ICC regime. The *Rules of Procedure and Evidence* (RPE), in particular, clarify that the court "may award reparations on an individualized basis or ... on a collective basis" (R. 97). The principle of collective reparations, even as an alternative to individualized ones, is thus set in an incontrovertible manner. We will return in more detail to the challenges of collective reparations in the next section.

Despite this fact, there does seem to be a certain bias in the court's regime in favor of individualized rather than collective reparations. The *Rome Statute* itself may be noncommittal in terms of the nature – individual or collective – of victims, and the main article in that respect, Article 75, reflects this. However, the overall regime that has been drafted beyond the statute – including the RPE and the TFV's regulations – suggests an attachment to the notion of an individual victim. One of the sources of that bias is the very definition of victims. Rule 85(a) of the RPE defines "victims" first as "natural persons who have suffered harm as a result of the commission of any crime within the jurisdiction of the ICC" (1995). Rule 85(b) also says that victims include organizations or institutions that have sustained direct harm to property (*Rules of Procedures and Evidence* 1995). However, that is not identical to stating that a group or a community are potentially victims as such, and already seems to frame groups as merely derivative of individuals.

Despite the fact that reparations may be awarded in collective fashion, requests for reparations are largely seen as emanating from individual victims. Rule 94 on the "upon request" reparation procedure, for example, stipulates the sort of "particulars" which "a victim" must include in her request for reparations. The particulars (e.g. identity and address of the claimant) leave no doubt as to the individual character of the application. It is hard to see how a group could directly ask for reparations in this context, and it is only as a result of aggregate individual demands that an image of the group's existence may come to the court's knowledge. Because most of Section III of the *Rules*, on victims and witnesses, is devoted to the role of victims during the procedure (and not just to the issue of reparations), the image of victims that tends to appear is that of individual participants. The whole gamut of measures anticipated to protect victims, for example, are clearly individual measures (*Rules of Procedures and Evidence* 1995). The rule as far as the TFV is concerned is that "all reparations collected through awards for reparations may only benefit victims as defined in rule 85" (*Regulations of the Trust Fund for Victims* 2005, par. 42). Although that provision does not exclude collective reparations, it does make it clear that there is no third category of victims beyond individuals and organizations (*Regulations of the Trust Fund for Victims* 2005). Even if reparations are awarded collectively, they must benefit individuals. Not even in cases where reparations are awarded from the Trust Fund's "other resources" (i.e. voluntary contributions rather than reparation awards) can they be any more collective (Art. 48). In the case of the ICC's first conviction, that of Thomas Lubanga Dyilo, the court focused quite heavily on beneficiaries of reparations as being individuals and their relatives (*Prosecutor v. Thomas Lubanga Dyilo* 2012 ICC-01/04–01/06–2904).

Even in those cases where the court "does not identify the beneficiaries" (*Regulations of the Trust Fund for Victims*, par. 60) of a reparation award, it does not follow that the award is necessarily a collective one. In other words, the court can make individual reparations to unknown beneficiaries, leaving it to the Trust Fund to determine who these beneficiaries should be (par. 60). In other places, lump sum awards may be deposited to the Trust Fund, but only when "it is impossible or impracticable to make individual awards directly to each victim" (*Rules of Procedures and Evidence*, r. 98.2), suggesting that the collective nature of awards in these cases is merely a stop-gap measure while victims are being identified. There is a sense, finally, that collective reparations are subsidiary and that the criterion for collective reparations is that they are "more appropriate" (*Rules of Procedures and Evidence*, r. 89.3) rather than simply appropriate, as if the default rule were always individual reparations.

Reasons for the bias

There are many reasons why the ICC has the reparations regime that it has, some historical, some conceptual and some ideological. One of them is a sort of cultural individualism that has been very influential within international criminal justice. Due to their breadth, international crimes often have an abstract dimension, which is hard to understand or convey. In this context, the historical construction of international criminal justice, thanks in particular to the media, has exhibited a fascination for "individual narratives" of suffering and plight. The radical evil of the perpetrator versus the radical innocence of the victim has been a powerful trope in the construction of the rhetorical apparatus of international criminal law, and has also helped sustain some of the discipline's aspirations.

It is also true that criminal justice is premised on an individualist ideology largely, ironically, as a result of its focus on the perpetrator. The individual – or as Alan Norrie put it "the ideological form of the abstract juridical individual" (1992: 56) – is the basic unit of the criminal law. This is in a sense only a manifestation of the liberal ideology's fascination with the individual, but it also has specific causes in terms of criminal law. Much of criminal law, for example, is a secularized version of canon law with its emphasis on sin, clearly a matter of individual behavior (Foucault 1977; Kamenka and Tay 1975). International criminal law has systematically and almost by definition focused on individual guilt. It is quite likely that this emphasis on the individual as perpetrator has influenced, by symmetry, a vision of the victim as individual: that it is another manifestation, in other words, of the "individuating tendencies of criminological thought" (Jamieson 1999: 132).

The influence of domestic criminal law conceptions is also visible in a particular conception of the victim as individual. By and large, domestic criminal law systems have been oblivious to the possibility that crime might be committed with entire collectivities as their targets. The sort of crime that is contemplated domestically is in a sense "normal" crime, i.e. crime resulting from ordinary social interaction, and the mix of contradictory passions it may generate. The emphasis is on crime that is of a private nature: individuals stealing, raping and killing, for a number of individual motives such as greed, lust and hate. Few criminal law systems traditionally anticipate crimes of mass, in part because such a possibility would imply such a failure of ordinary institutions as to be hard to contemplate for any society; nor do they contemplate crime that is fundamentally political in nature, especially when it would have to be committed by the state. One of the implications of a domestic criminal justice system's focus on private crime is also an inability to see victims of crime as being anything but individual. Victims, as a result, may be numerous – numbering in the dozens or even hundreds when it comes to particularly dangerous serial killers or criminal gangs – but they are not so typically (the vast majority of murders are single acts). Given the influence of domestic concepts and ideas on international criminal justice, it is probably no surprise that this individualism has crossed over into the field.

Finally, reparations rules and policy at the ICC have been heavily influenced by the international human rights framework, which is a regime traditionally very much focused on individual reparations. For example, the most influential international instrument in terms of reparations, the *Basic Principles and Guidelines on the Right to a Remedy and Reparation for Victims of Gross Violations of International Human Rights Law and Serious Violations of International Humanitarian Law*, adopted on 16 December 2005 by the General Assembly of the United Nations, has in mind human rights violations rather than international crimes as such. Although it notes that victimization may "also be directed against groups of persons who are targeted collectively" (2005: 4) it emphasizes that it is "essentially directed against persons" (2005: 4). Most of the forms of reparation (restitution, compensation and rehabilitation) are framed in a way that leaves little doubt that the UN has individual victims in mind. More significantly, with some exceptions that will be mentioned in due course, the thrust of international human rights bodies' reparative jurisprudence has been directed at individuals.

A short critique of the bias

There are many arguments in favor of individual reparations. From the victim's point of view, reparations obviously offer a measure of personalized attention, which also represents societal recognition of the suffering caused. Individual reparations offer a direct link with retribution, and provide the psychological and symbolic satisfaction that the perpetrator is being made accountable. One can see reparations as having a larger societal function as well, making it clear that in committing crimes one is not merely breaching a public order, but also causing definite social harm to actual people. This process of recognition can be seen as essential to justice efforts.

Nonetheless, individual reparations do raise a number of problems. First, individual reparations will often be hard to obtain in isolation, creating complex problems of coordination and duplication between victims, as well as potential frictions. The individualization of reparations and their link to specific perpetrators creates an added judicial or administrative hurdle in order to determine the merits of each and every case, which may only increase delays for the provision of reparations. Second, victims' frustration is likely to be heightened in cases where they have an expectation of individual reparation that is not satisfied, potentially creating considerable problems of legitimacy for the ICC if it fails to adequately manage expectations. Moreover, an excessive focus on individual reparations may create a perception that some victims have benefited more than others. The risk is that individual reparations will further reinforce a sense that the chance of having been tormented by an individual who happens to have been tried and convicted by the court greatly increases the prospects of obtaining reparation. For example, following the Lubanga case, it is not simply the case that child soldiers have been uniquely highlighted by international criminal justice as victims, but also that even among former child soldiers, some individuals will clearly stand to benefit more from the court.

More symbolically, excessive individual reparations may in some cases have the problematic effect of undermining some of the very solidarities that the prosecution of international offences is supposed to protect. Perhaps one of the most obvious points about individual reparations is that they emphasize the individual at the expense of the collective. In this respect, it is important to understand the extent to which "repairing" does not occur in a void, but is also an essential element in designating, identifying, and thus "constituting" the victim as a social construct. Culturally insensitive reparations might make the individual appear as isolated from their surroundings and their community. Such reparations may have the effect of "disaggregating" individuals from the group to which they belong, excessively privatizing a suffering that is incomprehensible for victims themselves (and the group) if one does not contextualize it within communal life. It can, in fact, fail to repair deeper and subtler wounds that were inflicted on the individual as a result of their belonging to, and through the victimization of, their community of belonging.

The case for collective reparations

As suggested, the ICC's reparations regime is not primarily focused on groups when it comes to victims, but it seems as if at times the presence of such groups is hard to escape. At the procedural level, for example, the possibility that victims may come to the court in great numbers (although not necessarily as groups) is something that the drafters of the statute and the RPE were keenly aware of. For example, "where there are a number of applications (for the status of victims), the Chamber may consider the applications in such a manner as to ensure the effectiveness of the proceedings and may issue one decision" (*Rules of Procedures and Evidence*, r. 89.3). Also, "where there are a number of victims, the Chamber may … request the victims or particular groups of victims … to choose a common legal representative or representatives" (*Rules of Procedures and Evidence* 1995: r. 90.2). These measures seem to be implemented only for the practical purpose "of ensuring the effectiveness of the proceedings" (*Rules of Procedures and Evidence*, r. 90.2), but they do have the effect of inscribing a sense of groupness in the proceedings.

Collective reparations are not defined in the ICC's regime on victims, which makes it sometimes difficult to know exactly what is contemplated. However, this lack of definition may also present an opportunity to construct the "collective" in a manner that is sound from the point of view of international criminal justice. The fact that collective awards in some cases will be "resources" from the Trust Fund does not mean that reparations could not be granted to some groups or group-representing institutions. Indeed, one could argue that what benefits the group necessarily benefits its individual members.

The Regulations of the TFV also evidence, at least in passing, a certain sensitivity to groups. For example, paragraph 55 mentions

> the size and location of the beneficiary group" (2005) as one factor to be taken into account "in determining the nature and/or size of awards, inter alia: the nature of the crimes, the particular injuries to the victims and the nature of the evidence to support such injuries.
>
> (2005: par. 55)

When the court makes a reparation award without identifying the beneficiaries, the Fund Secretariat "shall set out all relevant demographic/statistical data about the group of victims, as defined in the order of the Court" (par. 60). In order to do so, the Secretariat may adopt such measures as the

> use of demographic data to determine the members of the beneficiary group; and/or: (b) Targeted outreach to the beneficiary group to invite any potential members of the group who have not already been identified through the reparations process to identify themselves to the Trust Fund.
>
> (par. 61)

Although they are not defined, the *Rules of Procedure* tell us when "collective reparations" should be awarded, which is in itself an element of definition. Collective reparations, in this sense, are awards that are to be granted "where the number of the victims and the scope, forms and modalities of reparations" (2005: r. 98.3) makes them "more appropriate". Nonetheless, it remains unclear when exactly collective reparations would be "appropriate". In what follows, I highlight three levels of argument on the need for collective reparations: pragmatic, transitional and ontological, indicating a preference for the third.

Pragmatic arguments for collective reparations

Perhaps the foremost justification of collective reparations is a pragmatic one that seeks to make the best of a bad situation. The starting point in any analysis of reparations considered by the ICC is that funds available for reparations will always be limited. The amount available will often be small compared to the needs of victims, as a result of a combination of two factors. First, the ICC's regime focuses on reparations owed by individuals convicted of international crimes. Their assets are envisaged as the main source, at least theoretically, of reparation awards. Reparations obtained under the ICC's regime are not exclusive of a range of other reparatory initiatives that might take place (in particular those emanating from the state), but they have tended to displace the emphasis on such initiatives. The problem is that most accused in the history of international criminal justice have, for fairly obvious reasons, tended to be impecunious at least by the time they were convicted. In this context, the Statute and the court's practice do suggest one way in which funds might be supplemented, namely when the court orders the TFV to make available some of its autonomous resources to complement reparation awards (*Prosecutor v. Thomas Lubanga Dyilo* 2011 ICC-01/04–01/06–2806). There has been much debate about the wisdom of such a move,[3] but suffice it to say here that even if the court were to order such provisioning systematically, there is absolutely no guarantee that the TFV's autonomous resources will in any way match the needs of reparation awards. More importantly, there is no clear theory of the status of funds donated by the international community to the TFV, but very few people would argue that the international community is a sort of "guarantor" of reparation awards and has to foot the bill for crimes that it did not commit (Mégret 2010).

Second, in addition to the lack of "supply" of funds, there is of course an almost unlimited demand for them. Not only does international criminal justice run up against the familiar complications of seeking to compensate for what is, fundamentally, irreplaceable (even though it can be translated into a rough, often monetary formula), but the sheer scale of mass crimes creates challenges of its own. The multiplicity of individual victims of mass crimes, in particular, makes it even more difficult to envisage some sort of *restitutio ad integrum* – restoration to what would have been the position had no injury been sustained – for all. This has interesting, almost philosophical, implications: the idea that massive tragedies create such conditions that one can never fully compensate for them; essentially, mass suffering creates a debt that its addressee cannot shoulder (i.e. individuals' ability to do harm is far greater than their ability to compensate for it).

The bottom line is that the court will be operating under a very rigid economic constraint of scarcity. Of course, that may evolve in the future but it is hard not to envisage a situation where the availability of funds will chronically fall short of victims' needs. This is of course a situation not unfamiliar domestically, where the "chance" of who one has been victimized by has always had a role in determining whether one obtains reparation or not. In this context, collective reparations may at least provide a more abstract and symbolic way to deal with the reparative issue that makes the shortfall less glaring. For example, Carla Ferstman has argued that

> There is likely only to be a limited amount of funds for reparations awards when compared with the rights and needs of victims, and therefore collective awards may be, at times, the only method to bring a certain measure of justice to victims.
>
> (2006: 4)

Similarly, the ICC in its decision on the Lubanga reparations noted that "a community-based approach, using the TFV's voluntary contributions, would be more beneficial and have greater utility than individual awards, given the limited funds available" (*Prosecutor v. Thomas Lubanga Dyilo* 2012 ICC-01/04–01/06–2904: par. 274). By shifting the focus to the group, the awkward problem of the partial unavailability of funds for reparations can be at least minimized.

Moreover, collective reparations may simplify the process of determining and administering awards. In all likelihood, the ICC will not want to award individual reparations nor see itself suited to doing so, and even the TFV, with its more relaxed non-judicial rules, may find the rigid computation of individual reparation awards amounts to be a very complex exercise. Indeed, it would be problematic if the costs of actually assessing the amount of reparations turned out to be very significant in a context where one of the goals is to ensure that as much as possible of the reparations reaches their intended beneficiaries. Collective reparations, conversely, lend themselves better to lump sum awards by the court or the TFV, relayed by various organizations. By increasing the speed of awards, it ensures that reparations arrive as quickly as possible to victims. As the court emphasized, "this approach does not require costly and resource-intensive verification procedures" (*Prosecutor v. Thomas Lubanga Dyilo* 2012 ICC-01/04–01/06–2876: par. 274).

All these pragmatic arguments are significant, but they are not entirely convincing from the point of view of justice. Ultimately, the modalities of awarding reparations should not simply be linked to practical arguments. Reparations have a strong principled component – they have indeed been proclaimed as a right of victims – and the tension between a theory of reparations as rights and a practice of just making do with what is available will sooner or later challenge the very idea of reparation as anchored in principle. If there are not enough resources to fund reparations programs, that may simply be reason to think about how more resources could be found.

Transitional justice arguments for collective reparations

An argument can also be made that collective reparations can be harnessed more effectively to transitional justice goals than is possible with individual reparations. Transitional justice is typically understood as the "set of judicial and non-judicial measures implemented in order to redress the legacies of massive human rights abuses" (International Center for Transitional Justice 2013); in practice, it often deals with democratic or post-conflict transitions. The addition of individual reparations does not necessarily make for good transitional justice. The success of transitional justice, in particular, is not measured by the extent to which each and every individual has been more or less compensated for the harm separately suffered. Excessively individualized reparations might drive a wedge between different members of the group, creating a class of "super-victims" and thus unwittingly contributing to efforts to destroy or dissolve the group. Conversely, by identifying the group as such, collective reparations can reinstate the groups in its dignity by recognizing their suffering. Such reparations can, therefore, contribute to empowering groups in the post-atrocity context, highlighting them as prominent interlocutors and as the repositories of a certain collective legitimacy. Groups rather than individuals have historically assumed this role (one thinks of the role of Armenian and Jewish organizations in keeping alive the legacy of the Armenian genocide and the Holocaust), and individual victims' suffering has never been so well recognized as when it fell within the ambit of the victimization of a larger group.[4]

Moreover, collective reparations are the ones that best allow us to move beyond the notion of *restitutio ad integrum*, to a more dynamic, forward-looking concept of reparations. Individual reparations classically have a backward-leaning dimension (restoring the status quo from before the crime). This is not particularly problematic for ordinary domestic crimes, where the goal is to erase as much as possible the consequences of the crime, and where that crime is seen as an isolated, individual social aberration rather than a direct consequence of social structures. However, it may be wholly inadequate in the transitional justice context where the goal of reparations cannot simply be to put individuals back in the situation in which they were before the commission of international crimes, even assuming that was possible. The situation before international crimes may not be a particularly desirable one; moreover, it may reflect asymmetries of wealth and power that had their share in the dynamics that led to atrocities (see Manrique Rueda in this volume).

Rather, reparations in the mass-crime context should be much more goal and program oriented. For example, they must also involve a corrective element (avoiding the pitfalls of the past) and a preventive function. These functions involve changes that have a social or political dimension.[5] Reparations should aim more largely at creating the conditions for a society in which the repeat of the relevant crimes is no longer possible. This is apparent in the Women's Initiatives for Gender Justice presentation before the ICC in the Lubanga case and the focus on the need to "transform communal and gender relations" (*Prosecutor v. Thomas Lubanga Dyilo* 2012 ICC-01/04–01/06–2876: par. 13). The court itself has insisted that "reparations need to address any underlying injustices" (par. 192) and "should secure, whenever possible, reconciliation between the convicted person, the victims of the crimes and the affected communities" (par. 193). Otherwise the reparations will have only been an illusory attempt to erase intervening events, without any thought as to how to avoid their repeat. International reparations should aim to bring about changes in society rather than being a vain attempt to return to the society that led to the commission of crimes in the first place. Collective reparations can play an intrinsic role in breaking out of vicious circles of oppression, discrimination and violence.

Collective reparations also typically associate groups with the administration and choice of reparation programs. They can, therefore, help re-establish social solidarity, community cohesion and reconciliation. They are particularly relevant in cultural contexts where individuals are defined in terms of their membership in a group and where "understanding an individual's entitlements cannot be separated from those of their families, communities and environment" (*Prosecutor v. Thomas Lubanga Dyilo* 2012 ICC-01/04–01/06–2876: par. 64). Indeed, it would be ironic if reparations policy were to harm the groups whose members it is intended to assist by projecting a conception of the relations between members and the group that is not culturally sensitive. It should also be said that this description of who is affected by international crimes probably largely intersects with most victims' perception. Of course, individual victims are likely to feel to a considerable extent affected by their individual suffering. But in most cases, there will also be a strong sense that their suffering is a result not only of the direct harm inflicted on them, but of the suffering and degradation imposed onto the group to which they belong. The attack on the group will in most cases have been a particularly efficient way of attacking what makes individuals feel like individuals, namely their sociability, their ability to coalesce with others into human communities. To attack the group is to attack the individual's freedom of choice, his identity and his sense of self-worth.

The ontological case for collective reparations: an exploration

The key intuition of the argument in this section is that reparations policy cannot entirely claim autonomy from the regime within which it is embedded. One of the challenges, as we have seen, has been the mix of different regimes at the ICC, most notably the role that international human rights instruments drafted in a quite different context have had in shaping expectations about reparations. Once transposed in the international criminal justice context, ideas of reparation need to be adapted. The international community has decided to create a highly specific regime of reparations for international crimes that is first and foremost tied to a particular conception of these crimes' structure and gravity. It is important that reparations policy not contradict – in fact, that it be rigorously in line with – the existing conception of these crimes.

In this section, I will try to make the case that at least some international crimes are by nature collective crimes that target groups. One of the key questions for the purposes of assessing the appropriate beneficiaries of reparations has always been to actually define who is a victim of international crimes. Of course in both ordinary parlance and actual fact, individuals are almost always effectively victimized by international crimes. It would be shocking to claim otherwise. Yet this does not mean that they are the only victims or even, from a certain conceptual point of view, that they are the main victims. In fact, the targeting of individuals may often only be a means to attack groups or categories of populations. In such crimes individuals are rarely if ever attacked as individuals, but almost always as members of a particular generic category. More importantly, most international crimes require that this be so as a matter of ontology. It goes to the essence of what makes them "international" rather than mere ordinary, "domestic" crimes. To use one example, an epidemic of serious crimes that happened to affect individuals who were members of a particular group would not a priori be genocide; it is only because the group is targeted as such, and because in the process the perpetrators find it opportune to harm the group's members, that we have something genocidal at work. This is indeed a key difference from domestic crimes. Not only does domestic criminal law not anticipate large numbers of victims, but it does not particularly anticipate crimes, except in the case of hate crimes, being part of an attack against a group as such. Conversely, the element of "groupness" or "collectivity" in international crimes is very much at the forefront of the definition of crimes.

The case that international crimes are group crimes should not be overstated, and there are situations where the victim group is not one to which one would want to grant reparation as such. This is especially true of child soldiers, and obviously reparations in this case are of the sort that will allow children or former children to escape the "child soldier" group. In other words, not all groups are worth preserving as such. But even in the case of child soldiers, the issue might be simply of redefining the relevant target group, for example as "children" or a group of children who have been preyed upon because of their particular vulnerability, and who as such should receive reparations.

At any rate, many international crimes adopt a structure that makes them first and foremost crimes against groups and categories of population, which are then effectively committed by engaging in a number of crimes that may affect individuals also, albeit secondarily. This is most clearly evidenced in the definition of genocide, which, as is well known, consists in targeting a group with a number of measures that betray an "intent to destroy, in whole or in part, a national, ethnical, racial or religious group, as such" (United Nations 1948; art. 2). As Larry May has insisted, "genocide is primarily defined in terms of a harm to a group instead of to an individual" and it is as if the expression "as such" took "the individual out of the mix" (2010: 64; 66). Of the five ways listed in the Convention in which genocide can be committed, three specifically involve targeting the group as such.[6] Individuals may be targeted for killing or "causing serious bodily or mental harm", but this only becomes genocide if they are targeted because of their belonging in a group and in order to destroy that group. The International Law Commission has emphasized that "the intention must be to destroy the group as such, meaning as a separate and distinct entity, and not merely some individuals because of their membership in [a] particular group" (1996: 45, par. 7).

Indeed, while the individual offence of genocide under contemporary international criminal law has come to be understood as one that (for the rather narrow purposes of establishing individual guilt) can be committed even by killing a few individuals, this is a far cry from the canonical understanding of genocide as a crime very much aimed at groups per se. Rafael Lemkin, the originator of the idea of genocide, understood it as having a fundamentally communal rather than an individual aspect. As Lemkin emphasized "the acts are directed against groups, as such, and individuals are selected for destruction only because they belong to these groups" (1947: 147). Genocide could be committed not only through "the deprivation of life but also the prevention of life" (Lemkin 1947: 147): for example, through sterilization or the forced removal of children, in a way that would reduce the group's ability to thrive. Moreover, it follows that even persons who are not directly targeted by a genocidal attack can consider themselves and be considered victims if they belong to the attacked group since "attacks on individuals constitute attacks on the group because they are interpreted by those not attacked as affronts to 'groupness'" (Carpenter 2000: 220).

Although perhaps less evident, it is also clear that the structure of the characterization of crimes against humanity evidences a certain willingness to protect at least a particular category of the population, if not groups as such. For a long time, an entire strand of the definition of crimes against humanity, taking its cue from the Holocaust, included a discriminatory element. The Nuremberg Principles defined crimes against humanity as, inter alia, "persecutions on political, racial, or religious grounds" (United Nations 1950; Art. 6(c)). This definition was adapted for the International Criminal Tribunal for Rwanda (ICTR), whose Statute described crimes against humanity as "a widespread or systematic attack against any civilian population on national, political, ethnic, racial or religious grounds" (ICTR 1994; Art. 3). In other words, crimes against humanity, apart from the lack of intent to destroy the group as such and somewhat different underlying crimes, clearly manifested a broader approach focusing on groups.

Moreover, at least some of the ways in which crimes against humanity can be committed include a distinct "group" element. This is particularly true of the crime of extermination, which is the offence that comes closest to genocide, albeit one that does not require proof of an intent to destroy the group as such. In the Vasilijevic case (*Prosecutor v. Vasilijevic* 2002), the International Criminal Tribunal for the Former Yugoslavia (ICTY) required that "extermination must be collective in nature rather than directed towards singled out individuals" (par. 227). In addition, "persecution against any identifiable group or collectivity on political, racial, national, ethnic, cultural, religious, gender ... or other grounds that are universally recognized as impermissible under international law" (*Rome Statute of The International Criminal Court* 1998: Art. 7(1)(h)) is identified as a crime against humanity. In the ICC Statute, the crime of apartheid, as an offence characteristically directed at a group as such, is now incorporated into the general definition of a crime against humanity (Art 7(1) (j)).

This "sectarian animus" was not always required and has tended to be phased out as a general requirement of crimes against humanity outside persecution and extermination (Lippman 1997). The Nuremberg Charter also anticipated that attacks "against any civilian population" (United Nations 1945; Art. 3) would suffice. The targeting of a particular constituted group gradually faded during the 1990s as a result of changes introduced in the ICTY Statute and the case law of both ad hoc tribunals (see *Prosecutor v. Tadic* 1997, IT-94–1-T: paras 644, 652; *Prosecutor v. Tadic* 1999, IT-94–1-A: paras 281–305; Chesterman 2000: 327–328). Its role today has been marginalized, reflecting the contingent (quite often, the massive killing of civilians will occur because a group is targeted) rather than the necessary (the massive killing of civilians could occur outside a group being targeted) link between mass and group crimes. However, even if crimes against humanity are no longer characterized by a discriminatory element, in practice generalized and systematic attacks against civilians are often a result of some racist or similarly intolerant motive.

More importantly, the *Rome Statute*, like the statutes of all ad hoc international criminal tribunals,[7] does maintain that crimes against humanity have to be committed against a particular category of human beings, the "civilian population". It is quite striking that the most direct victim of crimes against humanity is a "population" rather than individuals as such, something which was underscored by the case law early on (see *U.S. v. Josef Altstoetter et al.* 1947: par. 40). As Egon Schwelb pointed out, "this indicates that a larger body of victims is visualized and that single or isolated acts committed against individuals are outside its scope" (1946: 191). International criminal tribunals have on repeated occasions stressed that they need to be satisfied that the civilian population is "the primary rather than an incidental target of the attack," and that the attack is "in fact directed against a civilian 'population', rather than against a limited and randomly selected number of individuals".[8]

One of the difficulties for this argument is that a civilian population is less a group than a category. It is, at least, less of a constituted, conscious group than a national or religious group, for example. Members of a civilian population may have little in common, and certainly do not normally see themselves as defined by their "civilian" nature. But that may also be true of groups under the

Genocide Convention, which may be more or less constituted and self-aware. Civilians are a category worth defending, a specific by-product of the project of separating those who do not exercise fighting functions from those who do. Indeed, in times of crimes against humanity, the civilian population may develop a keen sense that it is victimized as such and develop a newfound feeling of solidarity as a result. A civilian population is a relatively well-defined entity whose collective contours can be ascertained judicially for the purposes of reparations, in the same way they are assessed for the purposes of establishing perpetrator guilt. In prohibiting crimes against humanity, international law is prohibiting not only the concrete attack of civilians, but also a symbolic attack on the idea of civilians that aims, in a sense, to erase their difference.

The collective dimension of war crimes is perhaps the least evident. There is no doubt that a war crime can be committed against a single individual, so that there is not the same quantitative threshold as for genocide and crimes against humanity. However, two things are worth mentioning in this context. First, international criminal justice is never as interested in war crimes as when they reflect a massive character that brings them closer to the other core crimes than their strict definition would suggest. The *Rome Statute* includes a jurisdictional threshold whereby the court has jurisdiction over war crimes "in particular when committed as part of a plan or policy or as part of a large-scale commission of such crime" (Art. 8.1). Second, it is also clearly the case that individuals are not targeted as such in war crimes; rather, they are targeted (or insufficiently protected) as a result of or despite their belonging to the broad category of non-combatants, whether wounded combatants or those surrendering, prisoners of war and, again, civilians.

In a more jurisprudential sense, it is quite clear that the core definitions of international crimes are not particularly concerned with individuals per se. International criminal law, in that respect, is not simply a repeat of domestic criminal law, prosecuting for example murder or rape against individuals, not even the murder or rape of individuals with some aggravating circumstance such as a racist motive. Such an overlap between the domestic and the international would be largely incompatible with state sovereignty[9] and inconsistent with the idea of international law occupying a specific sphere as a legal order. Nor is international criminal law aligned with international human rights law, which focuses mostly on individual rights violations. Instead, international criminal law is about repressing either crimes that are massive or (which is often the other side of the same coin) crimes that target groups as such.[10] It is this particular pathology of violence and politics, which international criminal law has traditionally been interested in repressing, that makes the targeting of groups particularly central to international crimes.[11]

Again, this is not to say that individuals are not effectively targeted, but they are targeted less as such than as part of a plan to attack a population or destroy a group or category. The individual is merely a constituent of the collective, the group or the undifferentiated mass of "civilians". He is not targeted because of his individual characteristics (as in ordinary criminality), but is either targeted indiscriminately as a member of the civilian population, or discriminately as a member of a group. The perpetrator targets something over which the individual in ordinary circumstances has little or no control, and which at any rate, in the case of crimes such as genocide, may be defined arbitrarily by the perpetrator himself.[12] The individual victim in international criminal law is an instrumental victim, one that bears little relation to the highly particularized individual of ordinary offences. This also explains the relative distance of international criminal law from the international law of human rights. While the latter is historically premised on a very specific vision of the individual and his protection, the former seems more interested in large-scale phenomena of violence and pathologies of the body politic.[13]

The idea that if the damage is collective, then so should the reparation be is a strong one. The Inter-American Court, for example, has considered in the Mayagna Awas Tingni Community Case (*Mayagna (Sumo) Awas Tingni Community v. Nicaragua* 2001) that since the injury was communal then equity dictated a form of collective compensation.

This sort of logic suggests a larger representational function for international criminal justice: the idea that the reparations should reflect the harm, not simply from the point of view of just reparation, but also as a result of the criminal law's larger attempt at "representing" crime faithfully (see Mégret 2005). In the same way that international crimes are more than the aggregate of crimes against individuals, therefore, international reparations should be more than the accumulation of individual awards.

The argument for collective reparations is not one for neglecting individual reparations but, ultimately, one for understanding individual reparations within an overall theory of reparations in the ICC context. In most cases, it is argued, the collective is the first victim of international crimes. But the collective is always both the product of individualities and a means for individualities to prosper. If the collective is harmed by targeting its parts, then the collective can also be whole again by an attention to those parts. International criminal justice, however, should probably not seek to pre-empt each group's process of reckoning with how individuals were affected in relation to and because of their membership in the group. It seems important, as a matter of transitional needs and sheer logic, that the groups or categories that are the targets of international crimes retain the upper hand on understandings of what makes them unique.

But perhaps a broader point ought to be made here that relates less to who is entitled to reparations, as the problem is typically framed as part of a tradition of corrective justice, than to what ought to be repaired (Cunneen 2001; Wright 1996). In that respect, human rights reparations theory is still strongly indebted to a subjectivist understanding of reparations that almost systematically sees individuals or collectives as having an entitlement to reparations. This chapter has not entirely escaped that logic, although it has tried to refine our understanding of how international criminal law proposes to understand the relationship between the two. Yet the opposition between individuals and groups is also partially artificial. International crimes target the "groupness" that is in the individual, and the individual that is in the group. More than trying to offer reparation to groups and/or individuals as such, one may wonder whether a truly groundbreaking theory of reparations would not try to direct itself less at mending the subjects (individual or collective) than at the relations that exist between them and the rest of society. In the end, it seems that what is broken and torn apart by international crimes is not only the integrity of individuals or groups taken in isolation, but also their place in the world and the ties that bind them. In that respect, however, looking at groups, the place of individuals within them, and the place of the group within society, is already in itself a way of focusing attention on the relational aspects of reparations.

Notes

1 Article 75.1 ICC Statute: "The Court shall establish principles relating to reparations to, or in respect of, victims, including restitution, compensation and rehabilitation".

2 Regulation 67 ICC-ASP/4/Res.3, *Regulations of the Trust Fund for Victims*:

> The Trust Fund may decide to use intermediaries to facilitate the disbursement of reparations awards, as necessary, where to do so would provide greater access to the beneficiary group and would not create any conflict of interest. Intermediaries may include interested States, intergovernmental organizations, as well as national or international non-governmental organizations working in close proximity with the beneficiary groups.

3 For the views of the Victims Trust Fund on this issue and, in particular, the emphasis on reparations as owed by the convicted above all, see Registry Report on Reparations, par. 128. See also Ferstman and Goetz (2009: 346).

4 This is a point that has been made in the Inter-American context. See Martin (2006: 503–4) noting that

> decisions of this nature may spearhead a broader debate within states regarding the disadvantages faced by members of certain vulnerable groups in their ordinary lives. In the long run, awareness of these issues may contribute to ensuring that in multiethnic societies, such as those existing in Suriname, Paraguay, and Nicaragua, all the different voices are heard and represented in the process of consolidating democratic political processes in those states.

5 Reparations awarded in those decisions always have a broader impact than the individual case, particularly with regard to the amendment of existing legislation or the adoption of policies to regulate aspects that have not been contemplated in existing municipal laws or practices.

6 See Genocide Convention (United Nations 1948): Art. 2: "(c) Deliberately inflicting on the group conditions of life calculated to bring about its physical destruction in whole or in part; (d) Imposing measures intended to prevent births within the group; (e) Forcibly transferring children of the group to another group."

7 ICTY Statute Art. 5; ICTR Statute Art. 3.; ICC Statute Art. 7.

8 *Prosecutor v. Kunarac et al.* (2002) IT-96–23 & 23/1-A; *Prosecutor v. Jean-Pierre Bemba Gombo* (2009) ICC-01/05–01/08–424, 15, par. 77.

9 To use Larry May's analysis (2010), it would fail to satisfy the "harm principle" in relation to the international community.

10 David Luban (2004) is one of the authors who has most contributed to analyzing the anti-group and anti-civilian population elements as essentially parallel:

the population requirement in the definition of crimes of the murder type functions in parallel to the discriminatory intent requirement in the definition of crimes of the persecution type. Both requirements imply that at bottom crimes against humanity are launched against individuals because they belong to a targeted group. The difference between the two requirements is that the discriminatory intent requirement for persecutions and genocide limits itself to specific categories of groups (political, religious, racial, etc.), whereas a "population" can be any identifiable group.

11 See Luban 2004 on what has been described as the "population requirement", "those who launch crimes against humanity are targeting individuals on a non-individualized or collective basis" (2004: 86).

12 This is also reflected in the idea that the individual is targeted "for being born" into a group, i.e.: for pre-individualization characteristics that do not go beyond the mere fact of "being" or, at most, "belonging".

13 This is not to say that there is no overlap. For example, a genocide can be seen as both a multiplication of violations of the right to life and the right to be free from discrimination, as well as an attempt to destroy the group as such. However, the accumulation of individual rights violations does not simply add up to genocide, and the aggregate is clearly more than the sum of the parts.

References

Carpenter, R.C. (2000) "Forced Maternity, Children's Rights and the Genocide Convention: A theoretical analysis", *Journal of Genocide Research*, 2: 213–44.

Chesterman, S. (2000) "An Altogether Different Order: Defining the elements of crimes against humanity", *Duke Journal of Comparative and International Law*, 10: 307–43.

Cunneen, C. (2001) "Reparations and Restorative Justice: Responding to the gross violation of human rights", in H. Strang and J. Braithwaite (eds) *Restorative Justice and Civil Society*, New York: Cambridge University Press, 83–98.

Ferstman, C. (2002) "The Reparations Regime of the International Criminal Court: Practical considerations", *Leiden Journal of International Law*, 15: 667–86.

Ferstman, C. (2006) "NGOs and the Role of Victims in International Criminal Justice", paper presented at the Forum for International Criminal Justice and Conflict Seminar on the Evolving Role of NGOs in International Criminal Justice, Oslo, October.

Ferstman, C. and Goetz, M. (2009) "Reparations Before the International Criminal Court: The early jurisprudence on victim participation and its impact on future reparations proceedings", in C. Ferstman, M. Goetz and A. Stephens (eds) *Reparations for Victims of Genocide, War Crimes and Crimes against Humanity: Systems in place and systems in the making*, Boston: Martinus Nijhoff Publishers, 313–50.

Foucault, M. (1977) *Discipline and Punish: The birth of the prison*, New York: Pantheon Books.

International Center for Transitional Justice (2013) *Justice, Truth, Dignity*, available at: http://ictj.org/about/transitional-justice (accessed July 25, 2013).

ICTR (International Criminal Tribunal for Rwanda) (1994) *Statute of the International Tribunal for Rwanda*, available at: http://untreaty.un.org/cod/avl/pdf/ha/ictr_EF.pdf (accessed August 14, 2013).

International Law Commission of the United Nations (1996) "Commentary on the Draft Code of Crimes Against the Peace and Security of Mankind", in *Yearbook of the International Law Commission*, vol. 2, available at: http://untreaty.un.org/ilc/publications/yearbooks/Ybkvolumes%28e%29/ILC_1996_v2_p2_e.pdf (accessed August 7, 2013).

Jamieson, R. (1999) "Genocide and the Social Production of Immorality", *Theoretical Criminology*, 3: 131–46.

Kamenka, E and Erh-Soon Tay, A. (1975) "Beyond Bourgeois Individualism: The contemporary crisis in law and legal ideology", in E. Kamenka and R.S. Neale (eds) *Feudalism, Capitalism and Beyond*, Canberra: Australian National University Press.

Lemkin, R. (1947) "Genocide as a Crime under International Law", *The American Journal of International Law*, 41: 145–51.

Lippman, M. (1997) "Crimes against Humanity", *Boston College Third World Law Journal*, 17: 171–3.

Luban, D. (2004) "A Theory of Crimes against Humanity", *Yale Journal of International Law*, 29: 85–67.

Martin, C. (2006) "The Moiwana Village Case: A new trend in approaching the rights of ethnic groups in the Inter-American system", *Leiden Journal of International Law*, 19: 491–504.

May, L. (2010) *Genocide: A normative account*, New York: Cambridge University Press.

Mayagna (Sumo) Awas Tingni Community v. Nicaragua (2001) Inter-Am. Ct. H.R. (Ser. C) No. 79.

Mégret, F. (2005) "In Defense of Hybridity: Towards a representational theory of International Criminal Justice", *Cornell International Law Journal*, 38: 725–51.

Mégret, F. (2009) "Of Shrines, Memorials and Museums: Using the International Criminal Court's victim reparation and assistance regime to promote transitional justice", *Buffalo Human Rights Law Review*, 16: 1–56.

Mégret, F. (2010) "Justifying Compensation by the International Criminal Court's Victims Trust Fund: Lessons from domestic compensation schemes", *Brooklyn Journal of International Law*, 36: 123–204.

Norrie, A. (1991) "Criminal Law", in I. Grigg-Spall and P. Ireland (eds) *The Critical Lawyers' Handbook*,vol. 1, London: Pluto Press, 56–60.

Prosecutor v. Jean-Pierre Bemba Gombo (2009) ICC-01/05–01/08–424.

Prosecutor v. Kunarac et al. (2002) IT-96–23 & 23/1-A.

Prosecutor v. Tadic (1997) IT-94–1-T.

Prosecutor v. Tadic (1999) IT-94–1-A.

Prosecutor v. Thomas Lubanga Dyilo (2011) ICC-01/04–01/06–2806.

Prosecutor v. Thomas Lubanga Dyilo (2012) ICC-01/04–01/06–2876.

Prosecutor v. Thomas Lubanga Dyilo (2012) ICC-01/04–01/06–2904.

Prosecutor v. Vasilijevic (2002) IT-98–32-T.

Regulations of the Trust Fund for Victims 2005, ICC-ASP/4/Res.3.

Rules of Procedure and Evidence 1995, PCNICC/2000/1/Add.1.

Schwelb, E. (1946) "Crimes against Humanity", *British Yearbook of International Law*, 23: 178–226.

United Nations (1945) *Nürnberg Charter – Charter of the International Military Tribunal*, available at: http://avalon.law.yale.edu/imt/imtconst.asp (accessed August 14, 2013).

United Nations (1948) *Convention on Genocide: Convention on the prevention and punishment of the crime of genocide*, available at: http://treaties.un.org/doc/treaties/1951/01/19510112%2008–12%20pm/ch_iv_1p.pdf (accessed August 15, 2013).

United Nations (1950) *Nuremburg principles: Principle of International Law recognized in the Charter of the Nürnberg Tribunal and in the Judgement of the Tribunal*, available at: http://untreaty.un.org/ilc/texts/instruments/english/draft%20articles/7_1_1950.pdf (accessed August 14, 2013).

United Nations (2005) *Basic Principles and Guidelines on the Right to a Remedy and Reparation for Victims of Gross Violations of International Human Rights Law and Serious Violations of International Humanitarian Law*, available at: www.refworld.org/docid/4721cb942.html (accessed July 31, 2013).

U.S. v. Josef Altstoetter et al. (1947) *The Justice Case*, available at: www.worldcourts.com/ildc/eng/decisions/1947.12.04_United_States_v_Altstoetter.pdf (accessed July 27, 2013).

Wright, M. (1996) *Justice for Victims and Offenders: A restorative response to crime*, Winchester, Hampshire: Waterside Press.

12 Lands, wars and restoring justice for victims

Gabriela Manrique Rueda

The question of justice in societies devastated by armed conflicts or dictatorships, where large-scale violent crimes have been committed, is a complex contemporary issue. Public international law has a victim-oriented approach to justice, which conceives the crime as a violation of the victim's human rights. To a great extent, in international law, justice for massive crimes is defined in terms of bringing justice to the victims by ending impunity. Over the last two decades international principles of justice, such as the *Basic Principles of Justice for Victims of Crime and Abuse of Power*, have been adopted by the United Nations. These principles favor the criminal prosecution of offenders. Conceiving the passage from war to peace or from dictatorship to democracy as a kind of ritual transition from one moral order to another, punishment is viewed as a moral obligation to the victims in order to build a morally just and democratic social order (Huyse 1996). This assumption provides a basis for the idea that international law has a moral obligation to prosecute serious crimes (Parmentier 2004).

At the same time, however, the view has emerged that justice should be defined in terms of reparation for victims. An international consensus can be observed regarding the basic principles of transitional justice (Botero and Restrepo 2005). These principles, which link justice and reparation, were presented in 1996 by Louis Joinet, who was appointed by the United Nations' Subcommission on Prevention of Discrimination and Protection of Minorities to study impunity related to the violation of human rights. Joinet's 42 principles, the *Set of Principles for the Protection and Promotion of Human Rights through Action to Combat Impunity*, assigns three irrevocable obligations to states during the transitional process: 1) States must investigate, prosecute and condemn to penalties proportional to their crimes the individuals liable for gross human rights' violations. 2) They should promote the right to truth, which is considered a right of victims and societies. Acknowledgment and social knowledge of the truth are viewed in these principles as ways to prevent new victimizations. Truth is also considered a form of reparation and victims have a right to the truth. 3) States must also guarantee the victim's right to obtain full reparation for the harm suffered, including restitution, compensation, rehabilitation, satisfaction and guarantees of non-repetition (Botero and Restrepo 2005).

Reparation of the harm done to the victim is considered a fundamental mechanism in attaining justice. Justice means doing justice to the victim through the redress of harms. Punishment, truth and reparation are mechanisms aiming to redress individual and social harms. Joinet's principles were later developed by Theo van Boven and Charif Bassiouni, both United Nations' rapporteurs and professors of international law. The Van Boven and Bassiouni principles were adopted in 2005 by the General Assembly of the United Nations in the *Basic principles and Guidelines on the Right to a Remedy and Reparation for Victims of Gross Violations of International Human Rights Law and Serious Violations of International Humanitarian Law* (United Nations 2005).

While international principles on transitional justice link justice and reparation, one aspect that has received relatively little attention is the issue of justice related to the distribution of resources in societies where mass violence has taken place. The distribution of resources is often a source of disagreement in political and ethnic wars. In Darfur, for example, the acquisition of lands and properties is the main motivation for the Arab militias to attack the black Africans (Hagan and Rymond-Richmond 2009). In Rwanda, the elites and the farmers who participated in the genocide wanted to keep the lands from the Tutsis (Hatzfeld 2005). Mass violence and the unfair distribution of resources are linked. As we will illustrate, an unfair distribution of resources, especially an extremely unequal distribution of land, is a structural issue in these societies. Armed conflicts are often fights for the control of economic resources and lands, which frequently take place in agrarian societies where survival depends on land. International public law focuses on human rights and moral aspects of justice, but it does not address justice related to the distribution of resources. Building a moral order, punishing the offenders, the knowledge of the truth or redressing the harms done to the victims is not enough. A just distribution of resources could be viewed as an important step to prevent violence. Analysis of the distribution of resources requires returning to fundamental questions concerning what is justice and how to distribute resources.

In this chapter, we argue that justice should be pursued with distributive justice (DJ) mechanisms, in addition to those of corrective justice (CJ). The first part of the chapter discusses the basic notions of DJ and CJ. In the second part we analyze the problem of land and political violence in Colombia, showing that these two forms of justice are complementary and that both are necessary to provide justice for victims of war crimes. In the third part of the chapter we show how one can integrate DJ and CJ in order to restore justice for victims.

Corrective justice, distributive justice and reparation to victims

According to Aristotle (50 BC [2003]), there are different types of justice. In Book 5 of the *Nicomachean Ethics*, he writes about DJ and CJ. For the philosopher, injustice is what is contrary to proportion and justice is a kind of means to attain proportionality in human interactions. The type of justice depends on the nature of the interaction. DJ refers to the distribution of things that have to be divided, such as money or honor. When things have to be divided, the meaning of justice is related to merit but the sense of merit depends on the political regime. According to Aristotle, things in democracies are distributed among all eligible citizens (so-called free men). Thus, while certain groups such as slaves and women did not have rights and could not own property, eligible citizens would have equal say in decisions. In contrast, oligarchies allocate merit based on wealth or noble birth, while in aristocracies merit is defined in terms of excellence. Hence, oligarchies and aristocracies are models that place power unequally in the hands of a few, whereas democracies distribute power equally across citizens.

Aristotle defines CJ as "that which plays a rectifying part in transactions between man and man" (2003: 101). Whereas DJ concerns the distribution of things and the rules governing the fair distribution of resources, CJ has to do with the restoration of equality that has been disturbed in a transaction. The transaction can be voluntary or involuntary. Involuntary transactions are not reciprocal. Crimes like theft, assault, murder, robbery and abuse are involuntary transactions, and the aim of justice is to return the victim to the situation that they were in prior to the crime. Unlike DJ, which may distribute resources based on merit or equality, in CJ all parts are considered equal and treated as equal by the law. The role of the judge is to restore the inequality resulting from the injustice. Thus, for Aristotle, DJ and CJ are different.

DJ requires that one adopt rules for the fair distribution of resources. Morton Deutsch (1975) identifies different possible values as the basis for just distributions: equity, equality and need. Equity or merit means giving an increase in the distribution according to the value and contribution of the individual to his social group. Equality means giving an equal part of the distribution to each one. Need means providing resources based on not on performance but on what a person requires for their wellbeing.

Defining DJ in terms of the fair distribution of conditions and goods that affect individual wellbeing, Deutsch (1985) shows that DJ has psychological, physiological, economic and social aspects. Deutsch states that in any situation, the rules governing fair distribution depend on the kind of social goods and resources being distributed as well as on socio-historical circumstances (1985). For Deutsch (1975), equity should be the main principle of DJ in cooperative relations in which the primary goal is economic productivity. If the goal is the fostering or maintenance of good social relations, the dominant principle should be equality. If, however, the primary goal is the fostering of personal development and personal welfare, then need should be the dominant principle of DJ. Deutsch (1985) argues that equity and need are linked but that when personal integrity is at risk, need should prevail over equity.

The notions of DJ and CJ are useful when thinking about justice in the context of war. As war crimes are often related to the distribution of land, property and goods, DJ is highly relevant. At the same time, justice related to war crimes has to do with rectifying the damages done to the victims, which means that CJ is relevant as well. Deutsch's hypotheses regarding DJ can be used to think about which values should be considered in order to attain justice in societies after violent conflict. We argue that the principle of equity or merit is an interesting value of justice with regard to the distribution of lands and properties. According to this principle, lands should be distributed to the individuals who work land because of their contribution to the economy and their social groups. However, an important aspect to be considered is the stolen and lost lands and properties of the victims during armed conflicts, especially the lands of victims of forced displacement. As we are going to show in the case of victims of paramilitary groups in Colombia, when victims lose their lands they are also losing their incomes. As lands and properties have to do with people's history and identity, the crime also creates tremendous moral damage. These victims are no longer able to meet their basic economic and moral needs. In this sense, the principle of need should prevail over equity in the context of war. The challenge is to create a system of distribution that can promote equity while meeting victims' needs.

However, authors such as Pablo Kalmanovitz (2010) view DJ as an alternative to CJ and see these two forms of justice as being incompatible. Inspired by John Rawls' notion of DJ, Kalmanovitz (2010) argues that in the aftermath of massive destructive wars, DJ should be given priority over CJ. For Rawls (2003), political philosophy has the role of shaping a fair and reasonable society. A main question of political philosophy concerns the organization of fundamental institutions in order to promote freedom and equality of citizenship. Rawls (2003) proposes to conceive of society as an equitable system of social cooperation. Based on equality between citizens, the goal of social cooperation is to promote and foster enjoyable social relations. The organization of political and social institutions provides the society's basic structure and ensures social justice. The basic structure should promote equal access to opportunities. DJ is about the fair distribution of goods and services. Primary goods are seen as necessary in order to allow citizens to develop to their fullest potential. There are different kinds of primary goods such as basic human and civil rights and liberties, including freedom of movement, freedom of choosing an occupation, and income and wealth. In order for a system of distribution to be fair, the basic structure of a society's institutions, which distribute resources, must promote equal access. Inequality, according to Rawls, is only acceptable when they benefit the least advantaged members of the group. For example, affirmative action programs, which favor disadvantaged groups, would constitute an equitable system of social cooperation. The role of law is to regulate the acquisition of properties, favoring fairness or equality in the distribution of goods and services.

According to Kalmanovitz (2010), societies that have suffered situations of war should implement the Rawlsian system of DJ, instead of using mechanisms of CJ, which aim to return the victim to the situation prior to the crime. He believes that the principles of CJ that have been conceived to provide reparation to the victims in peaceful contexts should not be implemented during transitions from war to peace. He uses two main arguments to defend his position. The first one is that CJ aims to restore the status quo from before the crime without considering that the status quo may have been based on an unfair situation (e.g. the ownership of land by an elite minority) and that it is the status quo that may have led to the violence in the first place. In this sense, justice should avoid returning to the status quo and should instead invest in the construction of peace and justice. The second argument is that CJ is individualistic and is oriented towards the past. Kalmanoviz (2010) proposes that contrary to CJ, the Rawlsian notion of DJ has the advantage that is oriented towards the future instead of the past as it creates social institutions that distribute resources, benefiting the whole population.

Let us examine these arguments, their strengths and their limitations. They have the advantage that they highlight the (in)justice of the situation prior to the violation, which CJ does not address. An important question to consider is whether it is desirable to return a person to a situation that was already unfair. Also, returning to an unfair situation could reproduce the conditions from which the violence originated in the first place. In this sense, the redistribution of resources could be seen as a way to redress the conditions that led to violence and thus to prevent violence. Despite this, these arguments have significant limitations and negative implications that come from the lack of empirical evidence and of adequate understanding of conflicts. They fail to consider that landownership is often concentrated in the hands of a few and that a system of mutual exploitation of legal and illegal forces may propagate the violence to gain and maintain power. In the following, these shortcomings are illustrated as we consider the problem of land and violence in Colombia.

Political violence and distribution of land: the case of Colombia

The unequal distribution of land is a common reason used by insurgent groups to justify the use of violence against minorities in whose hands the ownership of land is concentrated, aiming to distribute the resources among the peasants. Likewise, violence is used by minority elites against the insurgents and civil movements in order to preserve their privileges. In Colombia, traditional political elites created paramilitary groups to attack peasants who had occupied lands in order to claim rights of property (Mazzei 2009). Reyes (2009) shows that in Colombian history, those who had the political power also had ownership of the best lands. According to Reyes (2009), changes in the distribution of power and land in Colombia were made using violent means. For example, during the colonial period, the Spanish had the monopoly of the rights over land. The structure of the division of land was called the “hacienda”. After the war of independence, the new political republican elites that replaced the Spanish monarchy inherited the rights of property over land, maintaining the “hacienda” institution. The government distributed land among those who fought during the civil war. In the first half of the twentieth century, the regional elites belonging to the two traditional parties, the liberal and the conservative parties, had a monopoly over rights to the lands. This created a situation of subordination of the peasants, who were unable to have access to the rights of property because they could not demonstrate that the land had been inherited from the Spanish monarchy (Reyes 2009).

In 1936, the peasants obtained the right to claim ownership of the land after having occupied it for 20 years. Nevertheless, the elites profited from this new law by making the peasants work for them and subsequently claiming the rights to the land for themselves. Furthermore, during this time the elites expanded their own lands by colonizing new territories. According to Reyes (2009), the best land in the country was colonized by peasants and then appropriated by the elites. At the end of the 1960s, the government of Carlos Lleras Restrepo supported a land reform that strengthened the peasant movement, promoting the creation of the Asociacion Nacional de Usuarios Campesinos. However, the land reform was frustrated by subsequent governments, which defended the interests of regional elites. This generated a massive occupation of lands by the peasant movement. Between 1971 and 1975, 2000 farms were occupied and claimed by the peasant movement (Reyes 2009).

The occupation of land had an effect on its distribution. In some regions, such as Montanas de María, the state gave thousands of hectares of land to create communal farms (Verdad Abierta 2010). However, this generated a violent reaction against the peasant movement. On the one hand, some of the old landowners used private armed groups to attack the peasants that claimed their lands. On the other hand, from the 1980s guerillas and paramilitary groups took control over territories, generating the displacement of civilian population. Paramilitary groups treated some members of the peasant movement as subversives, killing them and forcing their families to abandon their lands. Other peasants were displaced by paramilitary groups as a consequence of the dynamics of war.

As the limits between economic and political motivations became unclear, the context of the internal conflict in Colombia became even more complex with the participation of organized criminals (Kaldor 2001). As shown by Mazzei (2009), the formation of paramilitary groups at the beginning of the 1980s in Colombia resulted from an alliance between various actors: militaries promoting the creation of civilian groups as a part of the state's war against subversion; local politicians; landowners who have been victims of the guerrillas; and drug traffickers belonging to the cartels. The alliance with drug traffickers was a way to finance the groups, while the drug traffickers used the paramilitary groups to fight guerrillas and to gain control over territories. Drug traffickers fought guerrillas not for political reasons but because they were business competitors.

In the early 1980s, drug traffickers bought thousands of hectares of land in regions where landowners were attacked by the rebels. Their alliance with the paramilitaries allowed them to take control over land that was necessary to perform their illegal activities, while gaining legitimacy because of their alliance with political and economic elites (Reyes 2009). The creation of the Autodefensas Unidas de Colombia in 1997 by Carlos Castaño unified a set of regional paramilitary groups, obtaining the resources needed to expand over the whole national territory (Mazzei 2009). The expansion was made by committing hundreds of massacres against civilians accused to be subversives (Valencia 2007). Terror and forced displacement made the control over the communities, the land, drugs and other resources possible, thus benefiting a set of actors such as local politicians, local elites, drug traffickers and militaries. This resulted in the appropriation and concentration of land by illegal means for political and economical reasons. Half (52.2 percent) of cultivable land is in the hands of 1.15 percent of landowners. Drug traffickers and paramilitaries have appropriated the land of displaced people or it has been given to peasants supporting the paramilitary groups. In addition, multinational agro-industries have been buying these lands to produce biofuels (Summers 2012).

According to the mutual exploitation hypothesis, proposed by Tanner and Mulone (2013), mass violence is the result of a system of mutual exploitation in which a set of legal and illegal actors work together, using violence, in order to advance their own interests. In an article based on a case study in former Yugoslavia, Tanner and Mulone (2013) show how the state, allied with a set of private actors including criminal organizations, exercised violence in order to advance the state's plan of elimination. This hypothesis is very interesting in order to understand contemporary conflicts, including the Colombian war. The mutual exploitation hypothesis shows how the state benefits from organized crime and how, as in the case of Colombia, multinational companies take advantage of opportunities that have been created by mass violence.

The mutual exploitation hypothesis is also useful when we think about the problem of land distribution and DJ. Historically, the problem was one of land concentration by traditional and political elites. Currently, the appropriation and purchase of lands belonging to the peasants by organized criminals and multinational companies makes any possibility of land restitution or land distribution very complex and dangerous for the victims. In Colombia, the process of land restitution requires the dismantling of very violent criminal organizations in order to recover the lands and to protect the security of the victims who are asking for the return of their lands. Also, the law regulates the purchase of land by multinational enterprises in order to protect the property rights of the peasants who have been victimized.

Distributive and corrective justice: a complementary approach

Reparation of the harm done to the victims is a fundamental mechanism in attaining justice for victims. International principles on justice and reparation are focused on the redress of the harm done to the victims without considering the problem of justice related to the distribution of resources, which is also important in order to build peace and justice. Kalmanovitz (2010) argues that DJ has not been given sufficient attention in research on reparation for victims following violent conflict. History shows that the distribution of resources is at the heart of armed conflicts in agrarian societies where wealth and political power are concentrated in the hands of a small but powerful minority. In these societies, violence is justified as a mean to change a situation that is perceived as unfair and thus redistribute the resources held by those in power, such as elites, rebel groups and criminal groups. In the case of the Colombian victims of paramilitary groups, the problem of reparation can be considered a matter of DJ because it concerns the question of how to recover the resources that were appropriated by paramilitary networks (including drug traffickers and local elites) and how to distribute them among the victims. Thus DJ is important when restoring justice after violent conflict.

However, reparation is not just a matter of resources. It is also important to understand historical and contextual factors in order to restore justice in societies devastated by war. The question of justice and reparation also has to do with human relationships. Justice and reparation have to do with the past. An advantage of the CJ perspective is that it conceives violence as a human interaction having consequences on people's lives. Mass violence has deep consequences for the survivors and for the communities, since violence destroys social relations and lifestyles that communities have created over decades. When people are forced to leave their communities, they lose their properties and their jobs, but they also lose the way they interact with each other and their relationship with the territory they belong to. In Colombia, peasants who were forced to leave their lands and to move to urban areas were unable to use their agricultural skills, and they had to become part of the informal economy. It is very important to consider that their relationship with land and working the land is a central aspect of the identity of these people.

As we mentioned earlier, Kalmanovitz (2010) criticizes CJ because it is individualistic and because it looks to the past. One of Kalmanovitz's arguments against CJ is that it aims to restore the status quo, which may be socially unfair (2010). The problem with Kalmanovitz's analysis is that he considers only the economic aspects of conflicts and reparation while ignoring the moral consequences of the crimes. He fails to take into account that violence can be exercised by the elites against the peasants to make a counter-agrarian reform. In Colombia, violence against peasants was in part a reaction by local elites against the mandated redistribution of land by the state, which aimed to benefit the peasant movement. Thus, while violence may be used to change the status quo, violence is also exercised by local elites in order to oppose change and to maintain the status quo. The state-mandated redistribution of land in Colombia meant that many of the peasants were in a good situation before being victimized. Hence, the situation of the victim before the crime is not necessarily fair or unfair. The situation prior to victimization needs to be taken into consideration when restoring justice and should not, as Kalmanovitz suggests, simply be dismissed. CJ and the victim-oriented approach to justice, which is reflected in the UN Declaration, have the advantage that they favor respect for human rights and take into consideration the consequences of crime for individual victims and their communities. Thus corrective justice is also important with regard to the restitution of land following armed conflict.

Hence, DJ and CJ are both necessary to respond to war crimes. These forms of justice are complementary and related. In the case of Colombia, restitution of land can be considered a mechanism of CJ because it helps to rectify the harm done to the victims. This mechanism allows peasants to recover their source of income and to preserve their individual histories and identities as well as those of their community. The restitution of land in Colombia is a form of economic and moral reparation. It requires that the state is able to recover lands that have been appropriated by criminal networks. These networks have to be dismantled in order to protect the security of the victims participating in the process. Likewise, the purchase of lands by multinational enterprises has to be regulated by law in order to protect the needs and interest of victims and farmers.

At the same time, restitution of land is a mechanism of DJ because a process of land distribution existed prior to the commission of the crimes, and in this sense restitution favors a fair social distribution of resources. As for what constitutes a fair distribution, the distribution of resources should be based on equity. Land should be distributed to the individuals who work it because of their contribution to the economy. However, equity and need are linked, and when victims' personal integrity is at risk, need should prevail over equity. Following mass violence, victims' basic economic and moral needs are often no longer guaranteed and hence the principle of need should prevail over equity in the context of war. Thus both DJ and CJ can help to build peace and restore justice.

The restitution of land, however, remains a complex issue. In addition to making reparation to victims in a way that restores justice and respects their dignity and human rights, other issues may remain. After the demobilizations of the paramilitary groups, many victims returned to their lands and were killed for claiming their rights over the land.[1]

This raises another important question, namely how to protect the security of peasants who are reclaiming lands from new attacks by the violent networks that still exist. In this sense, reparation is not just a problem of redistributing resources with equity and respecting victims' right to property. It is also about ensuring the security and safety of victims by preventing new victimizations.

Reparation for victims is a key aspect of restoring justice after violent conflict. With respect to reparation, international law is victim-oriented, putting victims at the heart of international and domestic responses following violent conflict. In order to be sustainable, society's passage from war to peace must give priority to reparation and justice for its victims. The distribution of land should be based on the distributive principle of equity while prioritizing victims' needs and respecting their right to own property. In this way, reparation includes the fair distribution of resources as well as the historical and cultural importance of those resources for victims.

Note

1 Between 2006 and 2011 more than 70 peasants' leaders were killed.

References

Aristotle (2003) *Nicomachean Ethics*, Sioux Falls: NuVision Publications.

Botero, C. and Restrepo, E. (2005) "Estándares internacionales y procesos de transición en Colombia", in A. Rettberg (ed.) *Entre el perdón y el paredón: Preguntas y dilemas de la justicia transicional*, Bogota: Ediciones Uniandes, 19–66.

Deutsch, M. (1975) "Equity, Equality and Need: What determines which value will be used as the basis of distributive justice?", *Journal of Social Issues*, 31(3): 137–49.

Deutsch, M. (1985) *Distributive Justice: A social psychological perspective*, New Haven: Yale University Press.

Hagan, J. and Rymond-Richmond, W. (2009) *Darfur and the Crime of Genocide*, New York: Cambridge University Press.

Hatzfeld, J. (2005) *Machete Season: The killers in Rwanda speak*, New York: Farrar, Straus and Giroux.

Huyse, L. (1996) "Justice after Transition: On the choices successor elites make in dealing with the past", in A. Jongman (ed.) *Contemporary Genocides: Causes, cases, consequences*, Leiden: Interdisciplinary Research Programme on Root Causes of Human Rights Violations, 187–214.

Kaldor, M. (2001) *New and Old Wars: Organized violence in a global era*, Cambridge: Polity Press.

Kalmanovitz, P. (2010) "Justicia correctiva vs. justicia social en casos de conflicto armado", *Revista Estudios Socio-Jurídicos*, 12: 59–85.

Mazzei, J. (2009) *Death Squads or Self-Defense Forces? How paramilitary groups emerge and challenge democracy in Latin America*, Chapel Hill: University of North Carolina Press.

Parmentier, S. (2004) "La Commission 'Vérité et Réconciliation' en Afrique du Sud: possibilités et limites de 'justice restaurative' après conflits politiques majeurs", in D. Salas (ed.) *Victimes de guerre en quête de justice*, Paris: Editions l'Harmattan, 55–88.

Rawls, J. (2003) *La justice comme équité: Une reformulation de théorie de la justice*, Paris: Éditions La Découverte.

Reyes, A. (2009) *Guerreros y campesinos: El despojo de la tierra en Colombia*, Bogota: Grupo Editorial Norma.

Summers, N. (2012) "Colombia's Victims' Law: Transitional justice in a time of violent conflict?", *Harvard Human Rights Journal*, 25: 219–35.

Tanner, S. and Mulone, M. (2013) "Private Security and Armed Conflict: A case study of the Scorpions during the mass killings in former Yugoslavia", *The British Journal of Criminology*, 52: 1–18.

United Nations. (2005) *Basic Principles and Guidelines on the Right to a Remedy and Reparation for Victims of Gross Violations of International Human Rights Law and Serious Violations of International Humanitarian Law*, available at: www.refworld.org/docid/4721cb942.html (accessed June 5, 2013).

Valencia, L. (2007) *Parapolitica: La ruta de la expansion paramilitar y los acuerdos políticos*, Bogotá: Corporación Nuevo Arco Iris.

Verdad Abierta. (2010) "Cómo se fraguó la tragedia de los Montes de María?" *Verdad Abierta*, September 2, available at: www.verdadabierta.com/nuncamas/38-desplazados/2676-icomo-se-fraguo-la-tragedia-de-los-montes-de-maria (accessed November 12, 2012).

Waller, J. (2007) *Becoming Evil: How ordinary people commit genocide and mass killing*, New York: Oxford University Press.

13 Reparations through different lenses

The culture, rights and politics of healing and empowerment after mass atrocities

Hugo van der Merwe

Reparations are a primary justice concern for most impoverished victims.[1] Some have called reparations the "most victim centered of the various transitional justice mechanisms" (Robins 2011b: 6). Not addressing these concerns head-on results in other justice processes becoming delegitimized. Providing reparations is however a process that is complicated by the context within which it needs to occur, particularly when there are many victims and the country is impoverished.

In a context of mass violations, it becomes difficult to make sense of the range of needs, rights and demands for reparations that emerge from victims who have suffered a range of abuses. These calls for reparative intervention make different moral, political and rights claims that can seem overwhelming and difficult to juggle and prioritize. Which abuses are the most important to respond to? Which victims are most worthy of assistance?

To make sense of these competing demands, this chapter unpacks reparations claims through three lenses: needs, rights and politics. Each provides a different logic for prioritization of reparative measures. The chapter then examines how reparations advocacy processes engage with these lenses to bolster claims (and hopefully build democracy) in a post-authoritarian context. The chapter uses the policies and victim advocacy process in South Africa to illustrate the various approaches and tensions.

Reparations as addressing critical human needs

Transitional justice processes are about addressing a number of goals, but victims' needs are a key source of its validation and legitimacy. While transitional justice processes have achieved notable successes, victims have generally not benefited greatly from these interventions; in this sense they are hollow victories that present little substantive gains for those most directly affected by past injustices. Despite the rhetoric about their centrality to these interventions, victims do not generally feel they have been heard in many of the transitional justice processes over the last two decades, and reparations programs generally struggle to get off the ground, to contain substantial benefits or to reach a large proportion of victims.

Particularly in contexts where victims fear for their survival because of their economic situation, reparations are a key concern that does not seem to be adequately prioritized. Reparations in these contexts not only speak to the need for acknowledgement and justice, but can also contribute directly to addressing the victims' urgent survival and safety needs.

Evaluations of transitional justice processes (such as courts, truth commissions, etc.) show that impoverished victims often prioritize reparations as their primary justice demand when they live in contexts of severe poverty and disrupted survival strategies (Vinck and Pham 2008; Robins 2011a; Robins 2012). Immediate safety needs and basic survival needs clearly dominate the list of priorities in the immediate aftermath of war. This is confirmed by detailed studies in numerous contexts including South Africa (Backer 2005), Democratic Republic of the Congo (Vinck and Pham 2008), Uganda (Pham and al 2005), Nepal (Robins 2011a), Timor Leste (Robins 2012), and Kenya (Robins 2011b).

From a victim-centered approach, transitional justice's credibility rests largely on its ability to provide reparations. Initial evaluations find that victims judge the process positively based on issues of procedural justice, voice, etc., but down the line, when the expectation of substantive change (such as reparations) is not fulfilled, such credibility can be seriously eroded (Backer 2010).

Transitional justice policy debates in the immediate aftermath of conflict are often driven primarily by urban elites and high-profile victims, who have a strong moral voice and an ability to clearly articulate demands in terms of international discourse and law. These voices are, however, not representative and the marginalized voice of the more common victim experience emerges only from more comprehensive research efforts or through sustained mobilization processes of these sectors of society. The perspective that seems more appropriate for assessing appropriate justice interventions is thus not just the small percentage of victims who engage actively with the court or other transitional justice process, but the broader victim population affected by the violations. While the more affluent, urban, and prominent victims often prioritize prosecutions and truth, more rural and impoverished victims understandably prioritize economic survival needs (Robins 2011a, 2012). However, these voices are often not heard in transitional justice debates and are often not captured by evaluations that overlook local cultural perspectives (Viaene 2010) or that only target the local elites (Millar 2010).

Reparations are thus a necessary component of a transitional justice process that hopes to address victims' needs. The complexity of these needs – what reparation means in terms of personal and social reconstruction and where it fits into a transitional justice agenda – needs to be understood in relation to the various categories and circumstances of victims in a particular country.

It is very dangerous to assume we know the impact of victimization in general terms and simply need to calibrate our framework to take into consideration local particularities. While there may be fundamental physiological factors that provide for some commonality of experience of severe mass trauma, there are numerous factors that affect the way that victimization is experienced, what meaning it is given, and the way that recovery is sought. This variation applies just as much to those within a country as it does to differences between countries. For example, research in South Africa with victims working with the Truth and Reconciliation Commission (TRC) shows vast differences between the meaning of victimization (van der Merwe 2008), the healing potential of testifying (Picker 2005), and the relief provided by reparations (Makhalemele 2009) for different victims. Specific circumstances and victim characteristics directly shape how the abuse impacted on each victim and how they respond to different interventions. The impact of victimization and interventions depend on a range of factors such as gender, the type of victimization suffered (e.g. torture versus massacre), the need to clear one's name in public, and the relative urgency of immediate survival needs.

There are three critical issues that these diverse experiences highlight which underpin the need for a contextualized understanding of victimization and healing. First, as well as creating the need for psychological and physical repair, victimization also reshapes individuals' relationships, with their families and their community, and their worldview (their internal justice theory). Victimization impacts on how victims relate to those around them and how they see the world. Interventions hold the potential for shifting these relationships and perspectives.

Second, reparations serve very different purposes in terms of symbolism and survival needs. Reparations may be a direct delivery of a basic need (such as housing, money for food, etc.) and may also carry a message from those in authority about its relationship to citizens. In a context where the state had violated its citizens or had failed to protect them, the process of reparations delivery conveys a critical message regarding who is valued, what responsibilities the state takes on for caring and healing, and how it views the needs and rights of citizens.

Third, victimization often destroys community bonds, capacities and knowledge. Communities, cultures and identity groups are often transformed or destroyed by conflict and can thus be considered as collectivities of victims. The question then becomes whether we accept this sad reality and treat victims in their atomized state, or whether we seek through reparations to rebuild social capital, cultural resources and affiliations. Reparations can thus be designed (or perceived) as an attempt to restore such collectivities to some semblance of their original state or to strengthen newly emerging communities of support. Where victimization took on a collective character (e.g. attack on a particular ethnic group), reparations can thus be seen as serving a particular collective purpose, but the form that such collective repair would take would be very dependent on the nature of the damage and the local understanding of how such damage can be repaired.

It is particularly because of this communal impact that collective reparations should be explored as an important complementary form of intervention. In some conflict contexts where communities were attacked as communities, where the impact of the victimization is distributed throughout the community and where there is a surviving legitimate communal process for healing and rebuilding, collective reparations could serve as an appropriate response to address individual needs along with collective harms. But such examples seem to be the exception rather than the rule (see Mégret in this volume).

A useful framework for making sense of some of the variation in needs found among victims is Maslow's hierarchy. Wemmers and De Brouwer (2011) summarize the range of crime victims' needs identified by researchers as falling into five categories: medical needs, financial needs, need for protection, need for support in order to help them deal with the psychological effects of their victimization, and need for recognition and respect in the criminal justice system. They note that these converge with the hierarchy of needs as theorized by Maslow: physiological, safety, belonging and self-esteem. They go on to suggest that in accordance with Maslow, victims of mass violations, particularly in a context of extensive needs, would prioritize the primary levels such as physiological and safety needs before pursuing relief for other needs.

This provides an important starting point for understanding the basic distinction between immediate survival needs and other needs that can only effectively be addressed once basic needs are fulfilled. It helps to clarify why certain victims would prioritize particular needs over others (and to clarify contrasts such as that between rich, urban, educated victims and impoverished, vulnerable, rural victims). It could also be used as a normative guide for prioritizing certain interventions as more directly addressing basic human needs. Rather than framing this contrast as the needs of elite victims versus those of mass victims, Maslow's analysis presents these needs as universal and incrementally realizable.

While also culturally and contextually varied in how they are fulfilled, basic physiological and safety needs should thus be treated as universal priorities, which should prevail over belonging and self-esteem interventions. Local variations, for example regarding how food is produced and distributed and how safety is secured and managed, are still critical in determining appropriate interventions.

As has been discussed above, though, the way in which reparations are provided conveys critical messages that impact on other "higher-level" needs. How the state provides even basic services carries a message about belonging and self-esteem. Whose needs are prioritized and how the state consults, communicates and delivers can provide a foundational experience of belonging and recovery of some sense of dignity among victims and victimized communities. Maslow's hierarchy is thus perhaps a critical framework for prioritization of interventions, but it should not be viewed as a sequentialization of reparative measures, as interventions are likely to impact on various levels at the same time.

While Maslow's framework thus explains some of the variation in needs of victims and helps shape our understanding of priorities, we are left with a broad scope of variability of needs that still leaves a serious challenge for policy makers when facing a range of demands. Another framework that has increasingly been used in understanding victims' needs and which has been central in shaping priorities is the lens of human rights.

Reparations through a human rights lens

In a conflict environment where there are numerous claims and counter-claims about victimization and demands for redress, a legal framework to guide the assessment of worthy claims and allocate responsibility for intervention is usually highlighted as a critical priority. Rule of law is the new battle cry of many foreign donors and international experts. The most prominent manifestation of this approach is the human rights framework.

With different groups and cultures labeling the same event differently (i.e. crimes, acts of terrorism, martyrdom, etc.), human rights offer the possibility of providing a unifying framework. For example, Garcia-Godos notes that the Peruvian Truth and Reconciliation Commission's reparation plan

> Homogenizes the universe of victims, so that they are considered equally worthy of attention on the basis of their suffering. Discriminatory practices ... would no longer be applicable if an overall policy on reparations for the victims of the armed conflict is established.
>
> (2009: 81)

However, the human rights framework is not neutral in the value it places on different forms of suffering. It comes with particular values and priorities, which speak to an international audience and an internationalized culture of criminal law and social order. While it presents a neutral approach, which sees all citizens as equal before the law, it elevates certain forms of victimization and certain types of responsibilities above others. It introduces a new approach to understanding needs through a legal framing of wrongs and suffering, and it presents its own hierarchy of reparative priorities. While all torture victims (from different sides of the conflict) would be treated the same, a victim of torture would be treated differently from a victim of economic discrimination.

Claims for the state could be made by individuals (or groups) who seek state assistance to address victimization of competing rights. For example, individuals can present themselves respectively as victims of civil-political rights violations, victims of ongoing inability to access basic socioeconomic rights, victims of past socioeconomic rights violations, victims of civil and political rights violations, or victims of international crimes. They can claim victim status based on one or more of these violations of their rights. Their ability to frame their claims in relation to these various rights could prove critical in having their rights recognized as legitimate or their claims given priority. A legal framework effectively gives different weights based on where victims manage to locate themselves in this picture (Figure 13.1).

The framing of these different rights and their relative weights varies from one national (or international) jurisdiction to the next. At a national level, human rights are often incorporated into civil rights legislation. For example, a country's constitution includes the civil rights (and remedies) available to all of its citizens and presents some forms of prioritization of different potential claims.

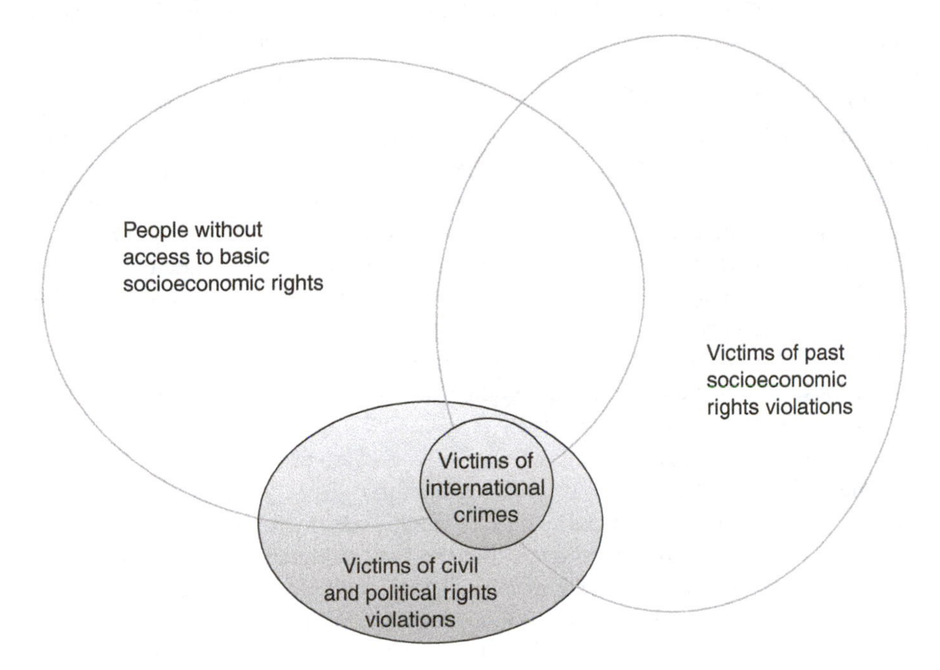

Figure 13.1 Human rights violations framework.

These national legal frameworks for rights provide localized prisms which shape how these and other categories of victim rights are framed and prioritized. Each jurisdiction thus presents a mix of local legal traditions and international obligations and developments.

The introduction of international criminal justice engagement to the national politics of redress complicates these debates further. International actors, and local actors funded by international agencies, have prioritized particular rights holders and increased the relative weight or authority of their claims. The legal framework at a national and international level thus presents a prioritization of different victim claims and judges the legitimacy and priority of claims in terms of how they fit these categories. A hierarchy of victims' rights emerges which elevates the needs of some victims above those of others.

This hierarchy is one that is subject to constant debate and contestation. Each country and each international mechanism presents a space where these are ordered slightly differently. In the expanding field of international justice, international crimes are particularly underscored. Transitional justice mechanisms, particularly those popular at present such as courts and truth commissions, have generally also prioritized redress for civil and political rights over redress for socioeconomic rights (Laplante 2008). Increasingly, however, transitional justice mechanisms are pressed to address social, economic and cultural rights (Arbour 2007). Transitional justice mechanisms are essentially backward-looking, addressing the violations of a past regime. This means that they focus on past abuses linked specifically to particular political policies rather than present abuses or ongoing social injustices, which are not directly ascribed to the former regime.

One thus finds that a narrow transitional justice framing of rights can prioritize the needs of certain victims over others. For example, in an effort to correct past injustices, the rights of corrective justice victims may be given priority over those of social justice victims (Kalmanovitz 2010; see also Manrique Rueda in this volume). The need for distributive justice and social transformation are thus often de-prioritized in the context of political transition. Consequently, victims tortured in the context of political persecution are treated as a priority while those tortured as regular criminal suspects are made invisible (McGregor 2013), and the needs of those dispossessed due to political persecution are prioritized over those who lost their land due to other policies such as making way for infrastructure development.

National and international law generally do not provide an unambiguous framework or justification for prioritizing certain rights over others. While some minimum standards are now more clearly spelled out, such progress relates more to rights to truth and prosecutions, while the right to reparations is struggling to achieve the same level of recognition. These standards leave reparations as a broad obligation, which is subject to various local circumstances. The failure to adequately deliver on reparations is thus often justified on the basis of balancing different demands on state resources.

A key challenge for the rights-based approach to reparations is the question of whether it maps onto (or speaks to) local experiences of violations and local victim needs. The way that a rights approach frames human experiences and offers remedies is often at odds with local frames of making sense of these events. Given that most of the contexts where reparations policies are debated and implemented are in countries without a human rights tradition, the way that people make sense of what happened – how they label it, explain its causes and propose solutions – is often done through a local political or cultural lens that does not necessarily use a human rights discourse.

Victims have their own sense of how different events impacted on their lives, how aspects of their suffering can be categorized together with that of other victims, and how different needs should be prioritized. These commonalities may be related to common ethnic identity, to having a perpetrator in common, having a similar type of loss, or having suffered during the same event or at the same time. What a human rights approach does is to impose a new framework of labeling and cataloguing individuals, events and entitlements. The positivist legal framework tends to flatten these multiple subjectivities and complex experiences into a simpler binary discourse of victims and perpetrators, violations and non-violations (Wilson 2001).

Sometimes this reframing provides a good match with local narratives and discourses; sometimes it doesn't. Similarly, victims' views of appropriate remedies can correspond with human rights guarantees, or not. In his study of victims' perspectives in Kenya, Robins notes that:

> Victims identified measures that, in some cases, correspond to the forms of reparations described in the ... 2005 UN Basic Principles, which are compensation, satisfaction, rehabilitation, restitution, and guarantees of non-repetition. In other cases, they specified measures – such as livelihood support, peaceful access to agricultural land and natural resources, or the return to their community's settlement – that would require a more fundamental overhaul of social and economic relations among and between Kenyans of different classes and identities.
>
> (2012: 7)

Recognizing that a rights framework is insufficient basis for prioritizing among the numerous worthy claims for assistance, some countries have complemented it with other moral principles. In Sierra Leone and Timor-Leste, reparations provisions have, for example, been guided by the urgency of victims' needs and their level of "vulnerability". The immediacy and/or severity of needs are thus used as guides for prioritizing particular services or particular categories of victims (Carrington and Naughton 2012). Among those with recognized rights claims, an additional prioritization, reflecting Maslow's prioritization of survival and safety needs (Wemmers and De Brower 2011), was thus used to determine state reparative priorities.

Given this complexity of demands and contrasting priorities, the challenge in post-conflict societies is to seek an inclusive framework for balancing the various demands, rights and priorities in a society. Correa and colleagues note that "a clear conceptual framework on reparations that is shared by the various actors in the process ... is crucial to moving forward on this issue in a positive way" (2009: 10). They add that "besides having a shared view of what reparations means ... it is important for all actors to have a clear picture of how this issue fits into a broader agenda of transition" (Correa *et al.* 2009: 10).

When the needs of all victims (international crimes, civil political violations, socioeconomic violations, those lacking basic services) are pooled as equally valid, or are seen as too vast to be addressed effectively in the short term, space is created for a political logic to take over the role of prioritizing services. Law may define individuals' human rights in a particular context, but it does not always provide an unambiguous logic with regard to their priority in the face of multiple demands. The legal framework, which gives content to particular rights, specifies types of violations and categories of victims who are entitled to reparations, but the application of these legal provisions is mediated through state institutions that are only partially swayed by this logic and that often actively resist these "imposed" obligations.

Reparations through a political lens

While there is clearly a justified concern about the resources that can or should be allocated to addressing all these needs, the dominant logic of addressing these obligations in contexts of vast needs and limited resources ultimately tends to be that of politics and power. Rather than being guided by human rights principles, the reparations policy process is fundamentally driven by the politics of fragile and traumatized new regimes. The interventions are therefore shaped by threats (e.g. organized and impatient ex-combatants), keeping or building alliances with ethnic groups, or key voting blocs or donors (particularly local and international business interests).

Nevertheless, all these reparative measures to address demands from various constituencies are often still justified in the name of human rights. It does not mean that these programs are illegal or illegitimate, but simply that the politics of power is a more persuasive logic for shaping policy when human rights guarantees are not sufficiently entrenched in law, when legal institutions are not sufficiently independent or when transitional arrangements and budgetary constraints trump legal obligations. Many reparations programs are, for example, prompted by court decisions setting a precedent that a government is loath to roll out for a vast number of victims.

We consequently end up with a set of policies that deal with reparative goals through a political lens, which only loosely map onto a human rights agenda. In the South African context for example, there are Truth and Reconciliation "urgent interim" reparations, Truth and Reconciliation "final" reparations, affirmative action, land restitution, land reform, repatriation of refugees, and a range of other measures that seek to address a complex legacy of abuses. All post-conflict countries have a similar plethora of programs that seek to correct the injustices of the past and to address the needs of particularly affected groups. Different types of abuses, or abuses that occurred at different times, are often treated quite differently, and there is often a lack of consistency in how victims are defined or the nature of benefits to which they are entitled. For example, a UN Special Rapporteur statement on developments in Tunisia (OHCHR 2012) notes that the various interventions in that context were ad hoc and event-based, resulting in different classes of victims.

As an illustration of the mismatch between a human rights framework and actual reparative measures, one could compare in South Africa how the categories of beneficiaries of the various reparative measures match the categories of victims recognized by the human rights framework. This fairly ad hoc link between reparative measures and rights promised by law raises concerns about what logic drives the implementation of these measures. While there may be no doubt about the importance of any of the measures taken in their own right, the prioritization was not one that followed a clear human rights strategy. Balancing different demands clearly contains a political logic.

Figure 13.2 gives a very simplified Venn diagram presentation of this mismatch. The different possible claims of rights to reparations (from victims of past socioeconomic rights violations; people without access to basic socioeconomic rights; and victims of civil and political rights violations) are only partially matched by the different intervention programs (e.g. repatriation of refugees; land restitution; affirmative action; ex-combatant reintegration; TRC reparations). Many gaps remain, indicating that not all reparations rights have

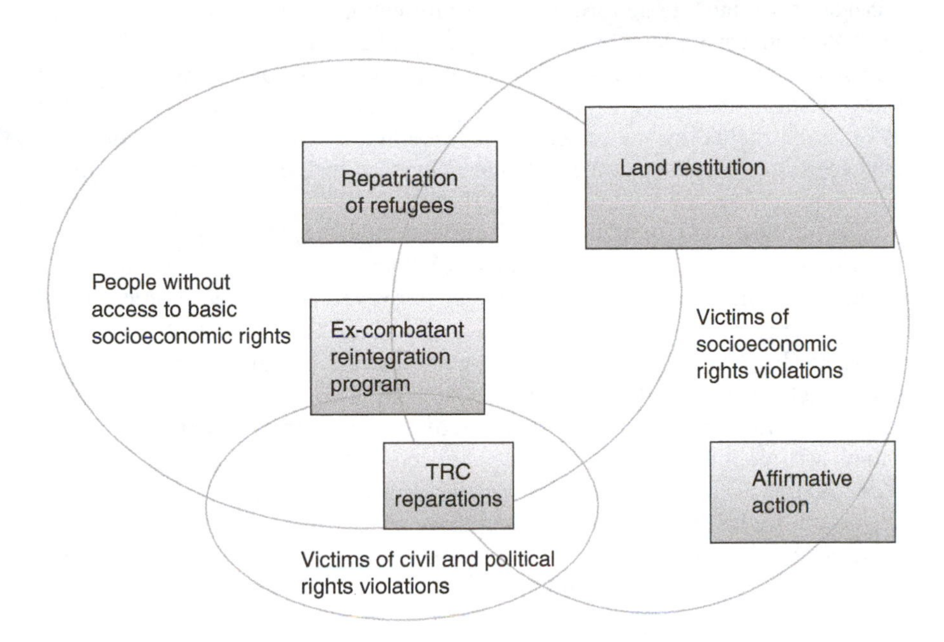

Figure 13.2 Overlap between human rights framework and reparative programs.

been addressed, and hinting that complex political dynamics lie behind the framing of reparative responses to specific rights.

In the process of implementing these new policies, the government in effect signals what suffering is recognized as particularly grievous and what injustices are considered particularly heinous. The symbolism conveyed by this set of policies says a lot about the moral landscape of the new society: whose needs are prioritized and whose remain marginalized. Particular programs to assist victims are often motivated in relation to the importance attached to the rights that were infringed. In practice, it is however impossible for reparative programs to provide comprehensive coverage for a whole category of victims. The selection of which victims in each category thus receive priority says something about how seriously the state takes these rights and which victims have their rights translated into actual services. What is perhaps most critical in the shaping of a framework for reparative interventions is the development of a transparent process and consistent justification for why certain needs are prioritized and why different classes of victims are recognized in different ways.

Reparations approached through a political lens can undermine human rights. When "human rights" is a vague collection of different promises that are only opportunistically used by government and selectively and disproportionally used by international agencies, it loses its value as a normative guide and a set of principles that society can use to prioritize needs and build consensus across political divides. This is particularly complicated by a context where most citizens are considered victims of one form or another of human rights violations and where the state is under pressure to respond urgently to a range of rights-based claims. A disjuncture between needs, rights and delivery of reparations can easily lead to cynicism about human rights as a value framework for guiding policy. This cynicism is fuelled by the selective use of rights to address the needs of those who are more politically connected, those able to offer a credible threat, or those who can mobilize international support for their cause.

The political logic of addressing needs can either compete with rights-based claims or can work in a complementary manner such that rights-based claims strengthen political claims. A key danger, however, is that the political logic simply trumps rights-based claims, particularly in a context of long-term conflict where the logic of power has been dominant and the institutions and culture of human rights are still in their infancy.

How victims engage with the tools and discourse of human rights when interacting with political institutions can play a critical role in promoting a rights-based approach to addressing reparations demands and thus building a human rights culture. It is not only government that makes rights real. The active use of these rights in policy advocacy also gives them traction and builds support for their significance in public culture.

The politics of reparations advocacy

The battle for reparations in South Africa has taken on various forms since the start of the TRC process. The strategies used by civil society and victims illustrate the way that human rights help shape, albeit in limited ways, state policies. Fennis, in her review of the reparations advocacy literature, finds that scholars highlight the importance of political pressure in the success of reparations advocacy efforts (2013). Brooks argues that the success of any claim is determined by "the degree of pressure (public and private)" exerted by a redress movement and admits that politics, rather than "matters of logic, justice, or culture", largely determine the success of a redress claim. He posits that even though successful redress movements have "reached the hearts and minds of lawmakers and citizens alike", legislators and thus politics is what really counts (1999: 6).

As indicated in figure 13.2, reparative claims arise in response to a wide range of violations due to apartheid and to subsequent denials of basic rights. As apartheid was a system that discriminated and brutalized the black majority, it could indeed be argued that the majority of the population are victims of human rights abuses. The TRC legislation, however, very directly highlighted the suffering of only a select group of victims of "gross human rights violations". These victims of politically motivated killing, attempted killing, torture and severe ill treatment were given particular acknowledgement in the process of national reconciliation.[2] The legislation also required that the TRC develop recommendations for reparations for these victims. The legislation was criticized for defining this category of abuses too narrowly, and the TRC was challenged to push the boundaries of how it categorized victims. Ultimately, though, the TRC legislation introduced a legal categorization of victims of gross human rights violations, which while roughly in line with international law framed it in a specifically South African context.[3] For example, while the UN recognized apartheid as a crime against humanity, the South African legislation did not.

While there has been subsequent debate about whether reparations provisions recommended by the TRC should be extended to a broader cross-section of apartheid victims, the TRC's definition of prioritized victims (victims of gross violations of human rights) has in effect marginalized other claims. While there were initial disagreements within victims' organizations and among civil society about this categorization and its narrow interpretation by the TRC, the general authority of the TRC's recommendations has increasingly focused reparations discourse on this narrow category of victims.

Reparations advocacy was an early component of the victims' concerns that emerged in the lead-up to the TRC and gained momentum during the TRC process (mainly carried by the Khulumani Support Group – a victims' rights organization representing over 60,000 members in South Africa). While reparations were often raised as a necessary component of a reconciliation process during the policy debates leading to the establishment of the TRC, the discussion of the details of such reparations was always put off until later (Colvin 2006). The TRC's mandate to develop recommendations for reparations was an early acknowledgement by the government of its own ultimate responsibility in this regard. While acknowledging this need, most particularly in the establishment of a Committee on Reparations and Rehabilitation within the TRC, a right to reparations was not formally acknowledged by the state in the debates about setting up the TRC. Indirectly, though, the state acknowledged its legal liability for reparations by ensuring that the TRC would provide indemnity from civil liability for any claims against the state arising from political violations. The legislation thus removed the state's civil liability for reparations by putting in place a body that was only empowered to make recommendations for reparations (Sec. 27(a)).[4]

The TRC itself, however, recognized that the responsibility for providing reparations was a government's obligation under international law (*TRC Report* 1998). Through various consultations with victims and civil society groups, the TRC sought to develop an integrated policy that would spell out how the state should fulfill its responsibility for providing appropriate and just reparations.

Rights-based demands on government were always part of civil society's strategy in campaigns for reparations, but were regularly presented alongside appeals based on empathy or threats linked to political power. The right to reparations had not been spelled out in the TRC legislation, and the legal basis for such claims under both South African and international law remained tenuous. While the language of rights provided a strong discourse of moral claims, advocacy efforts consistently sought to bolster these relatively weak legal claims through broader mobilization and advocacy efforts. There are thus (at least) three sources of power or authority which victims have used in advocating to have their needs addressed: empathy, coercive power and human rights claims.

Empathy is a central factor leveraged in transitional contexts, particularly where sections of a population have been dehumanized or enemies have been portrayed as less than human. New governments coming into power after conflict often present themselves as more caring and more humane – more able to empathize with those who have suffered (often linking this to their own suffering during the conflict or authoritarian rule).

Transitional justice mechanisms present an ideal opportunity for demonstrating this new commitment to those who have suffered and whose needs have been denied. A key claim for transitional justice mechanisms is that the power of revealing the truth will have a decisive impact on a country's trajectory. Many have thus attempted to reveal as explicitly as possible not just the facts about what happened, but also the stories and suffering of victims – to have them testify regarding their needs. The emblematic expression of this is the South African TRC's use of the concept of "ubuntu" – the recognition of our humanness through our interconnectedness with fellow human beings. No wonder then that voice, testimony and acknowledgement of suffering was so strongly emphasized by TRC commissioners. This interaction with victims was not only about the immediate process of engagement and empathy. It was also a form of advocacy by victims. After testifying, victims spoke of how good it felt to be listened to, but they also spoke of how the TRC now knew what their needs were and would be compelled to act because they had personally been touched by the suffering. This direct voice led to high expectations among victims of follow-through on reparations, as those with power now knew how much suffering had occurred and was still happening (Picker 2005).

Do processes that facilitate empathy produce support for assistance? In the South African case, it appears that is was successful up to a point. The commissioners who sat through almost 2000 individual direct testimonies of suffering came out with recommendations for very substantial reparations – much more that the state had anticipated when they gave the TRC the mandate to develop recommendations. Their reflections on the process indicate that victim perspectives were very influential in shaping their recommendations (Orr 2000). Empathy from the TRC did not, however, translate into empathy from the state. The recommendations were largely ignored, and public empathy gradually waned over time as other groups' needs became highlighted.

At the end of the TRC, the state remained silent on the question of reparations, seemingly hoping that it would simply be forgotten. When victims became more and more outspoken about the broken promises of the TRC, the state explicitly rejected individual reparations as an appropriate response, and publicly stated that victims were greedy and were in fact cheapening the legacy of the liberation struggle.[5]

As the limits of empathy as a persuasive tool became apparent, victims increasingly sought other ways of increasing the popular appeal of their claims to force the state to take notice. The state's rejection of the TRC's recommendations seemed to galvanize victims and they became more organized and outspoken. They realized that little progress would be made without a collective voice and without a broader coalition of social actors. Empathy was thus complemented by appeals to strategies that harnessed the collective power of victims and their allies.

Victims also increasingly framed their calls in terms of human rights – appealing both to the state's constitutional commitments to human rights and to its international obligations. As the international recognition of the right to reparations grew over this post-TRC period (2001 onwards), victims increasingly networked with international actors and drew on local human rights organizations to help frame their demands within this discourse. The fact that the South African state seeks to present itself as a bastion of human rights, both locally and internationally, makes this discourse a valuable currency.

Through this combination of empathy, power and human rights appeals, victims were able to secure an allocation to a Reparations Fund of about one billion rand (about $100 million), from which individual payments of R30,000 ($3000) were given to each victim recognized by the TRC. However, this was still only a quarter of what the TRC had recommended in its final report.

Ultimately, the South African state is still sitting on most of the money in the Reparations Fund and is seemingly at a complete loss as to how to spend it.[6] Victims continue to demand that this money comes to them in some form, as the initial individual payments were so small. They also demand that the class of beneficiaries should be opened up – to include all that qualify as victims of gross violations of human rights, not just those registered by the TRC. While the category of gross violations of human rights thus remains the accepted framework for who should qualify, victims and civil society groups have challenged the existing list of victims as too narrowly circumscribed by the TRC process of collecting statements. This battle is becoming increasingly legal in nature, with appeals to the government's human rights obligations (and implicit threats of court action) becoming the dominant discourse in submissions to government from civil society.[7]

These three sources of authority – empathy, coercion and rights – have always been intermingled. Tensions between different strategies and sources of authority and legitimacy are common in transitional justice and human rights advocacy efforts (Brankovic 2010). These tensions are illustrated in the following example. At a conference in December 2012, where a coalition of NGOs invited government representatives to a public dialogue on the reparations policy, there was extensive debate in the coalition over how to present a convincing argument to the state. Should the coalition allocate half of the two days to provide a platform for victims to tell their stories and show how they continue to suffer up to this day due to what happened to them under apartheid? Should time (and budget) be allocated to international legal experts to present the case for state obligations under international law? Or should there be more of a focus on drawing in church leaders, union representatives and other civic leaders to show broad public support for this cause? Each input has its place in a complementary strategy, but they also have their respective logics for what such reparations should look like and who are the most appropriate beneficiaries.

Coalitions involving human rights and victims' representatives need to find the appropriate mix that maximizes their complementarity in achieving particular outcomes. But it is not just immediate policy outcomes that are significant for deciding appropriate strategies. Given that reparations advocacy is part of a broader transformative process of seeking justice, the strategy needs to strengthen social mobilization processes. In this context, the role of international human rights experts may, for example, provide short-term advantages while removing political agency from victims and local activists.

Correa points to the importance of reparations processes not only delivering on the substance of victims' demands, but also empowering victims as a critical element:

> An important goal of reparations policies must be to empower victims to take control of their own future, which means that policies should not reinforce dependency. This suggests more than the obvious demand for participation in the definition and implementation of reparations and victims' right to be considered equal partners in future relationships.
>
> (2009: 290)

In a context of democratization after authoritarian rule, the process of developing and implementing a reparations policy conveys important messages both about how suffering is recognized and about how democracy will function. The way the state consults on such foundational policies can either nurture or circumvent active citizen participation in democratic processes of policy development.

Entrenching a rights discourse

At an international level, the language of rights is now clearly established in the discourse of addressing victims' needs around reparations (as well as around prosecutions and truth), and it has become the dominant (but not sole) language in certain local contexts.

Rights are still an alien language for many victims and also for many activists who work on projects of healing, dialogue and development in South Africa. The South African state also shows only a tentative ownership of the rights enshrined in its own constitution and it seems increasingly to feel resentful that its constitutional and international commitments constrain its ability to act with discretion in a complex political context where different sets of interests need to be balanced within a context of limited resources.

The language of rights is also gaining increased currency as a general language of popular struggle, both by apartheid victims and by others mobilizing for social change. For example, human rights litigation has also strengthened victims' rights to justice in terms of prosecutions and pardons processes (Van der Merwe 2012). These victories lend more credibility to the law and legal institutions as an avenue for pursuing rights in the face of a state that appears increasingly resistant to popular appeals for intervention or restraint. Litigation has also secured some important victories for other social justice causes in South Africa, and it is increasingly seen as more than just a liberal discourse or a tool to be used by elites or criminals. The right to HIV/AIDS treatment and the right to housing have for example been effectively promoted through legal challenges against the state by public-interest law firms. Even when not utilizing legal advocacy strategies, the language of claiming rights is a language that lends authority to particular claims of victim status.

A human rights framework for reparations has emerged in South Africa as a critical but contested tool for advocating for victims' needs. But this framework is one that is still quite static, narrowly framed in terms of the TRC legislation and recommendations. The lack of an open and engaged dialogue between the state and civil society has led to a hardening of positions and the framing of rights and obligations in terms of rigid categories defined by the law. The resort to a human rights discourse has resulted at least in part from the increasingly hostile attitude of the state to the demands from victims.

We need to reflect on the precedents that are being set by the mechanisms and policies being used to resolve reparations demands. Do truth commissions and courts provide an exceptionalist intervention that creates new rules specifically for the transitional period, or do they actually reshape our sense of how the state is held accountable, how victims are given space to express themselves, how we dialogue about painful issues and complex social problems? Do the transitions set society on a new trajectory where victims will be able to speak out, where they have expectations about being consulted, where channels for accountability and transparency are available; or will their needs be prescribed by legal categories of rights, and will they remain dependent on legal experts to come and save them when their rights are again trampled?

Conclusion

This chapter has highlighted the importance of understanding reparative demands in relation to addressing basic human needs and also understanding their full diversity and contextually framed nature. It is against this backdrop that reparations rights need to be understood as a proxy for addressing needs. A rights framework is a powerful lens, and one that is growing in importance, through which reparative demands are filtered and prioritized into legal discourse and legislative provisions. But ultimately a political lens provides a final layer of judgment regarding worthy claims and worthy victims.

In an ideal context one would want to ensure that victims' needs are appropriately and extensively voiced and heard, that the legal system provides a clear and morally acceptable framework for judging and prioritizing claims and responsibilities, and that the political system consultatively and transparently shapes a reparations framework and implementation plans that will allocate resources appropriately.

In the contexts of a divided society with limited resources trying to recover from mass victimization, we are likely to fall short of the ideal. As the South

African case illustrates, a strong victims' voice has an important role to play in ensuring that all these elements are brought to bear in meeting this vital transitional need. This role is of particular significance in a society dealing with an authoritarian legacy where the struggle for reparations also serves as a testing ground for democratic citizenship.

Notes

1 I use the term "victim" in this chapter to refer to those who have suffered human rights abuses. While the term "survivor" is generally preferable in terms of its implied sense of agency, this chapter seeks to question whether or when reparations policies do in fact facilitate conditions that encourage agency.

2 The legislation establishing the TRC, the *Promotion of National Unity and Reconciliation Act* No. 34 (1995), defined gross violation of human rights as "violation of human rights through (a) the killing, abduction, torture or severe ill-treatment of any person; or (b) any attempt, conspiracy, incitement, instigation, command or procurement to commit an act referred to in paragraph (a)".

3 The TRC introduced a definition of human rights victims that defined particular abuses as "gross" and which prioritized political motivation as key a consideration in its treatment of victims.

4 This abrogation of the rights of victims to civil claims against the state was confirmed by the Constitutional Court in its judgment on *AZAPO and others v. the President of the Republic of South Africa* (1996) ZACC 16.

5 President Thabo Mbeki, for example, said during a parliamentary debate on reparations (May 2000):

> Did our people engage in gigantic struggle, with some deciding to lay down their lives, with the prospect of financial reward in their minds? I have said and I will say it again, that any such suggestion is an insult to them and to all of us who now enjoy the freedom that they fought for.

6 Its draft regulations, published for public comment in 2011, suggest that it uses these funds to cross-subsidize the health and educations departments and disaster relief efforts.

7 See for example SACTJ (2011).

References

Arbour, L. (2007) "Economic and Social Justice for Societies in Transition", *International Law and Politics*, 40(1): 1–27.

AZAPO and others v. The President of the Republic of South Africa (1996), SACC: 17/96.

Backer, D. (2005) "Evaluating Transitional Justice in South Africa from a Victim's Perspective", *Journal of the International Institute*, 12(2): 8–9.

Backer, D. (2010) "Watching a Bargain Unravel? A panel study of victims' attitudes about transitional justice in Cape Town, South Africa", *International Journal of Transitional Justice*, 4(3): 443–56.

Brankovic, J. (2010) *Advocating Justice: Civil Society and Transitional Justice in Africa workshop report*, Johannesburg: African Transitional Justice Research Network and the Centre for the Study of Violence and Reconciliation.

Brooks, R.L. (1999) "Introduction: The age of apology", in R.L. Brooks (ed.) *When Sorry*

Isn't Enough: The controversy over apologies and reparations for human injustice, New York and London: New York University.

Carrington, G. and Naughton, E. (2012) *Unredressed Legacy: Possible policy options and approaches to fulfilling reparations in Uganda*, New York: International Centre for Transitional Justice.

Colvin, C.J. (2006) "Overview of the Reparations Program in South Africa", in P. de Greiff (ed.) *The Handbook of Reparations*, Oxford: Oxford University Press.

Correa, C. (2009) "Book Review", *International Journal of Transitional Justice*, 3(2): 286–93.

Correa, C., Guillerot, J. and Magarrell, L. (2009) "Reparations and Victim Participation: A look at the Truth Commission experience", in C. Ferstman, M. Goetz and A. Stephens (eds) *Reparations for Victims of Genocide, War Crimes and Crimes against Humanity*, Boston: Brill Academic Publishers.

Fennis, L. (2013) "Redress Movement Theory in South Africa: Civil society advocacy for the implementation of reparations programmes", unpublished thesis, University of Gothenburg.

Garcia-Godos, J. (2008) "Victim Reparations in the Peruvian Truth Commission and the Challenge of Historical Interpretation", *International Journal of Transitional Justice*, 2(1): 63–82.

Kalmanovitz, P. (2010) "Corrective Justice Versus Social Justice in the Aftermath of War", in M. Bergsmo, C. Rodriguez-Garavito, P. Kalmanovitz and M.P. Saffon (eds) *Distributive Justice in Transitions*, Oslo: Torkel Opsahl Academic EPublisher.

Laplante, L.J. (2008) "Transitional Justice and Peace Building: Diagnosing and addressing the socioeconomic roots of violence through a human rights framework", *International Journal of Transitional Justice*, 2(3): 331–55.

McGregor, L. (2013) "Transitional Justice and the Prevention of Torture", *International Journal of Transitional Justice*, 7(1): 29–51.

Makhalemele, O. (2009) "Still Not Talking: The South African government's exclusive reparations policy and the impact of the R30,000 financial reparations on survivors", in C. Ferstman, M. Goetz and A. Stephen (eds) *Reparations for Victims of Genocide, 110 War Crimes and Crimes against Humanity – Systems in place and systems in the making*, Leiden: Martinus Nijhoff Publishers, 541–66.

Millar, G. (2010) "Assessing Local Experiences of Truth-Telling in Sierra Leone: Getting to 'why' through a qualitative case study analysis", *International Journal of Transitional Justice*, 4(3): 477–96.

OHCHR (2012) "Tunisia: UN expert calls for human rights to be at the heart of the transitional justice process owned by the entire society", Statement by the United Nations Special Rapporteur on the promotion of truth, justice, reparations and guarantees of non-recurrence, November 16, 2012.

Orr, W. (2000) "Reparations Delayed is Healing Retarded", in C. Villa-Vicencio and W. Verwoerd (eds) *Looking Back, Reaching Forward: Reflections on the TRC of South Africa*, Cape Town: University of Cape Town Press.

Pham, P., Vinck, P., Wierda, M., Stover, E. and di Giovanni, A. (2005) *Forgotten Voices: A population-based survey of attitudes about peace and justice in Northern Uganda*, Berkeley: International Center for Transitional Justice and the Human Rights Center.

Picker, R. (2005)*Victims' Perspectives about the Human Rights Violations Hearings*, Johannesburg: Centre for the Study of Violence and Reconciliation.

Promotion of National Unity and Reconciliation Act 1995, Ch 34. Cape Town: South African Parliament.

Robins, S. (2011a) "Towards Victim-Centred Transitional Justice: Understanding the needs of families of the disappeared in post-conflict Nepal", *International Journal of Transitional Justice* 5(1): 75–98.

Robins, S. (2011b) *"To Live as Other Kenyans Do": A study of the reparative demands of Kenyan victims of human rights violations*, New York: International Centre for Transitional Justice.

Robins, S. (2012) "Challenging the Therapeutic Ethic: A victim-centered evaluation of transitional justice process in Timor-Leste", *International Journal of Transitional Justice*, 6(1): 83–105.

SACTJ (2011) *South African Coalition for Transitional Justice Comments on the Draft Regulations published by the Department of Justice dealing with Reparations for Apartheid Era Victims*, available at: www.khulumani.net/reparations/government/2011-regulations.html (accessed July 16, 2013).

Truth and Reconciliation Commission (1998) *Report of the Truth and Reconciliation Commission of South Africa*, Cape Town: TRC.

Van der Merwe, H. (2008) "What Survivors say About Justice: An analysis of the TRC victim hearings", in A.R. Chapman and H. van der Merwe (eds) *Truth and Reconciliation in South Africa: Did the TRC deliver?* Philadelphia: Pennsylvania University Press.

Van der Merwe, H. (2012) "Prosecutions, Pardons and Amnesty: The trajectory of transitional accountability in South Africa", in N. Palmer, P. Clark and D. Granville (eds) *Critical Perspectives in Transitional Justice*, Cambridge: Intersentia.

Viaene, L. (2010) "Life Is Priceless: Mayan Q'eqchi' voices on the Guatemalan national reparations program", *International Journal of Transitional Justice*, 4(1): 4–25.

Vinck, P. and Pham, P. (2008) "Ownership and Participation in Transitional Justice Mechanisms: A sustainable human development perspective from Eastern DRC", *International Journal of Transitional Justice*, 2(3): 398–411.

Wemmers, J.A. and de Brouwer, A.M. (2011) "Globalization and Victims of Crime", in R. Letschert and J. van Dijk (eds) *The New Faces of Victimhood: Globalisation, transnational crimes and victim rights*, Dordrecht: Springer, 279–300.

Wilson, R.A. (2001) *The Politics of Truth and Reconciliation in South Africa: Legitimizing the post-apartheid state*, Cambridge: Cambridge University Press.

Part V

Conclusion

14 The healing role of reparation

Jo-Anne M. Wemmers

The aim of this final chapter is to bring together the different ideas that have emerged from the preceding chapters. The authors all have different backgrounds, and across disciplines one word can take on very different meanings. Therefore, we first need to consider definitions. After addressing the meanings of "reparation" and "healing", the chapter discusses factors that can help or hinder victims' healing. This book follows the approach of therapeutic jurisprudence and aims to identify ways that justice contributes to healing. First, we identify victims' needs and the order in which they should be met in order to optimize healing. Second, we identify principles of justice that contribute to the restoration of justice for victims. Finally, these two concepts are considered together as we reflect on how reparation systems can be therapeutic.

Defining reparation

The central theme of this book is reparation, and therefore we need to closely consider the meaning of the term. Throughout the book various approaches to reparation can be found. These fall under two general categories: legal definitions and criminological definitions of reparations. Another approach to reparation that we find throughout this book is the notion of collective versus individual reparation. In the following, we will consider these different elements in order to arrive at a shared understanding of what reparation is.

Legal definition

Numerous authors in this book have referred to the *UN Basic Principles and Guidelines on the Right to a Remedy and Reparation for Victims of Gross Violations of International Human Rights Law and Serious Violations of International Humanitarian Law* (hereafter referred to as *Basic Principles and Guidelines*), which were adopted by the General Assembly of the United Nations in 2005. This legal document clearly identifies the many different forms of that reparation can take: restitution; compensation; rehabilitation; satisfaction and guarantees of non-repetition. The variety of forms of reparation highlights the flexibility and fluidity of reparation. The *Basic Principles and Guidelines* signify an important advancement in legal perceptions of reparation, which historically have largely viewed reparation in terms of restitution and compensation (in this volume see Goetz; Mégret; and Manirabona and Wemmers). The *Basic Principles and Guidelines* are also victim-centered because, regardless of the form, reparation is always defined in terms of what it offers to victims. As Manrique Rueda (in this volume) observes, the view has emerged in international law that justice should be defined in terms of reparations for victims.

Criminological definition

"Restorative justice" is defined as a process that is primarily oriented towards repairing the individual, relational and social harm that was caused by the commission of a crime (see Jones, Parmentier and Weitekamp in this volume). From this definition it is clear that restorative justice recognizes the harm suffered by the victim as a result of the offence. However, restorative justice takes a broad approach to harm, which corresponds with the domain of criminology. Consequently, some authors have criticized restorative justice for being offender-oriented and using victims to promote the rehabilitation of offenders (see Herbert, Rioux and Wemmers in this volume).

Reparative justice, in contrast, is presented as a victim-centered approach to reparation (see Goetz in this volume). Unlike restorative justice, reparative justice is only concerned with victims' experiences. Reparative justice, according to Goetz, defines reparation in terms of the UN *Basic Principles and Guidelines*. In addition it includes procedural rights aimed at providing victims with access to reparation. It also includes victims' perceptions of fairness and trust. Its focus on victims of crime, their needs and their perceptions means that, unlike restorative justice, reparative justice can be considered a victimological notion.

Victims' perceptions of what reparation is generally correspond with those described in the *Basic Principles and Guidelines*. The studies presented by Manirabona and Wemmers and by Jones, Parmentier and Weitekamp in this volume both demonstrate this. Unlike much of the work on restorative justice, which views it as an alternative to criminal prosecution, the victims in both of these studies emphasized the importance of prosecution as a form of reparation. The *Basic Principles and Guidelines* consider criminal prosecution a form of satisfaction for victims. Victims' perceptions are rather nuanced and they draw a distinction between external forces holding the offender to account and internalized recognition of responsibility by the offender. Both of these forms of satisfaction are significant for victims.

How much importance victims place on reparation is a function of the level of suffering they endured. The greater the degree of trauma suffered by the victims, the more important reparation becomes for them (see Jones, Parmentier and Weitekamp in this volume). In accordance with equity theory (Walster *et al.* 1973) doing justice for victims means balancing the victims' suffering (costs) with the costs or punishment imposed on the offender. As Danieli (in this volume) observes, it is what happens after the trauma that is crucial in the long term. Victims' ability to make sense of their suffering requires ending impunity and acknowledging the victim's suffering.

Individual versus collective reparations

The *Basic Principles and Guidelines* recognize both collective and individual victims; however, as Mégret (in this volume) observes, most forms of reparation are framed in terms of individual victims (i.e. restitution, compensation, rehabilitation). This tendency is particularly strong at the International Criminal Court. While the *Rome Statute* does not define reparation, Article 75 refers to reparation for victims, "including restitution, compensation and rehabilitation". The *Rome Statute* does not explicitly exclude collective forms of reparation, such as commemorations and guarantees of non-repetition, but it does not mention them either and this creates ambiguity.

Criminal prosecution can be viewed as an individual approach, as it targets individual offenders; however, the prosecutor represents the state, or in the case of the ICC the prosecutor acts on behalf of the Assembly of State Parties. Therefore, criminal prosecution has a strong collective component to it. However, victims who wish to participate in criminal cases at the ICC or receive reparation from the court must apply individually. At the same time, victims' legal representatives at the ICC can work on behalf of a group of victims much in the way the prosecutor works on behalf of the Assembly of State Parties. Hence, criminal prosecution can be viewed as a form of both individual and collective reparation.

Similarly, rehabilitation can focus on the individual or the group. For example, when a community is victimized, all group members may be affected, even members who were not yet born at the time of the events. The chapter by Jill Strauss in this volume is an excellent illustration of rehabilitation at the level of the group. While rehabilitation implicates the individual, measures that focus on group membership and the needs of the group can stimulate collective rehabilitation among group members.

Promoting healing

A second theme of this book is healing, and therefore it is important to reflect on what "healing" means. After discussing the meaning of healing at the individual and group levels, a hierarchy of needs is presented. The needs of victims of crimes against humanity can seem endless, and this hierarchy of needs is helpful in order to organize and prioritize needs. Justice is important for the wellbeing of the individual and for societal functioning. Different principles of justice are presented that may contribute to restoring victims' sense of justice.

Defining healing

Healing is often associated with the rehabilitation of the victim. Research with victims demonstrates that recovery does not mean returning to the way things were prior to the victimization. It is often impossible to go back. Recovery means successfully integrating the experience into one's life and giving it meaning (Hill 2004). Post-traumatic growth is a concept developed by clinical psychologists to describe how individuals sometimes grow emotionally following violent victimization and actually function better than they did before the crime occurred (Kunst 2010).

Although the *Basic Principles and Guidelines* and the *Rome Statute* both include rehabilitation, neither document provides a definition of rehabilitation. "Rehabilitation" in English means to restore to good health or good working condition. The *Basic Principles and Guidelines* do specify that rehabilitation should include medical and psychological care as well as legal and social services. Thus these services should be available in order to help the individual victim heal.

Without underestimating the importance of individual healing, when dealing with crimes against humanity, it is important to consider collective healing as well. Crimes against humanity can target entire communities. Collective healing is at the heart of transitional justice. It refers to a variety of measures, both judicial and non-judicial, implemented in order to redress the suffering following massive human rights abuses (see Jones, Parmentier and Weitekamp in this volume). Core components of transitional justice measures include accountability, truth, trust, healing, peace and justice (Jones *et al.* 2012).

While individual and collective healing are two distinct processes, they are also related. Each individual is also a member of one or more social groups. Victims are often aware of this distinction between their personal needs and those of the group. For example, in his work with victims of apartheid in South Africa, Hamber (2009) notes that victims sometimes spoke of the group's need to heal versus their own individual healing. The chapter in this volume by Jill Strauss on Northern Ireland illustrates how individual actions can impact group relations. The individual's social identity is the linking pin between individual and collective processes (Wemmers 2010). As we will see in the following section, belonging to groups, and in particular a group that is valued by others, is important for how we feel about ourselves.

Victims' pyramid of needs

After widespread and systematic violence, the needs of the people within the community can be so overwhelming that it is hard to know where to start. Maslow's (1968) hierarchy of needs can help set priorities with regard to meeting victims' needs in order to facilitate healing (Wemmers and De Brouwer 2011). Following a humanist approach, Maslow presents these needs as universal (see Van der Merwe in this volume). Maslow's hierarchy also indicates how the individual and the collective are linked within each person. In all, there are five different levels of needs. It is only after one level has been satisfied that the person can move on to the next level. However, any one reparative measure may impact several different levels of need.

Maslow's first level consists of physiological needs. This means such things as food, shelter and medical care. A victim who has lost everything and is unable to work due to injuries suffered as a result of their victimization will, in the first place, need medical care for their injuries, food for themselves and their family, and a place to stay.

The second level of needs identified by Maslow is safety. People need to feel safe and secure. Victimization can rob people of their sense of security, leaving them feeling vulnerable. Victims can be afraid of revictimization in general or revictimization by their aggressor in particular. An important question facing post-conflict societies is how to live together after mass victimization. This has been a major issue in in the states of the former Yugoslavia and in Rwanda. Many victims move and do not return to their homes out of fear (Parmentier and Weitekamp 2007).

The next level of needs is a feeling of love, belonging and acceptance. These needs may be particularly acute in the case of crimes that target a particular social group, because the very nature of these crimes is to exclude and reject a group of people based on of their social identity. Often victims of conventional crimes will find support in their informal network of family and friends (Wemmers 2003). This may be more difficult in the case of widespread violent victimization, where victims may have lost many family members. Those remaining may have experienced multiple victimizations, both directly and indirectly, as well as witnessing the victimization of others. They may not be in any condition to help others and may themselves need help. As Herbert (in this volume) explains, the need for formal support may be all the greater following widespread violence. Besides extensive trauma within the society following widespread violence, societies will sometimes stigmatize victims, shutting them out and rejecting them. During the violence in the Democratic Republic of Congo, girls were often kidnapped and forced to be "bush wives" for soldiers. However, when they tried to return to home after the violence they and their children were often rejected by their families, which added to their suffering (McKay and Mazurana 2004). Hence, victims need to find formal and/or informal support from others following their victimization.

The fourth level identified by Maslow is self-esteem. It is about feeling good about oneself. How individuals feel about themselves is partly based on their personal competencies and on the groups to which the person belongs (Lind and Tyler 1988). This is where the collective and the individual come together. People want to belong to groups that are valued and respected. People look for information about the value of their group in their interactions with members of other groups and with authorities (Tyler and Lind 1992). It is hard to feel good about belonging to a group that is looked down upon by others. Sensing that others do not respect your social group can lead to feelings of inferiority and helplessness (Hogg 2006).

The final level in Maslow's pyramid of needs is called self-actualization. The self-actualized individual is well-adjusted and functioning at their full potential. This is victim rehabilitation at its very best. Post-traumatic growth is a clear example of successful rehabilitation. The self-actualized individual does not have unmet needs. Their needs have already been met. A person's lower-level needs must first be met before they can achieve self-actualization.

Principles of justice that promote healing

Justice is intrinsically concerned with both individual wellbeing and societal functioning (Deutsch 1975), and as such it is essential for the healing of the individual victim after widespread violence as well as for the recovery of the society. Reparation can help restore justice for victims. In order to promote healing, reparative justice must provide reparation (see Van der Merwe in this volume). However, outcomes alone are not sufficient: how justice is done is equally important. In the following we will present four principles of justice that emerge from the various chapters in this book. These dimensions of justice are interrelated and not independent of one another (Greenberg 1993).

Distributive justice

Distributive justice refers to the distribution of the conditions and goods that affect individual wellbeing (Deutsch 1975). According to Deutsch, need-based distribution of resources fosters personal development and personal welfare (i.e. healing). When the value base underlying the distribution of resources is need, a fair distribution is one that gives priority to those with the greatest need. This principle is amplified in institutions that have the personal development and welfare of their clients as their primary concern (i.e. victim services). However, as Gabriela Manrique Rueda argues in this volume, it is important to bear the historical and cultural importance of those resources in mind as well. Hence, she argues for a system of reparation that is based on notions of corrective justice as well as distributive justice.

Procedural justice

A second principle of justice is that how a decision is reached is also important. Procedural justice refers to the perceived fairness of procedures underlying a decision-making process (Colquitt 2001; Blader and Tyler 2003). In other words, the procedures used to determine reparations should be fair. Procedural justice has been found to enhance victims' faith in institutions (Wemmers 1996) and their recovery from crime (Wemmers 2013). Fair procedures allow victims to have a voice or provide input into the process (Folger 1977; Wemmers 1996). For example, they would allow victims to express their needs and concerns regarding reparations (Wemmers and Cyr 2005). Other determinants of fair procedures are neutrality and consistency. As Wemmers (in this volume) stresses, it is important that rules and procedures are clear and applied even-handedly across all victims in order for procedures to be considered fair.

Interactional justice

A third principle of justice is interactional justice, which refers to the quality of the treatment of or interactions between people (Colquitt 2001; see also Wemmers in this volume). Several chapters in this volume have highlighted the importance of dialogue and interpersonal interactions between members of different social groups as well as with authorities. How victims are treated sends a message about their value to the group (Wemmers 1996). Victims need to feel supported in their interactions with others; when they fail to find support, this can augment their suffering. However, as Starzyk and her colleagues (in this volume) point out, people do not always react well to seeing others suffer and may blame the victim. Their research findings are highly relevant to how we can foster positive and supportive reactions to victims among members of the dominant (offending) group. Determinants of interactional justice include treating individuals in a polite manner, with dignity and respect for their rights and with empathy and concern for the plight of the victim (Greenberg 1993).

Informational justice

A fourth principle of justice is informational justice. The quality of the information and explanations that are shared with those subject to a procedure influences victims' justice judgments (their perception of whether justice has been accomplished; see Wemmers in this volume). An effective way of enhancing victims' perceptions of informational justice is by openly sharing with victims adequate social accounts of the procedures used and their outcomes (Greenberg 1993). In addition to providing victims with a sense of justice, Starzyk and her colleagues (in this volume) demonstrate that information also impacts how others react to victims. Presenting people with the facts of what happened while taking care not to invoke defensive processes is an avenue for increasing support for reparations among members of the offending group and third parties.

Information is also essential in dialogue, which is a key feature of restorative justice. Through dialogue people can learn about the other and their experiences as well as inform the other about their own experiences and views. Dialogue can transform relationships between members of different social groups (see Strauss in this volume).

Implications for reparation systems

In order for reparation to be healing, the mechanism in place for providing reparations should promote a sense of justice. Concretely, it should provide distributive, procedural, interactional and informational justice. It should also set priorities, and Maslow's hierarchy of needs is a useful tool in this regard. It allows the system to identify which needs have to be met first in order promote healing. At the same time, any one reparative measure may impact several different levels of need. Combining these two approaches gives rise to the following four-step system of reparation (summarized in Table 14.1).

Table 14.1 Four steps guiding reparative systems that promote healing

	Need	*Reparation*	*Justice principles*
Step 1	Physiological needs	Rehabilitation: medical services; social services (food, shelter) Compensation	Need-based distributive justice
Step 2	Safety and security	Satisfaction: criminal prosecution; apology Guarantees of non-repetition Compensation	Procedural justice Interactional justice Informational justice Equity-based distributive justice
Step 3	Belonging and acceptance	Satisfaction: criminal prosecution; apology; truth commission Rehabilitation: social services; legal services Compensation	Procedural justice Interactional justice Informational justice Equity-based distributive justice
Step 4	Self-esteem	Satisfaction: criminal prosecution; commemoration Guarantees of non-repetition	Procedural justice Interactional justice Informational justice Equity-based distributive justice

Basic physiological needs

The first step is to ensure that victims' basic physiological needs are met. Strictly speaking, this is humanitarian aid and not reparation as it is something that should be available to all human beings. International law such as the Geneva Convention requires that following a violent conflict, everyone, regardless of their role in the violence, has a right to basic medical care as well as food and shelter. Food, medicine and shelter should be available to all people and their access to these resources should be determined based on each person's need.

Safety and security

The second step is to ensure that victims are safe and secure. When victims do not feel safe in their own country due to widespread violence, they may find a sense of safety by leaving their country and becoming refugees. The large number of refugees leaving conflict areas illustrates victims' search for safety.

There are various forms of reparation that affect victims' feeling of safety and security. To begin with, criminal prosecution can provide victims with a sense of safety. Given the seriousness of the offences, the accused will typically be detained during the criminal justice process, and upon conviction they may be sentenced to prison. Knowing that the offender is not free can provide reassurance to victims. At the same time, however, criminal prosecution can be very stressful for victims. Victims who act as witnesses before the court may even face more risks for both themselves and their family (De Brouwer 2005; see also Herbert, Rioux and Wemmers in this volume). If the accused is not found guilty and is released by the court, victims may be very worried about their safety as well as that of their family. When determining who should be prosecuted, equity is a preferable principle of allocation: focusing on the most notorious criminals (see Jones, Parmentier and Weitekamp in this volume).

A second form of reparation that addresses victims' feeling of safety is guarantees of non-repetition. This form of reparation refers to structural changes in social institutions that are intended to prevent abuses of power from occurring again in the future. These measures can provide victims with a sense of safety and security because they ensure that such crimes will not happen again. The importance of guarantees of non-repetition for victims of crimes against humanity is evident in the interviews with Haitian victims in Manirabona and Wemmers' study in this volume. These victims wanted to see structural changes occur in Haiti in order to be certain that crimes against humanity would not occur again in their country. They were concerned that history might repeat itself because nothing had changed. Similarly, Woolford illustrates in this volume that without structural changes to the way the Canadian government treats First Nations people, the colonial relations that made the Indian Residential Schools possible in the first place seem to continue.

A third form of reparation that may affect feelings of safety and security is acknowledgement by the offender, for example in the form of a public apology. When offenders recognize the harm that they have done, this has a calming effect on their victims. Recognition sends victims the message that the offender acknowledges the wrong that has been committed and is therefore unlikely to repeat it (Wemmers and Cyr 2005; Strang 2002; see also Manirabona and Wemmers in this volume).

Another form of reparation that can sometimes help victims feel more secure is compensation. For example, money obtained through compensation may allow victims to purchase certain resources that provide them with a sense of security that they could not afford otherwise (e.g. move to a safer neighborhood).

Belonging and acceptance

The third reparative step is creating a sense of belonging and acceptance. Any form of reparation that provides a sense of recognition to victims may contribute to their feeling supported and accepted. What is important is that the victim is given a sense of recognition, validation and support. When executing reparation, whatever its form, authorities should be aware of the impact on victims. In doing so, it is important to not focus solely on outcomes or distributive justice and to remember that the way authorities treat victims will also contribute to their sense of justice and wellbeing. Whether victims are treated with dignity and respect or ignored and silenced will affect their recovery from victimization.

One form of reparation that provides a sense of recognition to victims is criminal prosecution. When police take victims' complaints seriously and lay charges against the accused this sends a message to the victim that society supports them and agrees that what happened to them is wrong and should not be tolerated. In the absence of support, their suffering will continue. Hence, criminal prosecution is not only important in providing victims with a sense of security, it is also a source of validation and recognition for victims. Criminal prosecution can make use of distributive, procedural, interactional and interpersonal justice in order to restore justice for victims. Fair procedures give victims voice; they are transparent; and they are applied consistently across victims. The lack of clarity regarding reparation at the ICC is a concern and may constitute a source of injustice for victims (see Wemmers in this volume). The court should develop principles for reparation in order to provide victims with procedural justice. It should also use its outreach activities to maximize the information given to victims in order to provide them with a sense of informational justice.

Another form of reparation that clearly addresses victims' need for belonging and acceptance is rehabilitation. Rehabilitation includes medical, legal and social services for victims. Psychosocial services aimed at providing support to victims are vital in order to meet the victim's needs at this level. Medical services not only meet victims' basic physiological needs, they also provide victims with a sense of support and encouragement. Similarly, legal services can provide victims with a sense of acceptance and support: for example, when a lawyer confirms the importance of their case and agrees to work on their behalf. Should, however, any of these services refuse victims, then this can augment victims' suffering as they fail to find the support and the validation that they seek. Essentially, any service for victims that recognizes their suffering and is supportive of them can help provide victims with a sense of belonging and acceptance.

Compensation is another form of reparation that recognizes victims and their suffering. Victims often consider the recognition provided by these programs more important than the money they receive (Feldthusen *et al.* 2000). However, the procedures followed by these programs can be very difficult for victims when they feel that their suffering is being brought into question rather than validated (Shapland *et al.* 1985; Greer 1996; Feldthusen *et al.* 2000).

Other forms of reparation that can provide victims with a sense of belonging and acceptance are truth commissions and public apologies. These can provide public recognition of the harm suffered by victim and openly condemn the crimes committed in the past. However, here as well process is important in order to ensure that victims feel fully recognized and that members of the offending group do not react defensively (see Starzyk, Gaucher, Boese and Neufeld in this volume). Essentially, any form of reparation that provides victims with a sense of recognition, validation and support can affect their need for belonging and acceptance.

Self-esteem

Step four is to improve self-esteem and, in particular, to help victims feel good about the groups to which they belong. Victimization constitutes a blow to one's self-esteem, and victims need reassurance that they are worthwhile and that their social group is valuable as well. Besides providing a sense of belonging and acceptance to the individual, many forms of reparation also validate the group. How authorities treat victims sends a message to them regarding their value to the group (Lind and Tyler 1988; Wemmers 1996; Wemmers 2010).

Many different forms of reparation affect victims' self-esteem and their perceived group-value. For example, criminal prosecution for crimes against humanity recognizes the widespread nature of the crimes committed. In the ICC the distinction is often made between victims of the situation (i.e. the group) and victims of the case (i.e. the individuals victimized by the accused) (Bitti 2011). In order to effectuate changes at the level of the society and transition towards stable peace and harmony (i.e. transitional justice), it is important to meet victims' needs at this level.

Other forms of reparation that recognize the group include commemoration and tributes to victims, and guarantees of non-repetition. A public apology can provide satisfaction to victims; however, the way the apology is made is critical for whether or not victims will consider it to be reparative (Ross 2008). If the apology talks about past wrongs without explicitly recognizing the crimes committed and the harm suffered by the victims, it may be rejected by victims. Through their respect for the group, these reparative measures can contribute in rebuilding victims' self-esteem and can thereby transform relations between social groups.

These four steps should guide reparative systems so that they can promote the healing of the victim and society. Reparation is an important tool in the restoration of justice for victims. The way victims are treated and whether they feel they have been treated with dignity and respect is crucial in order to restore victims' sense of justice. Recognition and accountability are prerequisites for reconciliation (Raymond 2010). In order to promote healing of the individual victim and the community, reparation should respect these principles of justice.

Conclusion

Crimes against humanity are among the worst crimes known to mankind. Recovery can seem almost impossible for the victims whose lives have been changed forever, as well as for the society as a whole. In this book we have looked at reparation for victims of crimes against humanity from different disciplines. This results in a multidisciplinary approach to reparation that combines elements of psychology, law, criminology and victimology to arrive at a victim-centered view of reparative justice in which victims' needs and the effects of reparation are fundamental.

Reparation has many different forms. Some forms target the individual, others target the group, and others carry a message for both the individual and their group. No matter the form of reparation, however, reparative justice should help heal both the victim and their group. In this book we have tried to understand when reparation is therapeutic and when it is not. When reparation restores a sense of justice for victims, it can be therapeutic.

Justice is a multidimensional concept. It is more than simply punishing offenders. It targets individual victims as well as their social group. The international community, and the ICC in particular, is currently at a crossroads regarding reparation for victims. The ideas presented in this book can help create a truly reparative system of reparation. Authorities will always be limited in one way or another in terms of what they can do for victims. However, when authorities treat them with dignity and respect, they can help restore justice for victims both individually and collectively.

References

Blader, S. and Tyler, T. (2003) "A Four-Component Model of Procedural Justice: Defining the meaning of a 'fair' process", *Personality and Social Psychology Bulletin*, 29(6): 747–58.

Bitti, G. (2011) "Les droits procéduraux des victimes devant la Cour Pénale Internationale", *Criminologie*, 44(2): 63–98.

Colquitt, J.A. (2001) "On the Dimensionality of Organizational Justice: A construct validation of a measure", *Journal of Applied Psychology* 86(1): 386–400.

De Brouwer, A.M. (2005) *Supranational Criminal Prosecution of Sexual Violence: The ICC and the practice of the ICTY and the ICTR*, Antwerp: Intersentia.

Deutsch, M. (1975) "Equity, Equality and Need: What determines which value will be used as the basis of distributive justice?", *Journal of Social Issues*, 31(3): 137–49.

Feldthusen, B., Hankivsky, O. and Greaves, L. (2000) "Therapeutic Consequences of Civil Actions for Damages and Compensation Claims by Victims of Sexual Abuse", *Canadian Journal of Women and the Law*, 12: 66–116.

Folger, R. (1977) "Distributive and Procedural Justice: Combined impact of 'voice' and improvement of experienced inequity", *Journal of Personality and Social Psychology*, 35: 108–19.

Greenberg, J. (1993). "The Social Side of Fairness: Interpersonal and informational classes of organizational justice", in R. Cropanzo (ed.) *Justice in the Workplace: Approaching fairness in human resource management*, Hillsdale, NJ: Lawrence Erlbaum Associates Publishers, 79–103.

Greer, D.S. (1996) *Compensating Crime Victims: A European survey*, Freiburg: Max Planck Institute, 374–400.

Hamber, B. (2009) *Transforming Societies after Political Violence: Truth, reconciliation and mental health*, Dordrecht: Springer.

Hill, J. (2004) *Guide de traitement des victimes d'actes criminels*, Canada: Ministère de la Justice.

Hogg, M.A. (2006) "Social Identity Theory", in P. Burke (ed.) *Contemporary Social Psychological Theories*, Palo Alto: Stanford University Press, 112–36.

Jones, N.A., Parmentier, S. and Weitekamp, E.G.M. (2012) "Dealing with International Crimes in Post-war Bosnia: A look through the lens of the affected population", *European Journal of Criminology*, 9(5): 553–64.

Kunst, M.J.J. (2010) *The Burden of Interpersonal Violence: Examining the psychosocial aftermath of victimisation*, Tilburg: Intervict.

Lind, E.A. and Tyler, T. (1988) *The Social Psychology of Procedural Justice*, New York: Plenum.

Maslow, A.H. (1968) *Toward a Psychology of Being*, 2nd edn, New York: Van Norstrand Reinhold.

McKay, S. and Mazurana, D. (2004) *Où sont les filles? La vie des filles enrôlées dans les forces et groupes armés pendant et après un conflit: les cas du nord de l'Ouganda et la Sierra Leone et du Mozambique*, Montreal: Droits et Démocratie.

Parmentier, S. and Weitekamp, E. (2007) "Political Crimes and Serious Violations of Human Rights: Towards a criminology of international crimes", in S. Parmentier and E. Weitekamp (eds) *Crime and Human Rights*, vol. 9 of *Sociology of Crime, Law and Deviance*, Amsterdam: Elsevier, 109–44.

Raymond, E. (2010) *L'expérience de la Justice pour les Victimes de Crimes Contre l'Humanité*, unpublished thesis, University of Montreal.

Ross, R. (2008) "Telling Truths and Seeking Reconciliation: Exploring the challenges", in M.B. Castellano, L. Archibald and M. DeGagné (eds) *From Truth To Reconciliation: Transforming the legacy of residential schools*, Ottawa: Aboriginal Healing Foundation, 143–62.

Shapland, J., Wilmore, J. and Duff, P. (1985) *Victims in the Criminal Justice System*, Aldershot: Gower Publishing.

Strang, H. (2002) *Repair or Revenge: Victims and restorative justice*, Oxford: Clarendon.

Tyler, T. and Lind, E.A. (1992) "A Relational Model of Authority in Groups", in M.P. Zanna (ed.) *Advances in Experimental Social Psychology*, vol. 25, San Diego: Academic, 115–91.

United Nations (2005) *Basic Principles and Guidelines on the Right to a Remedy and Reparation for Victims of Gross Violations of International Human Rights Law and Serious Violations of International Humanitarian Law*, available at: www.refworld.org/docid/4721cb942.html (accessed June 5, 2013).

Walster, E., Berscheid, E. and Walster, G.W. (1973) "New Directions in Equity Research", *Journal of Personality and Social Psychology*, 25(2): 151–76.

Wemmers, J.M. (1996) *Victims in the Criminal Justice System*, Amsterdam: Kugler Publications.

Wemmers, J. (2003) *Introduction à la victimologie*. Montreal: Les presses de l'université de Montréal.

Wemmers, J.M. (2010) "The Meaning of Fairness for Victims", in P. Knepper and S. Shoham (eds) *International Handbook of Victimology*, Boca Raton: Taylor and Francis Group, 27–43.

Wemmers, J.M. (2011a) "Victims' Need for Justice: Individual versus Collective Justice", in R. Letschert, R. Haveman, A.M. de Brouwer and A. Pemberton (eds) *Victimological Approaches to International Crimes: Africa*, Antwerp: Intersentia, 145–52.

Wemmers, J.M. (2013) "Victims' Experiences in the Criminal Justice System and Their Recovery from Crime", *International Review of Victimology*, available at: http://irv.sagepub.com/content/early/2013/07/11/0269758013492755.full.pdf (accessed August 8, 2013).

Wemmers, J.M. and Cyr, K. (2005) "Can Mediation be Therapeutic for Crime Victims? An evaluation of victims' experiences in mediation with young offenders", *Canadian Journal of Criminology and Criminal Justice*, 47(3): 527–44.

Wemmers, J.M. and De Brouwer, A.M. (2011) "Globalization and Victims of Crime", in R. Letschert and J. van Dijk (eds) *The New Faces of Victimhood: Globalisation, transnational crimes and victim rights*, Dordrecht: Springer, 279–300.

Index

Page numbers in *italics* denote tables, those in **bold** denote figures.

CPSIA information can be obtained
at www.ICGtesting.com
Printed in the USA
JSHW030307210722
28340JS00001B/1